LIFE REGAINED

By the same author

Memories
Julia
A Pacifist's War
Everything to Lose
Friends in Focus
Hanging On
Other People
Good Company

LIFE REGAINED

DIARIES
January 1970–December 1971

Frances Partridge

Weidenfeld & Nicolson

LONDON

First published in Great Britain in 1998
by Weidenfeld & Nicolson

A CIP catalogue record for this book is available
from the British Library.

ISBN 0 297 84246 3

Typeset by Selwood Systems, Midsomer Norton

Set in Perpetua

Printed in Great Britain by Butler & Tanner Ltd,
Frome and London

Weidenfeld & Nicolson

The Orion Publishing Group Ltd
Orion House
5 Upper Saint Martin's Lane
London, WC2H 9EA

FOREWORD

Among the motives for keeping a diary, one generally finds love of the truth and a desire to record it. Writers who enjoy powers of invention or fantasy will take to another medium and probably become novelists. I have often envied Emily Brontë, Anthony Trollope and Lewis Carroll (for instance) their ability to create an imaginary world and set it in motion. In the published notebooks of the great inventor Henry James, he reveals how his most elaborate plots were often fed by a stray remark at a dinner party, rising like a spring to create a river of words. While I remain chained to the truth, I have often regretted that I didn't start diarising earlier when life was full of excitement and thrills, instead of filling so much space with sadness and longing. Perhaps a little in *Good Company* and more now in *Life Regained*, I am aware that I am sending down roots and spreading stems of my *own*, though I miss Ralph and Burgo and the warm life of Ham Spray not a whit less and never shall. In this volume I go to three new countries – Poland, the Channel Islands and Corfu, and four old ones – Russia, Spain, France and Italy.

To
DADIE

DRAMATIS PERSONAE

BRENAN, GERALD, writer and hispanologist. He had been one of Ralph's greatest friends ever since they were together in the First War, despite rows caused by his making love to Ralph's first wife Dora Carrington and to disagreements over the Second War. He was married to Gamel Woolsey, American poetess, and had one daughter. In these diaries he is living in Alhaurin el Grande in Spain with Lynda Price.

CAMPBELL, ROBIN and SUSAN. Cyril Connolly had introduced us to Robin in 1948, when he was living near us at Stokke with his second wife, Mary (now DUNN). He had lost a leg and won a DSO in the war. After his divorce from Mary he married Susan Benson, writer of cookery and garden books, and himself joined the Arts Council. Robin and Susan had two sons, William and Arthur.

CARRINGTON, NOEL and CATHARINE, Dora Carrington's youngest brother and his wife (née Alexander). Ralph had been at Oxford with Noel, who became a publisher and designer, and died in 1989. They were country neighbours in reach of Ham Spray. Of their three children we saw most of Joanna.

CECIL, LORD DAVID and his family. We had known David's wife Rachel, daughter of our old friends Desmond and Molly

MacCarthy, since she was a schoolgirl, and travelled with her before and after her marriage. Their children were Jonathan (actor), Hugh and Laura. The whole family were very kind to me after Ralph's death and I often stayed with them.

COCHEMÉ, JOAN, painter, especially of children's portraits, and a faithful friend for many years. She hastened to be with me when Burgo died. Her husband was Jacques Cochemé, biologist, native of Mauritius, and a member of the Food and Agriculture Organisation in Rome, where they were living in the Sixties.

DUNN, LADY MARY. Our warm friendship began in 1948 when she was living (and actively farming the land) at Stokke with her second husband Robin Campbell. After their divorce she made an unhappy match with Charlie McCabe, columnist of a San Franciscan newspaper. The situation is complicated by the fact that her first husband, Sir Philip Dunn ('the Tycoon') lived not far away in Wiltshire. Philip and Mary had two daughters, Serena and Nell, friends and contemporaries of Burgo's. They eventually remarried.

GARNETT, DAVID, and family. Only son of Edward and Constance Garnett, the eminent translator from Russian, David was generally known as 'Bunny'. He married my sister Ray in 1921, the year that I was taken on as assistant in his bookshop, Birrell and Garnett. He was thus my boss, brother-in-law, and a great friend for life. When his first book *Lady into Fox*, won the Hawthornden Prize he left the shop to write over twenty more. Ray died of cancer in 1940, and in 1942 Bunny married Angelica, daughter of Duncan Grant and Vanessa Bell. He had two sons by Ray (Richard and William) and four daughters by Angelica; Burgo married the second, Henrietta, in 1962; the others were Amaryllis, and the twins – Fanny and Nerissa.

GATHORNE-HARDY, JONATHAN (Jonny) and SABRINA. The popular nephew of Lady Anne Hill and Eddie Gathorne-Hardy was at the time married to Sabrina Tennant, daughter of Virginia, Marchioness of Bath, and David Tennant, creator of the Gargoyle Club, and was launching a career as a writer.

GOODMAN, CELIA, one of the well-known Paget twins, who used as girls to make glamorous appearances at concerts and Glyndebourne. Her sister Mamaine married Arthur Koestler and died at only thirty-seven. Celia's husband was Arthur Goodman, who had spent a gruelling time in a Japanese prison in the war. They had two young children.

GOWING, LAWRENCE, painter of the Euston Road Group, had married in 1952 my 'best friend' Julia Strachey. She was eighteen years his senior, a gifted but very unproductive writer, an original, eccentric and at times difficult character.

HENDERSON, SIR NICHOLAS (Nicko) and LADY (MARY). Ralph and I had been friends of Nicko's parents, and he had come to swim in our pool as a boy. After he married Mary they came often to Ham Spray. He joined the Foreign Service when he was refused by the RAF on medical grounds. They had one daughter, Alexandra.

HILL, HEYWOOD and LADY ANNE (née Gathorne-Hardy). Our friendship began in about 1938, when they were both working in the famous bookshop in Curzon Street created by Heywood, and which still bears his name. When Heywood joined the army in the war, Anne kept the shop going with the help of Nancy Mitford. In the early Sixties the Hills were living in Richmond with their two grown-up daughters, Harriet and Lucy. Anne had four brothers, of whom the second, Eddie, had long been a friend of ours and a visitor to Ham Spray.

JACKSON, JANETTA (née Woolley, now Parladé). Ralph and I met her as a very attractive girl of fourteen, in Spain at the start of the Civil War. Young enough to be our daughter, she became instead one of our closest friends, and figures prominently in all my diaries. Her marriages to Robert Kee and Derek Jackson both ended in divorce. In this diary she is married to Jaime Parladé and living in Spain. Her three daughters were Nicolette (Nicky) Loutit, Georgiana (Georgie) Kee and Rose Jackson.

JEBB, JULIAN, grandson of Hilaire Belloc, to whose small house in Sussex he sometimes invited his friends. Always interested in opera, theatre and cinema, in 1963 he was a journalist heading towards television. An excellent mimic and raconteur, and an affectionate friend.

KEE, ROBERT, Oxford friend of Nicko Henderson, who brought him to Ham Spray soon after his release from prison camp in Germany, where he spent three years after being shot down while a bomber pilot in the RAF. He very quickly became one of our greatest friends, and before long married another – Janetta. They both figure prominently in my earlier diaries, but the marriage became stormy, and by 1963 they had parted and Robert was married to Cynthia Judah. He had one daughter, Georgie, by Janetta, and a son and daughter, Alexander and Sarah, by Cynthia.

He is a writer of novels and history – in particular of Irish history – and has also appeared in many television programmes.

KNOLLYS, EARDLEY, one of the three original owners of Long Crichel House, he was still living there in the Sixties, but had just decided to give up working for the National Trust in favour of his new love – painting.

MCCABE, LADY MARY, *see* DUNN, LADY MARY

MORTIMER, RAYMOND, writer on art and literature, at one time literary editor of the *New Statesman*, then for many years top book reviewer on the *Sunday Times*. Our neighbour when Ralph and I lived in Bloomsbury, he became a close friend of us both, coming often to Ham Spray and travelling with us by car in France. He joined his three friends at Long Crichel House soon after the inauguration. Travel and reading were his greatest pleasures.

PARLADÉ, JAIME, eldest son of a prominent Andalusian family. Ralph and I met him in the Fifties in Marbella, where he owned an antique shop, which afterwards developed into a decorating and architectural business. He is now married to Janetta.

PENROSE, LIONEL and MARGARET, and their extremely clever family. Lionel was an FRS and Galton Professor of Genetics; his wife Margaret had been my friend at Bedales School, Newnham College and ever since; Oliver and Roger are distinguished mathematicians; Jonathan was British Chess Champion for ten years; Shirley is a clinical geneticist. All addicted to chess and music.

PHILLIPS, 'MAGOUCHE' (now FIELDING). American by birth, her first husband, the famous Armenian painter Arshile Gorky, gave her her unusual name. After his death she married Jack Phillips. Later she came to Europe and lived in France, Italy and London with her four daughters (Maro and Natasha Gorky, Antonia and Susannah Phillips), in all of which places she made a great many friends. I got to know her through Mary Dunn and Janetta.

PHIPPS, LADY (FRANCES), widow of the diplomat Sir Eric Phipps; she had been ambassadress at Berlin and Paris. She and I made friends late in our lives but had quickly become intimate, agreeing on such subjects as politics, war and peace, sharing many tastes in books, opera, and even for driving Minis. She was a talented amateur painter.

SACKVILLE-WEST, EDWARD (Eddy) had become fifth Baron Sackville at the age of sixty, on the death of his father in 1962. His musical talent had already appeared at Eton, and after Oxford he became a music critic, as well as novelist, biographer, and poet. One of the three original owners of Long Crichel House, he still spent half the year there even after buying Cooleville House, County Tipperary.

SHAWE-TAYLOR, DESMOND, one of the three original owners of Long Crichel House. Writer on music and other subjects, in the Sixties, he was music critic for the *Sunday Times*.

STONE, REYNOLDS, and his family. We first met them as country neighbours during the war, and acquaintance became friendship later when they lived at their romantic rectory at Litton Cheney,

Dorset. Reynolds was a brilliant engraver on wood and stone, painter of trees and designer; Janet is a professional portrait photographer. They had four children: Edward, Humphrey, Phillida and Emma.

STRACHEY, ISOBEL, first wife of John (Lytton's nephew who had intervened in the Bussy inheritance), but long since divorced. Her only child Charlotte had been a great friend of Burgo's since childhood and was now married to Peter Jenkins. Isobel had published several novels and stories and was a dearly loved crony of mine.

STRACHEY, JAMES and ALIX (née Sargant Florence). James was Lytton's youngest brother. Both were practising psychoanalysts of long standing and James had translated the entire works of Freud in twenty-three volumes, indexed by me. Ralph and I felt towards them as though they were blood relations.

STRACHEY, JULIA, see GOWING

TENNANT, GEORGIA, daughter of David Tennant, creator of the Gargoyle Club, and Virginia, Marchioness of Bath. I first met her staying with Janetta in Alpbach, Austria, in the summer of 1961, and took a great fancy to her, which built up into a firm friendship.

WEST, KITTY, the painter Katharine Church. She had married Anthony West, son of Rebecca West and H. G. Wells, who had left her and made a life in America. She was living in a charming little Dorset cottage to which she had added a big studio, and had also opened a gallery and craft shop in Blandford.

ILLUSTRATIONS

I

1 JANUARY TO 28 DECEMBER 1970

4 January, Sunday

In bed, a dark morning and cold. Penetrating this new year has been very queer. London is a plague-stricken and deserted city. Voice after voice rings up, choked, to say they 'have flu, can't come'. Indeed, Mrs Murphy hasn't been since Monday (the day after I got back), increasing my solitude. The cold has been intense, and I am well aware that this year I shall reach the portentous age of seventy. What satisfaction I get out of my present life lies in making a sort of Chomskian 'synthetical structure' of it, stuffing it fairly full, and sometimes oddly. Work of course, the fag-end of Napoleon,[1] mopping up my flat sketchily but systematically, reading. At first I avoided public places – the flu epidemic is quite serious – then I gave up and went in one day to the coughing, sneezing hotbed of the London Library Reading Room, and also to *The Magic Flute* by myself. (The way other people impinge when one is alone! Ingratiating snarl of highbrow civil servant; Angelica, Fanny, Amaryllis[2] and Quentin's girls eating ices in the bar.)

I feel I have been unconscious for a week, a zombie stamping round but getting some pleasure from my own staunch stamping.

Georgie[3] has had a baby girl; I went to see her and was wrung

---

1 Translation from the French writer Gilbert Martineau, about Napoleon.

2 David and Angelica's four daughters were Henrietta, Amaryllis, Nerissa and Fanny. Quentin was Angelica's brother.

3 Second daughter of Janetta and first of Robert Kee, married to Jean-Pierre Martel.

and harrowed by the perilous mystery. Yesterday I drove down to see Alix[1] for lunch, and spent the evening playing records of *Walkyrie* with the score, which kind Desmond[2] lent me.

Julia [Strachey] is literally the only soul in London. I rang her up as soon as I got back. A loud wail of despair. 'Shall I come and cook you some lunch?' 'Oh, yes, DO.' I asked what she would eat. 'Nothing, really. Perhaps a little scrambled egg and spinach.' She did in fact eat *nothing*. And, my word, the business of being a bullied kitchen maid – memories of Lambourn – very quickly fills me with irritated indignation. 'Oh, no, no, not *that* saucepan, that's for eggs.' 'For heaven's sake, don't put water in *that* jug, it's full of germs.' A pretty girl came to clean the flat, and got the same treatment. Julia has arranged for someone to come every day. 'Good, then she'll do your shopping and perhaps cook a little.' 'Oh, no, it takes the whole time cleaning', and there followed a cascade of descriptions of carpets to take up and shake, fluff under beds, suitcases in piles. I fled, I'm afraid – the fuss, fuss, fuss too much for me. Yet I do see, though she does not, that having someone to find fault with is her great pleasure in life. On the telephone she nearly admitted it, and said unprompted: 'I HATE everyone!' 'Well, that can be a pleasure,' I said and she gave her new, diabolical chuckle and said, 'I think it can.'

I'm now going to pull on fur coat and trousers and go out into the cold, dark street for my Sunday papers while my coffee boils.

My Mini stood outside frosted all over like a Christmas cake. I got in and coasted round the block, lights on, peering owlishly through the obscured windscreen. Back to bed triumphant, with papers.

---

1 Strachey.
2 Desmond Shawe-Taylor was the music critic of the *Sunday Times*.

I went to lunch a few days ago with the Penroses and stayed to play trios. A short talk to Margaret afterwards. Dunyusha[1] had come to take Lionel for a walk. She comes every day, and Margaret admits she is 'a good nurse' and Lionel does what she tells him. But, 'She turns him against me.' Poor Margaret, standing shapelessly with a pregnant-looking stomach (the result of her compensatory stuffing with food), told me how Dunyusha had said to her, 'Please forgive me for *being young*.' And also that 'Lionel was very seriously ill, might die at any time, and must be allowed therefore what he wants.'

What amazes me, in a house of doctors, is Margaret's apparent uncertainty as to how ill Lionel is. She doesn't even know whether he's had a coronary or not, merely repeating that the 'cardiogram wasn't very good'. I don't understand this attitude. How can she possibly control his regime unless she knows the facts? Why not get in touch with his specialist, as the local doctor is said to be 'no good'? Why not get one who *is* some good? Perhaps she doesn't want to know.

8 January
The fearful cold goes on – the knife of the north wind goes straight to your throat when you step outdoors.

Mrs Murphy is back – extremely welcome – and I keep going all right, quietly working at the final touches to 'Little Nap'. Long pleasant conversation about it all with an intelligent woman at Murray's.

Meanwhile, I have got involved in a strange 'intrigue' – I feel it as that, though it may not be. Holroyd,[2] Paul Levy,[3] and the

---

1 A young Polish colleague with whom Lionel was having an affair.
2 Michael Holroyd, author of the Life of Lytton Strachey.
3 Biographer of G. E. Moore and later writer on music and food.

busybody Lucy Norton are trying to collect Bloomsbury material, letters, etc. for the library at King's. After telling Alix that hers might be worth £200,000, they now want her to donate them – virtually speaking – to King's. I felt worried, not knowing how comfortably off she was and whether she might not need funds suddenly for illness. Now I have been approached too by John Carter of Sotheby's, who previously wanted to sell my Lytton–Ralph correspondence.

Tomorrow I am summoned to meet Carter, Holroyd, Paul, Lucy, the librarian of King's and a solicitor from Lord Goodman's office at an hotel in Bond Street. It's really very odd indeed, and I have mixed feelings – principally that I have said my say to Alix on my last visit, and that as for my own fence I shall probably sit on it.

Very nice evening at *Don Giovanni* last night with Mary[1] and two pleasant Americans. I'm due to Stowell[2] this weekend, and as usual dread it. What is wrong with that world? They aren't serious enough. Unless they are giving off rattles of laughter, they don't feel alive.

9 January

I have just been to this extraordinary gathering to consider the possibility of Alix forming some sort of Strachey Trust with her collected papers, and handing them over to King's College, Cambridge. I got a distinct impression of a sort of conspiracy being afoot – the protagonists Michael Holroyd, Paul Levy and arch-spider Lucy Norton. What Lucy is after I don't know, but I suspect it is some instinctual gratification. Michael has a hare-

---

1 The house of Sir Philip and Lady Mary Dunn, known as 'The Tycoonery'.
2 It all turned out for the best in the end.

brained scheme to use the 'Trust funds', whatever they may be, to found a Union Catalogue (in computer form) of all manuscript material in private collections in England and the USA. I exonerate him from everything except perhaps hyper-idealism. Paul has this also in view, but I'm not sure what else. There were also present John Carter of Sotheby's, a bright little solicitor and the excellent Dr Munby of King's Library, who talked good sense and didn't even seem mad keen to get Alix's papers; there wouldn't be room at King's but he would sound out the University Library. Lucy viewed me with suspicion, knowing that I'd seen Alix lately and talked about the Trust scheme; she stated several times what were Alix's feelings and views (incorrectly, I thought, but I let it pass) and made one totally false statement – that if she were to sell her papers she would have to pay both capital gains and income tax in one year. I asked the solicitor if he could confirm this and he said, 'No.' 'I'm sorry,' said Lucy.

I hear the music of the three 'conspirators' straight from *Ballo in Maschera*. My main contribution to the meeting was to say, towards the end, 'I do feel we're talking as if we were all being very kind to Alix, and almost saving her money, whereas the truth is that *she* is making an extremely generous gift.' This was warmly seconded by Dr Munby. There was later some question as to who should go and explain to Alix what had been settled. Lucy, it was suggested, along with the solicitor. Michael said, 'I think it would be a good thing for Frances to go.' F: 'No, I don't really think so. I have absolutely no qualification except being devoted to Alix.' Lucy: 'We rather overlap, perhaps.' I was careful not to compete or contradict Lucy in any way, but I don't think that I took her in. I don't like her, nor greatly trust her.

The meeting had a curious sequel. Paul rang up at lunch-time and insisted on coming and wasting most of my afternoon, sitting staring at me from blue eyes out of his halo of orange curls with a worried and confused look. I was unable to find out what he was after except that I think my detached – or rather pro-Alix – remarks had suddenly made him see that the three of them hardly seem to be acting in Alix's interests. He appeared concerned as to what John Carter was 'up to'. I said I didn't understand what Lucy was 'up to'. P: 'I think she's a sort of Universal Aunt. She's always trying to protect Michael and me from people.' How can they bear to be deluged in the thwarted maternal feelings gushing from that vast, cushiony bosom?

15 January
Janetta has arrived, and looks very well and less harassed. She doesn't make an impression of great restlessness, though she is filled with a desire to travel, and has swept me into a plan to go to Warsaw and Leningrad next month.

18 January
Janetta and I have hurled ourselves into the net of preparations for Warsaw and Russia. I feel mezzo-terrified and mezzo-excited at the prospect. Will she love it as much as I did? We go first for a week to Nicko[1] at Warsaw. But what about the COLD??

Two evenings with her, the first at Chapel Street (with Rose,[2] Jonny[3] and Julian[4]) would have been simply delightful had it not been for the incursion of Sonia,[5] desperate, deplorable and drunk.

---

1 Henderson.
2 Jackson, her youngest daughter.
3 Gathorne-Hardy.
4 Jebb.
5 Orwell.

None of us could stand her shouting for long, and first Julian, then I, then Jonny fled from the dining-room. I felt ashamed afterwards and tried to atone by allowing her to 'bumble on', but it was thunderous bumbling, interspersed with deafening 'ER's about her new friend Decca Treuhaft (née Mitford), replacement for Mary MacCarthy, saying alas simply nothing, and losing sentence after sentence in midstream. Finally (guilt again) I let her talk for a full twenty minutes about Flaubert's 'use of three tenses'.

Much more shattering, though both events were collisions with a desperate human being, was a telephone call I made to Julia yesterday to ask how she was. After two words she started to blow me up savagely for not having found her an electrician. 'When you *knew* how cold I was and that my electric fires weren't working!!' Words literally failed me; uneasy guilt overwhelmed me. In the long and almost comic list of things, mostly mechanical, that she told me had gone wrong, and which she daily settled by telephone, I had detected persecution mania and doubted many of the facts. How pick out the electric fire? I had advised her to call in the GEC itself, rather than some little man round the corner, as she admitted when I reminded her.

After attacking me thus in trembling tones, holding me responsible (someone *must be*) for her sufferings, she said, 'I'm getting angry and rude. I'd better ring off.' That was impossible, so I told her I really did expect her to call on me for services. What else did she need? Well, her pension hadn't been collected for weeks. F: 'All right, I'll come round and do it.' J: 'You can't do that. It needs a witness to my signature and then someone to witness that you've witnessed it.' F: 'I'll manage, don't worry.' Then I asked if she wanted any food bought for her. She said a new French servant was coming in and had cooked her a huge stew, but of course bought the wrong sort of oranges. 'Just what I told her *not* to get. I'll tell you what I'd really like, but you must promise to let me pay for it. I've got money – some *pâté de foie gras*. Also some dressed crab and a little smoked salmon would be nice. And some thin-skinned oranges.'

Well, I've said I'll go on Tuesday morning, collect her pension and take some things. (I offered to go yesterday, but she murmured something about her typewriter.) 'For heaven's sake don't come too early, not before eleven. You've no idea what I look like before I've got my make-up on.'

I continue to think about Julia. Her request for sumptuous delicacies is of course a pathetic 'love test' and by getting me to bring them and then throwing them away (as she did the food I cooked her before) she will probably satisfy some part of her libido.

20 January

Prophetic words. This morning Julia rang up to say she thought perhaps she didn't want the dressed crab, smoked salmon and *foie gras* she'd asked me for. I told her I'd only bought the two latter, and the *foie gras* was in a tin. We then had an insane discussion about oranges. I explained that the very thin-skinned ones were not in season now, but I'd bought some Spanish ones whose skins were thinner than the Jaffas. J: 'The thing is, I've had so many of these oranges that they paint and then varnish over, and they're quite green and sour inside and have none of this carotin you know that oranges ought to contain.' 'Well, perhaps you'd rather I didn't bring them.' 'Yes, better not I think, and then the smoked salmon really doesn't agree with me, and I've got this big casserole of cooked food.' (Why did she ask for smoked salmon, then?) 'I'll keep that too, then.'

Could anything more exactly have followed my prognostications? She tried rather feebly to put off my going to get her pension for her, until a less wet day, but truth to tell I wanted to get it over, and destroy one of her grievances against me. But OOF, what a morning! She really is most horribly disagreeable to me. I tried to swallow my indignation when she contradicted me flat about what I had or had not said on the telephone, but not very successfully.

Had she got her pension book ready? Dear, no! 'I think it's in my bag . . . (scuffle, scuffle). Doesn't seem to be here. Do you know what it looks like?' F: 'No, I don't have one.' J: 'Well, I'd better look in my other bag . . . (more scuffle, scuffle). Not here either.' Finally three immense bags stuffed with papers and pills were brought and the contents emptied in a heap on the floor with a gesture of protest. J: 'Not here either.' She then looked in her first, current bag and found it. There followed a fantastic business over each of the five coupons. Though she had to put the same thing on each one it was necessary to start from scratch each time. 'Let's see now, what do I put here?' What she had taken to be the necessity for 'a witness to the witness' was designed for those able only to make a mark! Done at last after a full three quarters of an hour of frenzied impatience on my part, and several disagreeable remarks administered with a viperish look on hers, I left in the rain for the post office. 'You'll find this awful queue of course, and do be careful crossing Oxford Street, it's very dangerous.' No queue, no questions asked – but Julia had forgotten to sign on the front of three of the five coupons! I said to the assistant was this really necessary, as she was quite confused. 'Oh, yes! she ought to know. She must have done it dozens of times.' So back I trudged, raining hard now, and up her stairs again. She was apologetic this time, but I was determined to get the job done, and back I went, and back to her with the money.

Then the long trek home through Oxford Street, shiny, congested and hideous, to the welcome comparative sanity of my own flat.

This pattern of my relations with Julia must not be repeated – it is too squalid. I shall keep out of range of her banderillas for a while. She made no ghost of an attempt to detain me or talk of other things. When she has got one in the role of servant, only that aspect is allowed to exist, and I cannot and will not occupy it again if I can help it.

28 January

Swiftly the days rush by, all the more so now that my translation is done. I have begun to have Russian lessons and cram every spare minute with a struggle to pin a few words into the non-elastic substance of my mind.

At Crichel last weekend, news of a terrible drama. Pat[1] told us that Andrew Murray-Thripland's youngest brother was slowly dying of leukaemia, and that it was only a question of how long the process would take. If not too long, Pat hoped to carry Andrew off to Mexico. His mother sat by the boy's bed all day and said that when he died she would kill herself. On Sunday evening the telephone rang and Pat (returning from answering it) poured himself a large whisky. 'The boy has died,' he turned and told us, 'and his mother took a train to Brighton, cut her wrists and is dead too.'

8 February

What extremes of mood! Last week, a stunning performance of *Trovatore*, when the singers inspired each other and us and electricity blazed between audience and stage. I sat brimming with delight, and amazement that pleasure on this scale was still possible in this world of cruelty, stupidity and savage noise.

---

1 Trevor-Roper, brother of Hugh and an eminent eye specialist.

18 February

Andrew Murray-Thripland rang up and asked to come and see me. He was here over an hour talking about his ghastly experience. Might he commit suicide? Of course I wondered, but I don't think so. I heard the whole story – how his mother had shut herself away from life when his father had died ten years ago. 'She really committed suicide *then*,' I said. But, an intelligent woman, she had been responsible for her four boys, though wanting to shove them out into the world, *not* be a spider mother in fact. When the youngest, Patrick, aged sixteen, got this deadly and horrible disease she had decided what she would do. I think she might well have killed herself anyway when he was grown up. 'Any friends or lovers?' None, he said. She still carried on her archaeology.

Patrick died suddenly when she and Andrew were lunching near the hospital. They came back and were told. She thrust some papers at the nurse from her bag, and while Andrew went to telephone his brothers he told the nurse to look after her. When he came back he found she had dashed into her car, locked herself in and made off.

My attempted consolation was that with such determination he couldn't have stopped her. He might have that time, but she would have done it again. I instanced Carrington and the cruelty of bringing her round. *Not* being sorry for the dead in their peace. She had, in a sense, a right over her life. She had died ten years ago and been unable to come to terms with life. *Not* blaming himself, he displayed a classical reaction. He said he felt rejection, guilt, deep sorrow and fury on his mother's account, less on his brother's.

I felt utterly drained by the effort to produce real sense and consolation, followed immediately by a visit from Margaret to talk for some hours of her troubles about Dunyusha. 'I think the ambassador ought to know.' 'But what can I tell him?' 'Well, she's certainly up to something.' F: 'But what?' M: 'That's what we've got to find out.' These two agonising dialogues lasted for four hours without a pause. After which I lay beaten, a quivering wreck, scarlet-faced, with racing pulse, dreading next day's journey to Warsaw.

Dear old Eardley[1] provided a sedative evening.

Second visit to Russia but first to Poland.

19 February, British Embassy, Warsaw

My relief was great at finding myself human and calm on the morning of departure.

Only seven souls in our aeroplane and the flight was perfect. A pale blue day after yesterday's dark bluster. Looking out as we prepared to land, I saw a boundless snow-covered plain, with some patches like spilt tea that were really forests. Then we crunched down, buckled on our clothes (not the full quota reserved for Russia, but fur coats, caps, gloves and boots) and took a first breath of Polish air. Yes, it *is* certainly very cold, but crisp, dry and bearable. It doesn't seem to whip tears from the eyes, nor is it a knife at the throat. Nicko and Mary stood beaming there to meet us and we rolled smoothly off in their large Daimler behind a fluttering Union Jack, to this extremely ugly building, badly designed by the architect of the Post Office Tower. It is very warm and comfortable; there is a sweet young butler always bowing from the waist, called Casimir; the most inhabited room is sympathetically untidy with books and papers, hyacinths and

1 Knollys.

daffodils in pots. Janetta and I each have a typewritten programme of our days' events. Mary looks exhausted, with black circles under her eyes, yet after we'd had coffee she insisted on driving us out in her Mini to the Old Town – so-called, for it is entirely rebuilt, a macabre ghost of what the Germans deliberately destroyed.

All eyes as we drove, I saw strong, handsome people tramping purposefully along in leather coats, high boots and fur hats, and making Breughel-like groups against the rather dirty snow heaped at the sides of the road; houses painted dull yellow or sage green, an art and craft shop selling amber, striped rugs and wooden objects decorated with poker-work. There is a lot of space, wide streets and squares, and of course that universal deadness given by the funereal pall of snow. I think I shall soon tire of that, but feel intense excitement at being in a new country.

Quiet dinner and looking at photo albums. Then off to bed in a blurred confusion.

20 February

Those speculative ideas which are often launched by the first days abroad, where are they? There is too much still to discover about this Communist world. I felt shocked when Nicko said his junior staff and their wives were not allowed to mix with any Poles, for 'security reasons'. This is just what we used to complain of the Communists doing surely? There is a half-hearted appendix that it 'wouldn't be fair to the Poles'. But what is the use of having an embassy here at all? We aren't, after all, at war with these individually friendly and apparently admirable people. Surely every sort of intellectual and cultural contact should be kept going, and the embassy staff should be harbingers of peace and friendly relations, rather than gymnasts gyrating on the stiff climbing frame of diplomacy, while trying not to drop their secret information.

Almost opposite the embassy is a large and beautiful park in which is one of the few royal palaces still standing – Łazienki (Polish letter ł pronounced W). A visit there was our morning programme and we walked through the still, refrigerated air along paths of beaten snow. It lay quite thick on each side between the slender black tree trunks, and very tame and hungry red squirrels came hopping through the white silence asking for food. We were accompanied by two ghastly bores from the Ministry of Works, here to consider improvements to the embassy; one is staying in the house; both are square, bottled, unresponsive, navy-blue clad, and no one would guess to look at them that they spend their lives swooshing from Moscow to Ascension Island. The curator of the palace had a sensitive, intelligent face with the fine bone structure and good forehead that seem to be Polish, and lit from within (as a turnip by a candle) by the flame of his great creative passion to combat the damage the Germans had done to his palace, and faithfully, meticulously put it back just as it was. Just, in fact, as the Russians do. There's astonishingly much, even words, in common between the two countries. Yet the Russians have always been their dreaded enemies. I can't think about Russia yet.

Four guests to lunch, a Polish couple – a very attractive female paediatrician married to the translator of Shakespeare – and an Australian pianist and his girlfriend. He had a wild aureole of hair and piercing blue eyes behind owl specs; she, chirpy, engaging and mini-skirted, was now studying the flute but had before been a teacher of mathematics. Both made disquieting occult references to signs of the Zodiac, auras and emanations and were, I'm sure, very avant-garde.

I am handing over our travel arrangements to Janetta to an unprecedented degree and, with the utmost relief but feeling guilty too, lay on my bed reading about Poland's history while she went off to the Orbis Agency.

To *Tosca* in the evening, accompanied by our two plainclothes policemen – the Ministry of Works men – who sat woodenly showing no sign of either pleasure or pain. The large audience coughed and talked maddeningly throughout. The performance was moderate.

21 February, Cracow

Yesterday morning the long black car swept us in warmth and comfort to the National Museum, where we were handed over to two experts – a deathly pale girl with an appalling cold, and an intelligent and humorous bearded man. Both spoke English brilliantly.

Poor Mary looks more tired than ever after a three-hour session with the private detectives. In the afternoon, Nicko, Janetta and I took the train to Cracow.

Instant relaxation. We were alone in our carriage except for an ancient ancient man, during the five-hour run. After gazing out on the snowy wastes I began to long for green; then darkness fell, and we took to our equipment of hot soup, whisky and every other thing thoughtfully put up by Mary. Cracow station was crowded with short, strong, vital people, hurrying home in their fur hats, warm coats and boots. We found our rooms in a nice, old-fashioned hotel and walked out into the town – the silhouette of its massive sloping walls, towers and arcades looked very splendid. We descended into a drinking-place in a cellar frequented by university students, and drank a hot, delicious spicy wine made from honey, a sort of mead. Supper of Mary's collations in Nicko's room, whisky, wine, cold chicken, high spirits.

In the train I ploughed on through the horrifying nightmare of Polish history. It is appalling; worse far than Ireland.

22 February, Cracow

For the first time today I got a sharp twinge from the oppressive nature of the regime. On the whole I'm not greatly impressed by complaints of the 'poor quality of the things in the shops' made by Nicko in the style of Michael Pitt-Rivers. If they prefer to spend money in doing up their palaces and castles, all honour to them.

This morning a strong thaw had set in, but light snow was falling and gradually the snow turned to ugly slush and pools of blackish water. By daylight the ancient buildings reveal dingy, peeling walls and there is an all-pervading air of grimness. In the shops, faces are wooden and unsmiling. The answer is 'No' or 'No more' to everything asked for. In spite of the thaw, or because of it, it's bitterly cold. I'm longing for spring warmth, flowers, freedom, *green*.

My breakfast, got with some difficulty, was a glass of tea with a 'Pickwick tea bag' swinging in it, a leathery roll, bread, excellent butter and jam. We present coupons given us as tourists, and Janetta and I hope that hers and mine will pay the whole bill for the three of us.

The Daimler has arrived here mysteriously, and in it, with our Union Jack gazed at inscrutably by the dark figures in the streets, we rolled off to the Czartosyski Gallery, a collection of pictures and furniture made by a cultured Polish nobleman, including a superb Rembrandt and da Vinci's portrait of a girl with a ferret. Another charming and scholarly curator took us round. His English was pretty good, but he was stumped by one artist: 'It is by the Master of the Half Woman – no, that's not quite right.' F: 'Oh, you mean the Hermaphrodite?' He laughed heartily at this and when I saw the picture, which was of a well-developed bosom encased in red velvet, I felt rather sheepish. Good pictures too by Gozzoli, Lorenzo Monaco; splendid tents captured in Turkish wars; one of Shakespeare's chairs carefully encased. Janetta and I went on to Wawel Castle and saw more tents, tiled stoves – very tall and handsome – frescoes, rooms hung with Spanish leather. Our tiny, schoolmistressy guide clutched her shawl round her shoulders, lifted her square head backwards and spouted scholarly information like a dictaphone.

Lunch in our hotel, with a young Oxford undergraduate of Polish extraction doing a year's course here. The head of the English faculty came for a drink and Nicko was asked to visit him later, but, 'Please do not come in the embassy car if you don't mind.' They clearly must be living in fear, though it sounded extraordinary to hear Nicko ask the undergraduate, 'Are you *under much pressure?*' When asked if Polish girls tried to get him to marry them so as to get English nationality, he replied modestly that they did. Poor Nicko, who had spent the latter part of the morning at the university, suddenly looked quite exhausted, and Janetta and I begged him to have a rest and leave us to prowl in the town. After reading of the appalling horrors done by the Germans, it was strange to hear the sacristan of the Cathedral describing its famous altarpiece of brilliantly coloured, gilt and (it must be said) Germanic figures, to a group of tourists in the German language. In fact this town might be an Austrian one, and I'm not really bowled over by it, as one is supposed to be.

A longish rest and read, then conversation with Janetta in her rooms about faraway English things – Rose, Alexandra's relations with her parents. All these three sets of parents, Janetta, Magouche and the Hendersons, are sharply critical of the others' bringing-up of their daughters. But we agree that Nicko does his job as ambassador perfectly. Trouble-taking and kind, he conveys the impression that he represents a civilised country and is personally charming and totally unpompous. Very high marks indeed. We dined in a small, simple and good restaurant, where the portions were mountainous.

23 February, Warsaw again

Cracow looked more attractive on Sunday morning with snow falling on the people slowly oozing out of the church opposite my bedroom window. They are a religious race (RC) and in this the Russians have been unable to interfere. The large square had a new coat of snow over the slush, and old women were selling tulips and roses at ten shillings each for young men to give their girlfriends, as well as wreaths of immortelles of a drastic violet colour, prettily powdered with snow. Bought some grain for the hungry pigeons and at once had four or five pairs of fierce pink feet clutching my hand.

Started driving homewards in the Daimler. Of course I enjoy this regal comfort, being tucked under a fur rug by the chauffeur, this temporary assumption of luxe. The white landscape seemed more varied than from the train; we even crossed a low range of hills where the road became icy and slippery. I enjoyed the 'human interest': wrapped-up children, boys skating on a pond, skiers and tobogganers, a few horse-driven sledges – one with two ladies holding up an umbrella to the snow, another packed tight with nuns like a mediaeval painting – geese, a solid black dog sitting in the snow. We drew off the road up a farm track to eat our lunch and the chauffeur (returning from a pee) grinningly said that the military police had just shot by in their car, so presumably Nicko must have been tailed all the way from Warsaw. It is hard to take in this extraordinary and sinister mystery-game that is being played, and almost impossible for anyone used to rational behaviour to believe in it. We talked at length about Lionel and Dunyusha. Nicko, not knowing them, treated it rather as farce, but obviously thinks Margaret is probably right about Dunyusha's intentions, and that she is after British nationality. Also Lionel's money, for though Margaret never seems to realise it, I believe he is a rich man. Then talk of general ideas, theory of punishment, retribution, deterrent. The others both snoozed; I gazed. We passed through a large, hideous, rebuilt town, called Kielie I think, and Janetta suggested a stop in a café. N: 'Oh, you *can't*; it'll be appalling! Ghastly!' However, the chauffeur was given orders and with difficulty found one, full to the brim with cheerful people. Nicko and I drank fruit syrup, Janetta had a symbolic cognac. We had lots of drink with us in the car. When she again suggested a stop in a sordid-looking café attached to the petrol station where we filled up in the outskirts of Warsaw, Nicko opposed his will to her formidable one, saying we were nearly home, and this time he won.

Back in the warmth and comfort of the 'Residence' as it is called, welcomed by Mary and dogs.

I begin to dread our catapulting into the Russian maelstrom and wish the sky wasn't uniformly grey, day after day.

24 February

Ah! Out it came, the sun, and with it the sky turned pale blue over the sparkling, refreshed snow. There has fortunately been no wind.

Janetta has been so invariably sweet and considerate to the Hendersons (as well as to me) that I taxed Nicko yesterday, having once said how 'cross' she was. Perhaps she had changed, he admitted, but she could sometimes be really rude. I believe that this is quite unconscious, and comes from the concentrated pursuit of her own ends which temporarily blinkers her.

For lunch we had several English Poles from the university, a young Spaniard, the ex-Polish Ambassador to Paris, a dynamically attractive middle-aged man who seemed to be talking extremely freely at the other end of the lunch table, and afterwards absorbedly to Janetta in one corner of the huge and hideous reception room, leaving her stimulated and agitated. He told her that many things are much better now than they were. Where there was poverty, starvation even, shoelessness and illiteracy, people now have enough to eat, keep warm and dress well. Having got these things, the young have naturally begun thinking and talking about freedom. He had been a good deal in Russia and even there found young people whose flats were full of secretly printed literature, who knew that liberty throughout the Iron Curtain countries must come from them, from within Russia, but also that they had to bide their time. An Anglo-Polish student next to me said the standard of education here is now extremely high. But he was deeply depressed because, although his mother was Polish, the Polish students would not be friends, only acquaintances, and the very fact that he spoke perfect Polish made them suspicious. The poor Poles cannot for a moment risk a Czechoslovak disaster.

Today Janetta and I were taken peacefully and alone to another palace in the outskirts, baroque, charming, light and airy, with beautiful flock wallpapers; and after the lunch guests had gone, she and I and Mary walked in the Łasienki Park, our fingers and noses isolated into tingling blobs by the cold. But the air is crisp and invigorating and one's nose mercifully doesn't run.

Another student to supper. Ping-pong – I can still beat Janetta.

Music and talk about psychology with the student.

25 February

Day of the plunge. It could hardly have begun worse. Magouche, expected at ten-thirty last night, has still not arrived this morning. Telephoning the airport, Nicko was told that she had put down at Poznan, several hours away by train or car, because of fog. Janetta was strained and nervous, while Nicko and I rather heartlessly enjoyed *The Times* crossword puzzle. After further calls it seems she has probably stayed the night there. Apparently flights are often delayed or cancelled for fog or snow.

Oppressive all-overish pale grey sky. I don't care much for the look of the world.

Yesterday was a packed day. Janetta and I were taken to see the film of the destruction of Warsaw, sitting alone in a cinema in the square of the old town. Twenty restrained minutes of horror. Is it right to foster the necessarily furious resentment such things produce? Or rather, is it useful? Janetta and I argued it in the square. The sun had come mildly out, setting off the Poles' superhuman achievement of reconstruction.

But far the most striking tribute to their energy and intelligence was the College of Music, which we were shown around by an English student who had been at the Royal College of Music in London, and told us Warsaw completely outclassed it. The modern building was beautiful; the equipment incredibly good. Hundreds of practising rooms, all perfectly soundproof, the pianos all Steinways and Bechsteins, rehearsal rooms, libraries, elaborate recording and playing-back devices, by which a student can telephone to the basement for any recording to be switched to his practising room. They work there all day till nine at night; the course is five years. I was much moved by such a successful effort directed towards one of the great civilising influences in the world.

Lunch with Wapler, the French Ambassador here, another middle-aged charmer; an elderly female Bibesco and a delightful Polish composer (friend of the Berkeleys[1]). All sophisticated, amusing and civilised. Wapler depreciates everything. Going to Russia? 'Mais c'est *idiot!*' The composer told Janetta that the Berkeleys tried to persuade him to leave Poland, but he wouldn't. Someone must stay. All his friends were here. But he has lost his job and become poor because he spoke up against the invasion of Czechoslovakia. He came with us to the Madame Curie Museum, cracking ironical jokes and smiling with steel-trimmed teeth.

Some time this morning Magouche turned up in a taxi while Janetta was going the rounds of the stations in the Daimler. She had come on by train after a few hours in bed at Poznan.

26 February

Here I am in our long-thought-about, half-dreaded train to Moscow. I have got up from my sleeper and struggled along to the breakfast car to use my first coupon, brought me by the Intourist man in the middle of the night. A beautiful morning, with hot sun and a clear blue sky over virgin snow; but the night must have been cold as there was frost *inside* my window, and getting from one carriage to the next I stepped through rocking infernos of whirling snow blown up from the track. Breakfast was pale sausages, greyish mashed potato, a glass of tea, and bread and cheese.

Our fears of having to get out and change carriages or even trains at the frontier in the middle of the freezing night were

---

1 Lennox, the composer, and Freda.

groundless, though both Russian and Polish travel agencies mis-informed us, and might well have driven us to do so out of mutual hostility. We started the night in a grubby, second-class Polish sleeper, but moved to a first-class one going right through to Moscow. We didn't cross the frontier till about 1 a.m., after a frightening invasion of military officials in fur hats with impassive faces. All money and traveller's cheques were examined, gold objects listed, and then a young man with blazing blue eyes flashed his torch under my bed. And a strong, cross Customs woman pointed fiercely at the Polish apples in my basket and said proudly, 'No fruit allowed into the Soviet Union.' Huge arc lamps fixed at a great height made it seem even more as though we were going into a concentration camp.

So here we go into this vast and extraordinary country, and hardly a human being have I seen out of my window.

27 February, Moscow

It is a disappointing fact that it is less of a thrill being here just because it is the second time. Moscow is actually *familiar* – a place I know. 'Being in Russia' is no longer a miracle; nor does such snow as there is make much difference – it is dirty, urban snow. 'I suddenly see,' Magouche said, as we walked to the Kremlin. 'Everyone *is* the same. They're all equals.' I'm not sure if she meant it as criticism – a little, I think. The universal winter rig is much like that of the Poles: fur hats, good warm coats with fur collars, boots. In this they look more attractively and suitably dressed than in summer. Though I respond with admiration to this equality, I wish they could be more eccentric without losing it. For equality needn't be identity.

After breakfast in the train yesterday I fell peacefully asleep on my berth. Woke and joined the others for lunch, and it didn't seem long before we arrived at Moscow station, an hour late at five o'clock. We were met by an Intourist man with the ears of his fur hat flapping. Like children being greeted by a master at school, we were on this list, our names known. We were to go to the National Hotel, where Kitty [West] and I were last time. Our taxi driver thought otherwise, and firmly took us to a scruffy-looking one called the Berlin, but he was obliged to toe the line. Everyone addresses us in German, and there are many of them about. Janetta's tactics for communication are to speak slowly and softly in English and if they don't understand *'one word'*, as they generally don't, she seems to find them stupid, like a conventional Englishwoman.

Our rooms were well warmed, bathroomed, unattractive slits with no outlook. Both Janetta and Magouche have an instantaneous desire to get things bettered, set people running about on their behalf, put up with nothing. They at once tried to change rooms. Impossible – in this country they have probably met their match. They are both extremely kind to me and for the most part make allowances for my seniority, but last night they insisted on walking for miles in the cold night looking for the Georgian restaurant which, when we at last got there, slammed its door in our faces. Back, therefore, to the restaurant of our hotel, huge and unattractive with a thumping band, four couples revolving in an old-fashioned clinch, and food taking hours to come.

28 February

Janetta finds the bridle of regulations extremely irksome. She likes to ignore them, and would rather eat in a special restaurant where you pay in dollars than use our coupons. This we did last night after an intensely enjoyed performance of *The Three Sisters* at the Moscow Arts Theatre, beautifully staged and acted so that there was complete realism, perfect illusion. They all seemed to be living through these events before our eyes for the first time. Afterwards we drank vodka and ate caviare.

The morning had been gloriously beautiful with a bright blue sky, and we spent it in the Kremlin. The museum and one of the churches were shut; a new little church, very beautiful indeed, had been opened, and we explored at our leisure. Slow but quite good lunch afterwards in an old-fashioned and un-touristy restaurant. Then, I left my two more energetic companions and walked home, buying stamps and postcards.

1 March

I realise I am to some extent irritated by Janetta's claims to special treatment, just as she probably is by my submissiveness. Our food arrangements all today were significant. Breakfast can now be had on trays in our rooms, but we overslept and barely had time to snatch a biscuit and a glass of home-made tea before the private car and guide we had ordered came to take us to Zagorsk. We ended our sightseeing at about one-thirty, but it was a holiday, and our expectation of eating in the good restaurants I remembered there was frustrated. There were huge crowds of people. Outside the tall white wall of the monastery were a lot of booths where healthy, good-humoured females in peasant dress were selling food of various kinds. 'Oh, look!' said Magouche. 'Cold chicken, hard-boiled eggs!' So I bought enough for us three, and our guide and driver. Meanwhile Janetta was eating a small portion of coleslaw out of a cardboard plate and offering it to us on a spoon. 'It's delicious! Oh, *do* have some! Wouldn't you like it?' The fact that our guide and driver had gone back to the car and obviously wanted to be off affected her and me in opposite ways. And not only did Janetta refuse to touch either chicken or eggs, but the force of her personality made Magouche refuse to touch them too, though it had been her idea to buy them. Our guide nibbled a bun, and the remaining store hung about, to be pecked at by me at odd moments during the next two days. Janetta refused to eat any of it, even when we came in so late one night that we could get no food anywhere else. I was reminded of Ralph's account of how she had to invent skiing for herself and would not take advice even from the instructor they had hired. Here, she is inventing Russia for herself. No sooner had we got back to our hotel about three-thirty than Janetta and Magouche went off to the dollar restaurant and came back saying triumphantly that they had got 'delicious food and paid in *roubles*'. I rather unkindly pointed out that the food was exactly the same in all the hotel's several restaurants, and that it wasn't so very clever to buy in roubles what we had already paid for in London in coupons.

The day ended, and the opera over, Magouche suddenly and firmly said she was going straight to bed and Janetta and I were left to eat our delicious caviare and drink our delicious vodka in exactly the same restaurant where they had paid in roubles – but paying in coupons this time. What she eats must be *special*, must be eaten *late* and must be her own deliberate choice. She has already said this morning, 'Let's have lunch *late*, like we did today.' But if you aim at three your food comes at four, by which time my appetite has gone.

And that is quite enough about Janetta and food. Of course she can, and always does, mollify one with her positive sweetness.

Zagorsk: Well, there it was, just as I distinctly remembered it. The thrilling view of the onion domes and tall blue baroque tower seen over the great white wall. New this time was the nipping cold that pierced boots and gloves and made it impossible to stand still for a moment out of doors. And the crowds! Mothers' Day had brought a horde of old women swathed in greyish scarves and booted in felt. 'You'll find all Communist countries smell of hippos,' Nicko had told us – and here we were in the thick of that smell, unable to get into churches without squeezing past these squat, rank-smelling figures, all in putty-coloured clothes, creeping along, propped on sticks, kissing the walls and floors.

Last night's opera, *Don Carlos*, was in the huge new glass theatre inside the Kremlin. The size of the auditorium and of the stage itself meant that the singers could only make themselves heard by throbbing and straining away in front of a long row of microphones. Better draw a veil on this despondingly vulgar and unmusical production. It was turned into a pageant for the masses and the score and even the plot cut about to suit. The audience ate, made love and chattered as if at such a pageant, and when they rushed out in their hordes to the inevitable 'garderobes' it was like being in some frightening public uprising, and ropes had to be thrown across the foyer to keep back the oncoming waves of assault. I noticed that the audience knew enough to applaud the most famous arias, but not to be critical of the atrocious screams of the Italian 'prima donna from La Scala'. We cannot face this vulgar place for the ballet tonight and go to *Uncle Vanya* instead. Snowing as we came out.

2 March

Uncle Vanya was almost, if not quite, as enjoyable as *The Three Sisters*. What a magnificent play! It went on snowing most of yesterday with a cold, searching wind. The coughing in the theatre was dreadful and we hear that there is a lot of flu about. To the Pushkin Museum in the morning. Magouche and Janetta came out discussing whether it was right for the 'masses' to see these masterpieces, and what they got out of it. Janetta thought it was for them just a place to keep warm. She seemed upset, almost speechless and near tears, while Magouche appeared to think, as I do, that many of the young people who go there are studying the pictures with care and intelligently – not holding hands or giggling at all. It is an education, even if they have not got very far with it. You might as well say children should give up arithmetic because they can't understand long division at first sight. Janetta is evidently appalled by what she calls, characteristically, 'IT'. There have been many IT's in her life, and the Russian classless society fills the part perfectly.

Lunch at the Georgian restaurant pleased everyone; there was a huge and varied selection of hors d'oeuvres, on which we stuffed ourselves.

I find walking about, head down, Angora scarf wound round my face, no joke in this bitter, snow-laden wind, so I left my friends to visit St Basil and went back for a sleep.

When I woke this morning it suddenly became clear to me that I never in my heart of hearts wanted to come to Russia this time. I've never cared for snow, nor the shrivelling effect of cold. And I think I knew some of the excitement would wear off on a second visit. Why didn't I hand over to Magouche? Partly because by then I had accepted the challenge never to say NO to an experience, and was deeply involved with tickets, etc. Before that I didn't want to disappoint Janetta, who was so excited by the idea, and Magouche only made up her mind at the very last moment. I saw (rightly) what a splendid bolster-banister she would be. For some curious reason it's a fortifying relief to realise this – that I never wanted to come, I mean.

Of course I am enjoying many things enormously – our

morning in the Kremlin, the Pushkin, the two Chekhov plays, Zagorsk.

3 March, Leningrad

Yesterday was another cold morning, snowing. I packed my bags and set off in a taxi with Janetta and Magouche to the Novadevichi Monastery. This was an item on my own special list, but alas, the church was shut. The taxi man was amiable and agreed to come back for us in an hour and actually did. No *nyet*-man he. Janetta and Magouche wanted him to wait for us, a typical form of extravagance, but he said he couldn't do this. A bus-load of German tourists were also plodding round. We penetrated the long hall of the monastery where two bodies laid out for burial were more sweet-scented than the old hippo ladies and priests crowding the passage outside. Then we walked through the snow, down towards the river Moskva lying invisible under the general whiteness. Crocodiles of healthy children, rosy and well-wrapped little bears, a sleeping swathed baby being pulled on a sledge, boys doing flat skiing. We seemed suddenly to be in the country. Rather a good lunch at the Metropole; it is grander than the Europa. Afterwards we pounded about through the endless halls of GUM, where the proletariat were avidly buying things, and sparrows chirped stridently in the glass roof. Magouche and Janetta shopped enthusiastically, chiefly for children's felt boots. I found nothing to buy.

The blessed white witch vodka turned our departure in a flurry of snow into an adventure. Fur-hatted figures paced the platform under the high vault of the station and soon the big red train steamed in. A woman knocked off the icicles hanging from the letters ЛЕНИГРАД on its side, and they jangled to the platform. There were two berths reserved for us in one carriage, one in the next, where I was quickly joined by a small Russian female tub. Janetta and Magouche most sweetly offered to change, but I felt a moral obligation not to be too fussy, and stayed with my tub.

4 March

How greatly I prefer Leningrad and its inhabitants to Moscow and the Muscovites. They smile at us, they show desire to help rather than stubborn non-response.

We are at the old Europa and all have identical suites of the sort that Kitty and I had in '65 – hall, large bathroom, bedroom and alcove. My companions, however, cannot be satisfied with anything; nothing is quite good enough for them. I think their creative impulses must be starved! Magouche had to move her bed out from the wall to get more light, not noticing that the light swivelled; she turned round her writing-desk, and sent for 'Bolshoi' light bulbs. (A large friendly woman has just brought me tea and lemon, toast, delicious blackcurrant jam and butter.)

At first sight, under a pale blue sky, Leningrad looked warmer than Moscow in the snow. But our walk up the Nevsky Prospekt soon showed us that it was not. Not only is the *fond de l'air* extremely cold, but an icy wind sweeps round corners and grips one's throat. My Angora scarf is a godsend. My hottest outfit is thermal underwear, jersey and quilted jacket, thick tights, woollen trousers, fur coat, boots, gloves and hat. A lot of this has to come off and be put on again at every visit to a museum or restaurant. It is splendidly warm indoors. Near the Hermitage, groups of charming little 'bears' were happily playing in the snow.

It was a delight to take the Hermitage slowly – today the

Poussins, Chardins, Watteaus – and this time I noticed the rooms and furniture more.

Magouche and Janetta have been shopping and returned with jams, tea, tisanes and Nescafé. They have two little boiling outfits and spend hours brewing various hot drinks, their eyes blazing with obsessional pleasure. I hear the bubbling and hissing whenever I go into their rooms. I stick to whisky, which I prefer. We have taken to Scrabble in Janetta's room. They have just told me that in Moscow a boy asked them to change money to send to his relations in England. He said he liked England, that the police were 'bad here'. They told him they couldn't, and he said with deep feeling, 'For GOD's sake do it.' It must have been harrowing, but they didn't give in; I don't quite know why.

5 March

Almost imperceptible snow falling yesterday morning, when we set off rather late to the statue of Peter the Great and St Isaac's (shut). To the Hermitage with Janetta, where we lost each other in the lavatory. Glorious Rembrandts, sordid cafeteria snack, Rembrandts again. One can now get *The Times* here, from under the counter and at a cost of six shillings. Dropping with exhaustion, I staggered back, lay on my bed and read it.

In the evening to Mussorgsky's *Khovanshchina* at the Kirov Theatre, reopening after its redecoration. A special gala occasion, and it was wonderfully pretty in its new dress of gold and baby blue. The opera superbly put on and well sung. Though enjoying it enormously, we were quite unable to follow the complicated plot and came away before the end to avoid the rush for transport or a cold, long walk home. Russian basses are splendid. At eleven-twenty, with one and a half acts still to go (and not a bite or sup since lunch) we squeezed into a crowded bus smelling strongly

33

of drink; fur hats were nodding round us and I saw hardly anyone insert their 'honour' payment into the automatic machine. It was indeed almost a physical impossibility to reach it. (This was the only occasion when I induced my companions to use public transport.) The fur hats woke up and got out at their stop, to my amazement.

6 March

A blue sky appeared early; by lunch-time there was brilliant sunshine and it was thawing fast. Now and again the ice in huge pipes broke up suddenly and disgorged an excremental sausage onto the pavement with a crash. Men shovelled snow from the roofs and we walked in danger, but on the shady side of the Fontanka the roofs were still white and fringed with long, glittering icicles. A feeling of spring cheerfulness infected the crowds in the streets and many were buying flowers and fruit (expensive apples and oranges). We took a taxi to Peter and Paul's Fortress. Thence Janetta guided us deftly to Peter the Great's wooden house. To the Astoria for quite a good, dilatory lunch, and walked home along the Fontanka.

Janetta, who was feeling unwell, cried off the evening's entertainment – a concert of folk music. I enjoyed its high spirits, the talented balalaika player and singers, cheerful colours, and very genuine if humble audience. All round us were the barrel shapes and stout legs of women who looked as though they had been shovelling snow all day. They loved the traditional music and the high, clear voices singing comic songs; there was no chattering and moving about, only utter absorption. I would have liked to stay to the end, but deferred to Magouche's obvious feeling that half was enough. We had been driven there by a sweet young taxi man with a rosy face and dimples who absolutely refused to take a single kopek for his fare. What can have inspired him? Desire to be friendly to foreigners? When Janetta and I were in the main bookshop trying to get translations of Chekhov, a young man with a sensitive, intelligent face asked in excellent English if he could help us. He told us he read a lot in English. What did he like? Oh, Dickens and Shakespeare of course, but 'many, many – Hemingway, Kingsley Amis'. We would have liked to offer to send him English books but didn't dare.

7 *March*

My realisation that a second visit is less exciting than the first obscures the question: has IT deteriorated or improved? 'Things in the shops' are no better; 'they' perhaps look more prosperous and well-dressed; one can get *The Times*. Janetta is very much disgruntled and depressed by IT – I sometimes fear she is disappointed and emotionally upset by the whole adventure. I have woken this morning embarrassed by realising this and feeling that it was partly my enthusiasm that fired her to come, and that though I truly came chiefly for her sake, it is she who is now unhappy. I spoke to Magouche about this; I'm not quite clear what she feels, as she is so anxious to please. I don't think Janetta will regret having come, however.

We used our half-day trip coupons on an afternoon guided expedition to Tsarskoe Selo in a bus with a young English couple. Our little female guide was intelligent, and answered all our questions about wages, living conditions, with apparent frankness. As we drove through the hideous blocks of flats (she lives in one), she said that before the Revolution this region had been covered with peasant shacks, where they lived without water, light, sanitation and transport. Now they have all these, and two bedrooms, sitting-room, bath and kitchen per family.

The great palace looked wonderful, standing in bright blue state in the snow. As we walked in the park, the guide and I talked about books. She told me how she adored Dickens (their favourite English writer, it seems) and I told her how I loved Turgenev. So did she, but her daughters found him too old-fashioned. Members of her 'groups' had given her a book on Nicholas and Alexandra to read. Her criticisms were sharp, but we all thought fair. It was 'sentimental', and she 'almost laughed when she read about the *poor* Tsar dancing with tears in his eyes after his coronation, because owing to an error a few hundred peasants had been shot by his soldiers'. She thought him the 'most irresponsible of all the Tsars'. I would have thought 'incapable' was nearer the mark.

8 March

After various tussles with Intourist we left for the Hermitage, with an introduction from a Russian botanist Magouche knows who has telephoned the director or his secretary, to let us see the Scythian gold. We were shown into the office of a gentle, scholarly, washed-out elderly woman, who treated us with unmixed kindness, talked to us in French – though her English was quite good – and promised to take us into the basement after lunch. Saw the Cézannes and other modern French pictures; some of the Matisses have been sent to Czechoslovakia. A girl student, an American, approached Magouche and told her she had been here nine months. What was it like? Hard. The work? Yes, that, and the life too. They slept in dormitories. But she loved it here. Did they manage to have some fun? Oh yes, *lots*; but it was all in private houses and apartments.

The Scythian gold was both extraordinary and beautiful. Along with it was a collection of precious objects, jewels and jewelled boxes from Tsarist times. Having exhausted our admirable guide and ourselves, we crept home and I fell on my bed feeling I would never rise again. But I did, and washed my hair, and then at Magouche's bidding rushed across the road to a Beethoven concert in their chief concert hall. We were in the front row, under the grand piano, looking at the unlikely lower half and 'pig's-trotter shoes'[1] of the female soloist pressing the pedals. The orchestra sat up very straight and stiff, holding out their violins as if they didn't belong to them, the pudgy unathletic hands of the second violins hardly ever leaving the first position. They played the 'Pastoral' Symphony in an academically correct and unemotional style.

9 March

I misjudged the weather yesterday; today the searching wind came through and froze me to the marrow, so that I ended my day tucked in bed with *Middlemarch*, and missing dinner.

13 March

Woken at six (soon to become four by western time) and driven to the airport, arriving far too early, for a short, tranquil and empty flight.

Coming over the Kentish coast with my thoughts focused on grass and green (*Verde que te quiero verde*) I looked down and saw it as white with snow as Poland or Russia.

Round and round we went above London (no snow here) with the sun first on this side then on that, till at last we swooped down through the opaque clouds with that strange feeling of not altogether unpleasant finality.

---

1 A phrase of Molly MacCarthy's, the writer and wife of Sir Desmond MacCarthy.

So what remains of this visit to Russia for me personally? The conviction that it's my last, for one thing. And several characteristic sounds: the clickety-click of the abacus in the restaurant, the high, wild, repetitive singing on a record I bought for Sophie, the noise of shovelling snow.

14 March

On the eve of becoming seventy, I have been feeling it something obscene and to be ashamed of; then came the determination to be more realistic. In the event I have been deeply touched by the kindness of friends. Janetta has just given a delicious lunch for me at Wheeler's, with Jaime[1], Robert and Cynthia[2]. I have had flowers from the Campbells, a treat at the theatre from Margaret tonight (*Uncle Vanya*) and a most unexpected telegram from Lennox and Freda Berkeley. So the dread occasion has been gently eased past as it needs to be, and this great and friendly kindness has made it tolerable. But I have thought a lot about death recently, even more than usual, and my awareness that there isn't so much further to go is not sad at all.

17 March

Good Lord, I've said nothing about Julia, yet now she is in the foreground of my thoughts. The first news I had on my return was that she had finally sent an SOS to Margaret to say she was too weak from lack of food to go on any longer. Kind Margaret hurried round, was shocked by her white, thin, ill appearance and asked if she would like to go into hospital. Unqualified YES. So she is now in the psychiatric ward of St Pancras Hospital, resting in bed, eating

1 Parladé.
2 Kee.

better (so they say) and all completely free. I've seen her twice, the first time very briefly, but my second visit yesterday preys on me. Not that she seems unhappy; in an extraordinary way it appears to have been an immense relief to her to give up, not to pretend to be all right, and leave all the business of life to others. She isn't mad, though she gets a little muddled and looks dreadfully ill; but the others in her ward are. They mostly get up during the day and go to the 'badminton and television room', but Julia very wisely refuses. So she has the light, quite pleasant ward mainly to herself. But a crazy little sprite haunted it yesterday, sitting on her bed sobbing and rocking herself, talking to imaginary people, sometimes on an imaginary telephone. And suddenly while I was talking to Julia a prostrate figure was carried through to an inner room by fierce black nurses. An attempted suicide? I could see her being laid out on the bed and hear the nurses saying crossly, 'Now then, Ada, what have you been up to, eh?' Julia's face expressed only a mild surprise. Indeed it expressed very little on the whole – not the ghost of a smile, merely a gaunt despair which I found dreadfully tragic. She told me how she had fallen and hurt her chest while trying to get to the lavatory in the night. She talked almost in a whisper, and said her chest hurt, and in every way behaved like someone whose least movement was agony and effort. I fetched her water, propped her pillows, but her sad, dead expression didn't change. Yet she *didn't* (wonderfully enough) *complain*. I drove off to dinner with the Campbells feeling shaken and rather crazy myself. It is always necessary to her to blame someone for her sufferings, and if Lawrence is the First Villain, I believe she has cast me for the Second.

Bunny[1] has just been to lunch. Discussing Janetta and Mag-

---

1 Garnett.

ouche in Russia, as I do partly to pin down and clarify my feelings, he suggested that they were manifestations of Veblen's 'Conspicuous Waste', and I remembered that this had often been at the back of my mind in Russia. Although Bunny himself is extremely generous and hospitable, he says he has always disliked it, and so did Maynard Keynes. It is the philosophical implications that interest me; also the odd fact that both Magouche and Janetta have experienced being very short of money.

19 March
Like a cow, I often go on chewing the cud of recent experience, at least when it has coagulated in such a form as my Russia-provoked thoughts about privilege, conspicuous waste and self-indulgence.

Today I visited Mary,[1] whose mood was antipodal to my own. I found her discussing with a tall man, rather attractive in a smooth way, the renting of a yacht for the summer. Her questions about Poland were all directed towards embassy life and palaces with footmen behind your chair and I felt, rightly or wrongly, the implication that everyone must always long to mix with the rich and the grand.

21 March
I can understand the impulse behind those pathetic novels by immature young men – Isobel[2] showed me one – which merely describe futile attempts to write a novel, and ultimate failure. They long to express something for expression's sake, but hardly know what. The ego, struggling in a morass of rich and partly

1 Dunn.
2 Strachey.

horrible experience, wants to respond to as much as possible, and usually fails. The cosmos is extraordinary, enormous, stimulating, yet – seated in the midst of it all – one suddenly wearies and craves oblivion, wants to forget. The death instinct? Perhaps what is needed is just a rest – not to think about it for a bit, but play spiritual Bingo and switch on the television of memory, rather than spur oneself on. Why? Out of a deep conviction that life itself is important, is good, is meant to be lived – even if the world as a whole is none of these things (accepting that life is part of the world). I do feel guilty when I do the first, yet as one grows older it's probably necessary to throw a handkerchief over one's face now and again and take a nap, and set aside the deep conviction that it's desirable to employ all faculties, all the time, as fully as possible, sense-perception, thought, speculation.

Oh, the plight of those of us who have nothing ahead but the increasing obscenity of old age. Where's the way out? How to escape without giving others a painful sense of guilt (quite undeserved) or the equally painful duty of identifying one's body?

Friends die and will go on doing so as long as one lives. There are fewer and fewer people one is effortlessly at ease with. What is left, then, when making social efforts becomes too much? Self-love – but at the moment I dislike myself thoroughly.

Chekhov on death: 'It's a cruel thing, a disgusting punishment. It arouses something bigger than terror . . . It is disgusting to think of it.'

I found a book about him, reminiscences by various friends. What an angel he seems to have been, nothing in him one can't admire – sensitive, realistic, kind. Tolstoy said of him, watching him walk on the lawn with his daughter: 'Ah, what a beautiful magnificent man; modest, quite like a girl. He's simply wonderful.'

On Sunday at Kitty West's, sweet spring weather. I went alone to pick daffodils in the wood. The birds set up a tirra-lirra, her cat prowled off into the undergrowth, the twigs sparkled with buds, and there were even pink flowers on the peach. How soothing the English country is.

24 March
The Berkeleys, Magouche, Eardley and Michael Holroyd to dinner. I thought Michael was pretending to be more cynical than he really is.

26 March
Another visit to Julia in her psychiatric home yesterday. Finding her bed empty, I was looking about when a tall, good-looking, youngish man asked if he could help. He turned out to be her doctor, Alan Gardner. When I asked, he said, in some ways she was better, but they were worried about her physically, and taking all sorts of tests. I found her in a sitting-room upstairs reading the paper, her eyes curiously suffused with pink, as I now remember – perhaps she's using them more than before. It was a largish, impersonal room with a circle of chairs in which one or two stout dummies were sitting in absolute silence. A young, rather attractive girl came in briefly and addressed Julia by her christian name. Julia said, 'He always does that.' 'It's a she,' said the dummy next to us. 'I must remember that,' said Julia. I can't get over the feeling that she's *extremely* ill – indeed it increases. She spoke quietly and indistinctly. I did my best to guess at what she meant, but sometimes it was impossible. At other moments, mind and voice cleared together, and she would answer some question about Chekhov quite sensibly. But the impression is as of someone who has had a stroke. There are signs of intolerance of her

surroundings – the food is appalling, quite uneatable, cabbage with all the vitamins boiled away, etc. I was surprised she had expected anything else. The tea is undrinkable and she can't bear the canteen. Her companions are all terribly depressed and she has nothing in common with any of them. 'None of our class,' she said in a whisper, 'not a single one, and many of them awfully disagreeable.' All of this is too true. Perhaps it's only to her completely sane visitors that the insanity of the other patients would seem the worst feature. Our dummies were quiet enough, but there were occasional wild yells from down the passage. When I left she said she would go back to her ward. 'I'll come with you,' I said; but she wouldn't take my arm, only leant heavily on the banisters and climbed the stairs like a child, a foot at a time. She insisted on going *up*stairs, and said, 'Yes, this is my bed,' but the alarmingly black face of a negress nurse said, 'This isn't yours – it's the men's ward,' and down we had to go again. 'But I mustn't forget your chocolates,' she said, scrabbling under the chairs. I had taken her none, only some glossy magazines.

Every day a lot of time passes in discussions about her, between her four props – Margaret, Cynthia, Susan[1] and me. Cynthia and Susan are off to the country. Margaret and I will have to work overtime meanwhile. I feel so terribly guilty now for past irritation with her and for not taking her sometimes impossible behaviour just as a symptom that she is extremely ill. She reminds me painfully of her Aunt Marjorie, who dwindled away after a life of affection, high spirits and many interests, into soured nothingness.

---

1 Campbell.

Easter Monday Crichel

Here are Des, Raymond, Tam,[1] and Julian's friend Bryan Walsh, whom I like extremely; he is sane, interested, kind, intelligent, and all this dawns on one after an initial impression that is somewhat unattractive – bearded, plump, too short in the leg, inclined to bubble and giggle. Desmond and Tam listened to music endlessly; for me there was a surfeit but I could always withdraw. There were outbursts as usual: to Tam who had mishandled a libretto, 'Oo-OH, I see you're a crumpler!' A frenzy was aroused by the new burglar-proof windows which Desmond was unable to unfasten, and dismay by the newspapers ('Drugs in Easter Eggs!! It's really TOO awful!') and then a relapse into a look of such pink despairing loneliness as tore one's heart. But I think he enjoyed the weekend. At least he said with feeling that he wished it could go on for ever. For me it wasn't one of the very nicest. I had a feeling of a frothy soufflé layer on top of uneasiness, and experienced symptoms of withdrawal, thinking a lot about Julia and wanting to get back to London to atone by kindness to her. Then Raymond suddenly admitted that he was 'feeling awfully unwell', though he had been delighting everyone by his angelic and funny persona. Tam? Well, I thought she was restless too. Her smoking is incessant and suicidal. When once she thought Bryan had gone off with her cigarettes she became almost violently angry. She was like someone suffering from a fever only to be assuaged by listening to music, flying to the piano for short spells, and rushing out for walks. I would have guessed that she had something on her mind except that she talks freely and nothing emerges. I asked her a bit about David Gillies – he must have been an extremely important source of emotion, pleasure

---

1 Girlfriend of Julian, later Murray-Thripland.

and pain. They never now meet. Of Julian she said, to my astonishment, that she was pretty sure he would revert to being a
Catholic. Bryan has already had a heart attack at thirty-six, and
doesn't lead the life the doctors say he should, according to Tam –
that is: take walks, lose weight, smoke and drink less. But he is a
balanced man.

Cold, beautiful walks with dog Moses and other companions
in varying permutations. I took Tam to the wood to look for signs
of spring; there were almost none under the great arching trees.
I do not think, though, that her eyes are much use to her for pure
pleasure.

So I suppose the trouble about the weekend was that there
were many reminders of the human predicament, while nature –
it was fearfully cold – didn't oblige with its expected balm.

31 March

To see Julia again. She had had a lonely Easter and was glad to see
me, and much more like her old self, talking without mumbling,
and going astray less often, though she still forgets which is
upstairs and which downstairs, and thinks she has been in hospital
one week instead of three. The result is that she is now entirely
concerned with *getting out*, and feeble and muddled as she is, I
sympathise. As I reached the hospital a girl of about fifteen,
shoeless, was struggling on the gravel drive between two nurses
who were helping her up; weeping and throwing herself about,
she uttered desolating cries in a tone of heartbreak between her
sobs: 'I ca-a-an't slee-e-ep! Oh, God!' The bitter unhappiness of
the mad is really unbearable, and the more normal Julia gets the
more she notices it, of course. Otherwise there was just a
Madame Tussaud of eccentric dummies sitting about, most of
them too shut away to read or speak. The few visitors looked

frightened and, as no doubt they were, longing to be off. Julia has taken up her old 'knitting' – how to arrange her life in her flat, with someone to cook at £10 a week for four evenings. No sign of traumatic horror at returning to loneliness there. Indeed, how could it be worse than where she is when she becomes fully aware of her surroundings? 'And there's nowhere to work,' she said suddenly.

2 April

I'm shaking like a leaf and have taken to the whisky bottle. Peter Jenkins[1] has just rung up. It has been clear for some days that poor Charlotte[2] is near her end, and now it seems as though she might not last out the night – how I hope she does not. Peter wanted me to get in touch with Isobel, and find out how much she realises. I said I'd try and get her here tonight, and at once – but she won't come. So I've had to be content with saying I'll go round to her at any moment and be ready – to do what? Once again there is this agonising desire to help, and lack of certainty how.

Later: Peter rang almost as I was writing this. 'Charlotte has just died.' Terrible, pregnant words. Death is truly as Chekhov said, 'a cruel thing, a disgusting punishment'. I told him I would go to Isobel at once, and as I drove off in my Mini of course I felt the echo of a journey over six years ago. It is unsafe to assume that people react to grief in the same way; this is what puts a peculiar strain on the comforter. She has to intensify her sensitiveness and stretch her powers of apprehension to the utter-

---

1 Journalist and friend of Burgo's.
2 His wife and the only daughter of Isobel Strachey; she had had leukaemia for several years. From early childhood she and Burgo had been great friends.

most to see what the other person wants or needs. I have on occasion failed in the past to realise that they wanted to talk and weep out their horror and dismay. With Isobel I'm sure I was right in taking the cue that, while not shirking the facts, she didn't want to give way to emotion. She took to a punt, not a boat with a keel. And I got on board with her, sparing myself the depths of sadness when possible, but I noticed as so often before that sad grammatical sign of using the present tense: 'Charlotte has . . .'

Lovely visit to Anne and Heywood last weekend. Lucy[1] came and we had a brief glimpse of her new boyfriend with whom she is going to India – a dark, quiet Scotch Geordie, with gentle and reliable aura. Lucy is obviously mad about him and I've never seen her look so happy, which was a nice thing to be able to say to Anne and Heywood. There's still very little sign of spring in the grey-green grass and grey-brown ploughed fields. Only a melodious twittering when my train stopped at country stations, and prowling round the garden I saw a few bursting buds and blue and yellow flowers.

17 April

Visit to Julia. As I went in, an almighty banging began on the glass door into the ward opposite hers. Nurses gathered like bees: 'STOP THAT!' A patient was bashing with her plate because she wanted some more sandwiches. Julia appeared, nervous and desperate-looking, and at first I think took me for Margaret, who was on her mind. 'Terrible things are going on here! Do you know about them?' I shepherded her into the waiting-room, but she was quivering so that she couldn't hold her tea without spilling it, and her eyes full of tears. She talked at random; she

---

1 The Hills' daughter.

wants to go away and no one will listen to her. No wonder, as Dr Gardner is away for a week. She 'began at the beginning', saying that she had come there on the understanding that she would be free to leave, that she was to be fed up and gain weight (but of course the food was inedible). There were signs of indignation against Margaret. I worked hard for an hour trying to get the perspective more favourable, a very important thing being (so I feel) to say, 'Of course you can go when you want to,' for I think she only *half* wants to. Open the door of the cage and the bird doesn't fly out. Sometimes she is puzzled by the effort to latch on to what one is saying, and answers what one hasn't said. Once or twice she thought we were being spied on from behind the waiting-room door. It upset me dreadfully to see her so distressed; her tearful, quivering face was pitiful, but I think I did reassure her a bit. It's a pure toss-up whether one is subjected to maniac behaviour, screams, antics, or none – as yesterday, when I just saw a husband arrive to see his wife and take her outside to sit on a bench in the faint spring sun. The mad are not only terribly sad, but also rather horrid; or else it is that we sane manage to hide our horridness.

Long discussion with Margaret afterwards. Susan reports that Lawrence has gone about looking like death since first he heard the news. (He rang me up a few days ago and I gave him the facts as clear and unloaded as possible.)

Julian last night; lovely evening, and a lot of talk about Tramores. He doesn't think Janetta is well, though the trouble is obscure. What? It makes me very anxious. And he says that her obsession with the *horror* of Russia never wavers. She even said that one of the awful things about it was that nothing grew there. How could it, in the snow? Ivan Moffat had been at Tramores; his wife has gone off with that rather caddish Peter Townsend.

20 April

Spring fever driving down to Lambourn, and almost ditching myself at the sight of minuscule lambs, flowering trees, etcetera. Lunched with splendid Alix and her brother Philip – Alix's animated face and sparkling eyes show that she has come to terms with life. Talking of Julia's fear of being alone, she said she enjoyed it. Philip talked with refreshing rationalist extremism about *not* going to church.

24 April

Too much of too various things. I have been suffering from spiritual indigestion, but I am now just off for a week to the Slade and Alderney and I hope that a sauna bath of natural beauty will restore my perspective.

The Julia crisis has been frantic. Margaret working overtime to find somewhere for her to go, telephoning and writing.

A moral struggle to force myself to go and see Julia. I said I would like to present her with two weeks in a luxury nursing home pending arrangements. Julia, firmly: 'I don't want to go.' What about the private room at the end of the public sitting-room, I asked. No one had told her about it, said Julia, and obviously envisaged a comfortably furnished, tastefully decorated flatlet, for when we peered in and saw a bright little square room with large window looking onto the daffodils, she said, 'It's rather bleak and hygienic, isn't it? Not quite the sort of furnishing one would like.' When I suggested a table to type or write at might make it habitable, she brightened a little. But there were signs of the old pernickety, tart Julia – complaining of 'terrible draughts round one's legs'; not having any of her clothes washed; of her distress because of Dr Gardner mentioning her 'confusion', 'when he was talking to *you*'. 'But I've never talked to him!' I cried. I think she confuses me with Margaret. Of visitors arriving without notice 'interrupting her work'. (Her 'work' was reading an illustrated magazine) . . .

Last night came Peter Jenkins, a very balanced and stable bereaved husband. I respect and admire his rational approach to the problem of Amy,[1] his obvious deep grief for Charlotte, admiration of her 'extraordinary bravery and elegance', and yet the realism with which he talked of his 'girlfriend'. I hear she is Polly Toynbee, daughter of Philip.

26 April, the Slade

Came down here with Eardley, jabbering all the way, and also here, except when with total ease we both dip into books or go off on our separate occupations. Yes, undoubtedly he is one of my friends with whom I feel most entirely relaxed. Tomorrow we go to Alderney, but my God, what are we in for? The cold today is appalling. A violent southwest wind, raging like an angry lion, has this morning veered to the north. All nature stands still; at least the woods we gaze at from our windows are an unrelieved furry brown. I walked off to them yesterday; the wind blew my eyelids shut and nearly capsized me. It is *disgusting* weather. A few primroses, violets and wood anemones have made their shamefaced appearance, but the daffodils in the garden are blown to the ground. How horribly impossible it is to ignore what *IT*'s up to in the country – something one should be thankful for in London. I do feel the relief of not being on the Julia assembly line, though she returns to my mind whenever I close my eyes. Here at the Slade everything is simple, cooking, looking after ourselves. I am preparing myself to be a sensitised photographic

---

1 Daughter of Peter and Charlotte Jenkins.

plate in Alderney. If only – if only – this raging north wind would give over . . .

27 April

So off we go and thank heavens for a blue sky, though it's still cold. The beech buds opposite my window are in a state of readiness to burst that is painful to look at, like a very pregnant woman. I am determined to examine this little island with loving and scrupulous thoroughness and get to know every corner of it, like a strange flower brought back from the mountains.

Last night there was a programme about Leningrad on the television which, though not particularly good, brought a gulp of emotion rising in my throat. It had caught certain things about the Russians and their way of life, rather than the beauty of the town – their serious devotion to rebuilding their splendid buildings, and to the ballet, theatre and education; their simple-looking, rather ugly but well-meaning moon-shaped faces; their gloriously happy healthy children; the sense that their country and their life and their town was theirs, so that they didn't want to mess it up, felt responsible for it – the essentially peaceloving, friendly and trustful nature of the Leningraders.

4 May

Back now from my breathless week in Alderney, and have stepped into full summer. Yes, Eardley, Dadie[1] and I *did* get to know our island; from the moment we saw it spread like a soft green map beneath our tiny, slim, yellow eight-seater aeroplane on Monday to the similar view on Saturday, by which time it was thoroughly

1 Dr George Rylands, Professor of English at King's College, Cambridge.

known, understood and absorbed into my being and I saw it left behind with a pang.

We were out all and every day, three of them magnificently sunny; we lunched twice on grassy ledges on the cliffs; we walked round every bit of the coast and down every lane. It was a great success for all three. We all loved it in the same way and wanted to do the same sort of thing. Dadie was tremendous fun and constantly enjoyable as a companion even when being the complete scoutmaster. 'Wholesome' is his favourite word, used half ironically. He walked me off my legs, going at a spanking rate, and often six yards ahead of Eardley and me, his comically purposeful figure, head poking forward on his rather sloping shoulders in a floppy windcheater, striding and striding. On our hot days he was happy to lie and read, and I searched for flowers; when the mists closed in he managed to make me walk much faster than I wanted to, for all my determination not to. What would he have said if I'd asked, 'Why so fast?' We all liked whisky, buying postcards, discussion, jokes, Scrabble. Dadie made his own rules for this, and was wildly competitive; however I beat him, in spite of his firmly squashing any word he hadn't heard of, like 'almug', all colloquialisms and words of foreign origin, etc. There was hardly time for me to list and look up my flowers, or read, and none at all for this book.

6 May

I visited Julia again yesterday. Little change. She is coherent one moment, muddled the next. We took a rather alarmingly wobbly walk together across the zebras to 'the shops' where she wanted to berate 'White' the newspaper man (really 'Brown') for continuing to send papers. She leant across the counter and did this with snakish sharpness; but the shop was obviously used to the hospital patients. Once she shot at me, after her soft voice had failed to get through the thunder of the traffic, 'Are you deafer than ever?' I replied that thank God I was not in the least deaf, which is true, and I think she was confusing me with Margaret once again.

Getting home, I heard from poor Susan the terribly upsetting news that Robin [Campbell] has had a heart attack and is in hospital. The blows fall thick and fast on all sides and above this tragic scene lowers a new political cloud of unspeakable horror in the East. That brute Nixon, out of wickedness or futility, has spread the Vietnamese war into Cambodia. I can hardly bear to read about it, it makes my heart beat so fast. What a nightmare world! I begin to dread what Philip [Dunn] may say on the subject next weekend, as I feel it is not something to be treated lightly and he's sure to take the unspeakable view.

How tiny, vulnerable and unimportant seem my own activities in face of this world horror and the sinking of various friends into death or confusion.

By way of contrast, Gerald [Brenan] has written me one of his most unsympathetically boastful letters – complaining of his architect ('I think I can get him to yield, especially as he speaks of me as his best client and has a respect for me and my books'), jealous of a young man who had been spending hours with Lynda ('There was absolutely no occasion for it as she is not and could not be attracted to him . . . in the past two years she has not liked any of the few we have seen except Peter Townsend, who is irresistible to girls. But the moment she felt an attraction to him she avoided him as, seeing his character and her life with me, she did not intend to get mixed up with him. In any case he had too much regard for me to have made up to her.') Then he envisages the future – 'Some day she will leave me, if I live long enough.

Life without her would be worse than death for me and then I have never been left by any woman in my life, if one excepts Carrington, and such a prospect rouses in me an almost crazy pride. I know what I should do if that happens – vanish to Mexico or a Greek island and never write to anyone again. I could not hold up my head again without her.' Later he says, 'I often think of the injury I did Ralph at Watendlath. Innocence, immersion in Shelley on ideas of love and so forth. But it was betrayal.'[1] I'm glad he has realised *that* at long last. One of the first memorable things Ralph said to me was that he had discovered the futility of pride. 'I was as proud as Lucifer once, and it did me no good at all.' Perhaps Gerald's betrayal did the trick.

From Cynthia I hear that Patrick Woodcock has been to Julia's hospital, and told Cynthia that the position is hopeless. She has 'senile dementia'. Cynthia sounded quite shattered, and I have maligned her in thinking her unable to accept illness. She is merely too soft-hearted to do so.

15 May

Julia is back at Percy Street. She came to dinner last night with Bunny and Eardley. She told me she had 'learned her lesson', which is, I hope, to drop purple hearts and keep on eating. With her return to sanity comes a good deal of her old tartness. I asked if she liked her new maid. 'No, not much.' And when I said I'd been to see Pansy,[2] she said, 'Oh, bad luck.' About her sister Barbara she is ambivalent; half piqued that she won't have her to

---

1 Brenan is referring to making love to Carrington shortly after Ralph's marriage to her. See *Memories* (Phoenix).
2 Lamb, wife of Henry.

live with her for ever, half desirous to prove that it would be awful to live with her for three months.

On my way to tea with Pansy yesterday, forcing my Mini through the gut of Kensington Road, constipated with smelly shining cars, a distaste for it all rose and overwhelmed me – the ugliness, clatter, futility and the toothache I have had on and off for several weeks. *What* to put on the other side of the balance sheet? The exquisitely pale and feathery green of the trees in the park? But while registering it I think: how many times has all this come round; and though not exactly a stale sensation, it has an element of sadness.

17 May, Litton Cheney, abed Sunday morning

How the Stones[1] pamper one and treat one as 'special' – impossibly so – resulting in guilt feelings. My fellow-guest is that gross object Leslie Hartley, who has become so repellently fat, and such a dedicated full-time hypochondriac and insomniac that it is surprising to hear him say something perceptive or funny, as he often does. His fat can hardly be thought of as such, but is more like liquid in a silken container. Can he be unaware of the impression he makes, and is it in spite of or because of it that he tries to ingratiate himself by pawing, patting and nuzzling up? I had just pounded quickly through his last book, a hopeless affair, when he rang the front doorbell (the Stones had gone out) and stood there, mottled and perplexed, in front of one of the bearded thugs he employs to drive him, and whom (he told me later) he had just quarrelled with and sacked. Since then he has slept and talked about not sleeping so much that I have retired with relief to the third eleven of insomniacs. He has thrice said to me in a

---

1 Reynolds, an engraver, and Janet.

meaning, confidential tone, 'I think my insomnia comes from *below the belt*', my eye naturally gliding to what is there – a great smooth rounded protuberance which must have caused his tailor much difficulty.

We were a large party for dinner – the delightful Hubbards,[1] both of whom I find immensely attractive, and Sylvia Townsend Warner with her white pointed face like the Queen of Diamonds and absurd diction. I sat next to John Hubbard at dinner and talked about Chomsky whom I had been reading in the train. He (J.H.) has a delightfully quick darting mind and his eyes blink as he leaps from stepping-stone to stepping-stone. Sylvia Townsend Warner was unexpectedly forthcoming and talked to me intimately on the sofa about the death of her female mate.

Chomsky's neo-Kantianism is partly attractive, but he pushes it too far, so that he assumes that every child of whatever nationality is 'born with a knowledge of the highly restrictive principles of universal grammar'. Nor does he attempt to prove this, but merely points to it as an observable fact. Some uneducated people seem to me to go on all their lives acquiring speech and current locutions in an ape-like manner, yet I believe that *some* of what we take for the perceptual world really belongs to the structure and dimensions of the perceiving, knowing mind, to the camera rather than the landscape it is pointed at. I wish I knew where the line should be drawn, but I can't accept Chomsky's version of it.

20 May

We are not out of the Julia wood yet – oh, no. The weight of her troubles and the inability to deal with them have produced the

---

1 John and Carol.

same heavy, hag-ridden tones of voice in Cynthia, in Margaret and in me. Cynthia rang up last night 'extremely worried'. Julia's attack of 'suicidal loneliness' must literally have seized her ten minutes after she got back to her flat from the Penroses. Then Robert fetched her out to Kew for the evening and they hardened their hearts and sent her back in a minicab, although she had brought her nightdress. But though cogent, they thought she was desperate, talking of her need for 'some drug to change her mood'. Her letter to Lawrence had produced a very friendly reply enclosing a cheque for £150, which she told me about. I didn't detect – what was apparently true according to Cynthia – that she was at first furiously angry and talked of returning it and has now returned to her old daydreams of Lawrence rejecting Jenny and Laura[1] and returning to her.

21 May

Julia 'received me', no other word for it, in her flat yesterday, sitting opposite me in front of a table spread with her 'writing'. I was dumbfounded by her strikingly affected, unfriendly and unreal manner, and had the feeling I was being interviewed by my headmistress and could only gape while she rolled her eyes and allowed a series of extraordinary expressions to cross her face. Meanwhile she talked on and on and on about Lawrence, obsessionally and virulently. What would he think when her book came out describing his behaviour to her; how he had destroyed her? It might take three years to finish, of course. She would have to consult a solicitor about whether it was libellous. She didn't think he would like it much. She ran through a number of conversations and exchanges which he wouldn't be pleased to find

---

[1] Lawrence Gowing's second wife and their child.

made public. I sat with curdling blood. Then she told me he had sent her a cheque for £25 and answered her invitation 'too enthusiastically. I only wrote out of idle curiosity to see Laura. I didn't expect all this *enthusiasm*, all this talk of secret longing.' I read the letter; there was *no* mention of secret longing, it was friendly, affectionate and concerned. I remarked that she'd told me before the cheque was for £150. 'Oh, yes, I do believe it was.'

She *seemed*, however, completely on the spot – on the very odd spot she had chosen for her *querencia*. She told me Margaret had found her a new doctor. 'But of course I can't get on without purple hearts.' I exclaimed in dismay and asked how she got them. 'Through my old doctor.' So the old brute is already undermining the nine weeks' rescue work that was done in hospital!

I had been careful not to disagree with anything so far and when she pitched violently and at once into Julian ('So second rate. Why does he like awful commonplace people like Angus Wilson and John Betjeman? Why *does* he do it?') and Margaret ('She really looks so fat and awful. I do think she ought to take more trouble, with her husband involved with a younger woman') – when she did this, I thought the only thing was to change the subject before I began showing my feelings, so I said nothing, but of course the horrible rejoinders I could have made rose to my mind, like 'Taking trouble about your appearance doesn't always prevent husbands from going off with a younger woman.'

I did, however, feel that as her friend I ought not to let her reference to purple hearts pass. So I begged her to see the new doctor (she had said she might go in two or three weeks), and said I couldn't help feeling horrified that she was returning to the regime that had destroyed her appetite and health. By now I was passionately longing to go. I felt her dislike of me, expressed by this showing-off performance she was carrying out, and knew full well that beneath her criticism of Julian and Margaret were barbs aimed straight at me – *I* am much too uncritical, like far too many second-rate people, etc. *I* let myself look old and unattractive.

I hung on for a bit, digging my nails into my palms, and then went to see Robin in Bart's Hospital. The noble building, with its grey scholarly walls and air of deep seriousness, its vast empty corridors and the kind pretty faces of the nurses, may be reassuring but it seemed very much the antechamber to the tomb, and one's nose is rubbed in mortality. 'We lost two more last night,' says Robin with a quiet smile, having taken the plunge of 'accepting' its closeness. Oxygen cylinders stand by almost every bed. A young man with dark hair and moustache was having a blood transfusion in the next bed, the rusty-coloured life essence trickling down a tube into his arm. As I left I ran into a white-coated assistant clasping three little bottles of blood to his breast. It was *almost* too much – I knew for instance that I should have asked Robin exactly what his heart attack had felt like, as Cyril[1] apparently did, but it was too near the bone; I couldn't. I left moved, impressed, but shaken.

This morning I rang Julia to say I couldn't, after all, manage tomorrow evening together, chiefly (which I didn't say) because I didn't feel I could bear it so soon. She had quite forgotten about it. Then she said, 'I want to read you a lecture about purple hearts. I want you to ponder over the fact that they did me no harm at all during the ten years I was with Lawrence, and it was

---

1 Connolly.

only when my husband left me that I lost my appetite and couldn't eat.'

22 May

To Christopher Mason's film about Charleston and Duncan. A gathering of the Bloomsbury relics – Bunny, Angelica, Angus Davidson, Little Barbara, Quentin and Olivier, Raymond, Desmond, Carringtons, Penroses. Everyone was enthusiastic and indeed it is a great thing to have done. He has very sensitively caught the atmosphere of activity, peace, tremendous fun, beauty, and comical ramshackleness; he has suggested through their portraits the personalities of the dead – Roger, Maynard, Vanessa. Not enough about Clive. After the film a bar was opened and a jolly party developed. Bunny, Magouche and I dined along with a beautiful American called Jane Gunther, who talked to me with love and admiration about Anthony and Lily West. She says Lily is absolutely 'brilliant' but I didn't gather in what way.

25 May, Bank Holiday, at Iden

Spring weather in full bloom, speckled, spangled and sparkling. Bloom too, bluish, on the distant views of the Romney Marsh and its sheep. One is always looking over something here; over a very low gate to an eye-level field with sooty black cows in it; over the clipped hedge where one of these same black cows is snuffling and shuffling and rolling a bloodshot eye; over an apple orchard to the marsh. I had forgotten how still the flowers in a garden look as it grows dusk; apple blossom falls on the lawn already sprinkled with daisies; birds chirrup their hearts out; cats prowl (but are the enemy, digging up Judy's[1] seeds). In the wood

---

1 Rendel, my eldest sister.

down the lane I came across a badger's earth and in the pond some frogs said to be imported from France were setting up an incredibly loud CO-AX! All this might sound like country peace, but there is a ceaseless stream of motors hurrying almost nose to tail to the sea and back, with a restless hubbub.

26 May, London

Janetta is here. The more restful life she has been leading, with gardening her chief occupation, has had a wonderful effect in smoothing out her dear face, and it was a delight to see and talk to her yesterday.

The Seagull was impressive, extraordinary and rather disappointing. The sets deliberately battered and unattractive, whether or not to emphasise the down-at-heel nature of the nobility of the time – the acting a trifle hysterical and over-emphatic. The stage within a stage blocked the view mentally and physically.

It was nice going there as Old Russian girls; we came back for supper at Chapel Street and I heard that Janetta is thinking of taking part of it off Magouche's hands, so as 'to be with Rose more during her last year at the Lycée'. I'm all for it, selfishly.

One of the first things Janetta said was that she was appalled and indignant at being told by Ran Antrim that she had 'hated Russia'. This wasn't true AT ALL, she said. She discriminated then between the journey and IT. I have looked back over my notes in this book and I think she *did* hate it, but I never thought she regretted having gone. Of course not. Then there was Julian's emphatic report after his visit to Tramores. I didn't withdraw, even under Janetta's anxious insistence, my impression of her not having liked Russia. As for enjoying the *experience*, well, in a sense I've never doubted that she did, but one cannot enjoy a place that one is repelled by as much as one that sets one alight.

29 May, Crichel

Some, but not much, conversation with Julian talking of love. He surprised me by saying that of course when one loves someone, one must abnegate all possessive desires and simply want them to be happy (or words to that effect). 'Easier said than done,' I said, and went on to declare that withdrawing from the complete involvement of mutual love was acutely painful and often only possible by way of an interval of hatred or indignation. (Julia has stuck in that stage for years, which most people don't do.) Julian looked and sounded aghast, and I wondered if he had ever experienced intense mutual love. I don't think so. And as I haven't ever had to dig up my roots from it except for death, I don't quite know why I feel so sure about this, but I do.

5 June

To Glyndebourne with Janetta to see *The Magic Flute* – a peculiarly magical production on a magic evening, the great green downs swelling majestically on either side of the bus that rattled this odd collection of polite and uncongenial ladies and gents to their fun. Janetta had been trying out her new white Mercedes. We ate our picnic in a sunny, windy corner of the garden, watching the confident, privileged classes sweep inelegantly past in their hideous clothes.

Janetta has suggested asking Julia to come out to Spain when I do. I rather think she will refuse, and am not sure that it would be a success if she accepted; Janetta prognosticates that she would vent her criticisms of her way of life on me, which is highly probable.

Even Margaret's infinite good nature is beginning to wilt under

Julia's constant expectations that she will take on every task like a camel and bear endless criticism at the same time.

Janetta has just been to lunch and started talking at once; we talked for two hours, interestingly, poignantly, which left her with a look of serenity she has not had for years. With this has come an air of youth and enhanced beauty. I say for the twentieth time: she is a uniquely valuable, rare and fine person – and I love her most deeply.

Goncourt journals so nearly finished that I dwell on every sentence, belatedly, since I have really not appreciated them. Today I looked up the parody in the last volume of Proust – but it is so much better than Goncourt himself. If only he had Proust's power of visual elaboration, instead of chucking one an occasional, highly coloured sentence. Or if only his sentences were longer. Or less concerned with chitchat. Proust has caught his tricks of style, but so could any *New Statesman* parodist.

10 June
The heat! *On étouffe.* After Janetta left me yesterday, having drunk wine at lunch, I fell on my bed and dozed off, to be woken by an unearthly clap of thunder, a few heavy drops of rain and the strong, evocative stench of wet dust.

13 June, Lawford, for the Aldeburgh Festival
Came here with Raymond yesterday; he told me he had been worried and distressed by Julia, who seemed in a sleepwalker's haze all the evening we both dined with him. They talked for a long time about Matisse before he discovered she was really thinking of Bonnard.

I feel motherly tenderness and protective feelings towards

Raymond, who told me he was 'dreading' coming here, I don't quite know why.

NB. When he says, 'Ah!' in response to some remark, one knows it has bored him.

I was pleased to see Phyllis[1] stalking along the platform with a more birdlike gait than ever, partly because – poor creature – she has been suffering excruciating sciatica from a ripped nerve in the spine, and this constant pain has also increased her hair-shirted St Sebastian air.

The marvellously cloudless yet fresh blue and green June weather goes on unstintingly, and we walked out into the garden, whereupon a speckled thrush and a hen blackbird, both clearly well-known characters to Phyllis, at once advanced and took food from her hands while she sat with a look of satisfaction that was a pleasure to see. Where she has got with her other ideology, and without Phil's[2] guidance, I don't know, but I suspect God and the next world are in for good, also spook manifestations. Politics? After our evening drinks she talked excitedly of the wickedness of estate duties, and how she might '*have* to go and live in Guernsey' like her mother. I feel such reasoning must be bosh.

Leslie Hartley, our other fellow-guest, dreaded by both Raymond and me, has made no will, silly old bugger, although he has a worse life than any of us. Round as a ball, he arrived, driven by his same scoundrelly Figaro, rather late for dinner. All, all is the same. Endless talk about insomnia and sleeping pills, even the same remark about insomnia coming from 'below the belt'. Fairly drunk last night, he became grossly repellent, with his odd way of loudly smacking his lips. This

---

1 Lady Nichols.
2 Her husband.

morning he was somewhat humanised.

Dinner with the Gladwyns. Lots to drink, delicious food, Gladwyn less formidable than usual, and railing against both Powell and Heath; the 'Telephone-Dolly'[1] got up as a jolly clown, in a funny hat and with brightly painted face. Her great amiability is disarming. Dicky and Denis[2] next night, good as gold but talking compulsively about themselves. Two Shuckburghs, ex-ambassador from Rome, civilised people, to lunch.

But alas, poor Leslie! What a deplorable man he now is, whatever he once may have been. After describing his sleepless nights in every detail every morning at breakfast, he announced on Sunday that he didn't feel well enough to go to the Shos-takovich concert and would get his *funeste* 'man' to fetch him from Lawford instead, thus selfishly putting out everyone's plans, especially Raymond's, who was to have driven back with him. He was no great loss, but when Phyllis and I returned at midnight after a whole day at the Festival we found an immense written message from the butler: 'Mr Hartley has left behind the key to his own sitting-room' (presumably taken to protect his booze from his 'man'). 'Would Mrs Partridge bring it to London and the "man" would fetch it from her flat. Would her ladyship,' etc., etc. Reading his last book but one – *The Betrayal* – has filled me with disrespect for him. It's about a near-seventy-year-old spoiled baby of a bachelor who expects and receives devotion from loving women – aunts, would-be wife, and servants, only to be betrayed by a blackmailing secretary. The hero is a faithful self-portrait and it's impossible to imagine that Leslie expects his readers to find him attractive. Yet I'm sure he does, and I believe the real

---

1 His wife, Cynthia.
2 Chopping and Wirth-Miller.

L.P.H. has many devoted friends. I can't imagine what they get out of his company.

16 June, London

Feeling remarkably well and sure of a good report on my check-up from Dr Monynihan, it was disconcerting to be told that my blood pressure was up, too high in fact, though 'it had been higher'. Inevitably my foundations received a little shake, part of which functions as a way of reconciling me to the inevitable. But I like and trust him. He is giving me stronger pills. Damn.

Rattling round, unmoored by work, but so occupied that I am at the moment glad to be so.

20 June

I am off to Spain in three days, and feel less like any single person or thing than a pack of cards that is being constantly shuffled. *Six-thirty*, Julia has just been here, bringing letters and envelopes and brown paper and purple hearts, one of which she has swallowed in order to give herself strength to combine them together. One letter was a scrawled 'stinker' to the matron of her hospital, complaining of her having described her as 'confused', but proving that she is by, for the hundredth time, referring to her 'four weeks' in hospital, when they were really nine.

21 June

Yet again – failure, *total*, with Julia. Yet again she flounced out of my flat banging the door and saying that we are constitutionally unfitted to get on with each other. I must accept this, and failure too, which is always disagreeable.

I think her mental state is by no means all right. She told me she wanted to ring up Margaret at Thorington, and I discovered that the reason was to find out the address of the hospital she had been in. When I said I could give it her, she admitted that she hadn't the least idea where it was, not even that it was in London. All she wanted to do in my flat, which could not be done in hers, was tie up a parcel of some clothes she had borrowed and put the letters (substituting a milder one to matron) in envelopes. She had no idea how many stamps went on a letter.

23 June

Beside the stupendous eccentricity and incoherence of what's called ordinary life, flying seems regulated and normal – a return to a baby's existence, where one is fed, pushed in a pram and carried from place to place without volition or effort.

Aeroplane less than half full; soothing, untraumatic flight.

24 June

Janetta was waving from Málaga Airport terrace, and in no time we were purring along the familiar yet ever-deteriorating coast road in her magnificent white Mercedes. It is incredibly luxurious, privileged and comfortable. I capitulated to its grandeur at once and delighted in her delight in it. At Marbella we drew in beside Jaime's little old house, now doomed to be pulled down, and looking forlorn and dwarfed by a huge skeleton block of flats going up next door. Enter suddenly Jaime in a red check shirt disgruntled by a business lunch. We didn't linger but set off for Benahavis. The country isn't nearly so parched and papery as in August – there's a lovely lot of green and some flowers. Very smoothly and tenderly Janetta took her superb car through the ford and there we were met by Georgie, Jean-Pierre and their sweet little Chloe, laughing and with forget-me-not-blue eyes.

Janetta has a huge staff. There are a married couple, dark,

beaky-nosed Temi (who has a wry intelligent expression and rattling talk); there is the washerwoman, 'Auntie'. We live therefore in old-fashioned luxury, and as Janetta shops and cooks, it's hard to know what the servants do. 'Almost nothing,' she says. But they are a happy community, and this is invaluable to her, even though they eat mountains of food.

The house has not changed, but blossomed and burgeoned, putting out new embellishments everywhere – plates, jugs, pictures. Every time Jaime comes he brings it a 'present'. (Last night he had a glass picture of the Virgin under his arm.)

I had merely nibbled my one o'clock aeroplane lunch so hunger began to gnaw before our ten-thirty dinner. I slaked it on a few ripe strawberries while picking them; then whisky. A first swim in the pool. I mean to do this every day, also to be as accommodating as I possibly can to Janetta's way of life and other people's feelings and desires – probably to quiet my conscience for my recent failure with Julia, and prove to myself that I'm not an entirely selfish irritable old brute. Luckily adaptation seems so far effortless. Everything here is so perfectly designed to soothe, comfort, rest and content the spirit that I can't envisage getting bouts of prickliness or doing anything but revel in my surroundings. All to bed soon after dinner: it's not, oddly enough, very hot.

25 June

Woke to the sound of rain. Or was it the fountain? Behind my four-poster bed with its lace curtains there is actually a BELL, and when I press it Temi appears within three minutes with a tray of coffee, bread and home-made marmalade. Was it rain, I asked? Oh no, nothing but a little mist. It is, however, raining quite hard. My room is darkened by a dense screen of creepers to keep the terrace cool.

Jaime disappeared early and I settled to correct the proofs of Robert's book[1] on the terrace.

A first dip into the beach life and the sea itself – pellucid and warm. Janetta, Jaime and myself – the young were expected to join us but didn't – bathed and lunched off *pez de espada* and *chanquetes* at a quite attractive beach restaurant, where only the human beings were vulgar and garish, exposing the glistening meat of their bodies.

Very much hotter, crushingly so. Arrived home, I got at once into the pool and then sat solidly at Robert's book, which needs an unexpected amount of correction.

In the cool of evening I walked alone up the stream and climbed uphill through dry maquis plants and pines. The three young dressed up considerably in preparation for a descent on the town. Georgie is loving and compliant towards Jean-Pierre, who seems to be champing for something to do. Left alone, with darkness falling, Janetta and I naturally discussed them all. Later we sat out at a candlelit table beside the gurgling fountain under an infinitely remote black velvet sky sprinkled with tiny stars.

1 July

A ghost has begun to haunt our paradise – the ghost of Georgie's unhappiness. Impossible to go on as if it weren't there and I now see more reason for Janetta's anxiety, though still inclining to feel that the only help we can give this pair of wretched children is to bolster Jean-Pierre's ego and somehow include him in the party more than we do. He doesn't make it easy, though.

---

1 *The Green Flag.*

Ed[1] arrived last night, beaming, friendly, with Jaime and a mysterious Spaniard who played softly and very beautifully on his guitar through most of dinner – and so the evening wore on. Finally 'Curro' was summoned and, putting his face close to the guitarist's, he sang with a crude, fierce intensity unlike his usual softer style a song about '*los siete colores del Tinto*'. Rose had by now gone to bed and the Spaniard sang a gentle serenade outside her door and went off with Jaime into the darkness.

Today it is very hot. I'm waiting for it to cool sufficiently for me to take a walk. I've begun to take more interest in the flowers. Yesterday Janetta and I found a slender delphinium and a flower the colour of purple stained glass (throatwort) growing among the rocks.

4 July

Janetta, Jaime, Ed and I went on a projected weekend trip to the National Park at Cazorla. It was late already and night fell as we wound up the endless lacets of the Ronda road, entering the town at its last moment of *animación*. Crowds in impeccably clean summer clothes filled the streets, and the air with the harsh sound of their voices. The façade of the old bull-ring gleamed white in the lamplight. As we sat eating in a small café, I felt tired. But afterwards we drove on through the darkness, reaching the parador at Antequera in the small hours.

5 July

The night was appallingly hot and the Antequera dogs indefatigable. Oh, those dogs of Antequera! All night long, bass, tenor, treble and counter-tenor dogs performed tirelessly in

---

1 Gilbert, architect-decorator.

every possible combination – solo, duet, trio, quartet or full chorus. I half stifled myself with my head under my sausage pillow and contrived to sleep a little. We started early next morning and drove through such beauty that it was impossible to feel tired; rolling plains of pinkish-white earth, sown with olives, large and small, in varying patterns, and finally up through pinewoods to the new parador at Cazorla, a National Park where people come to shoot deer and wild boar. Janetta and Jaime have a large room overlooking the famous view and commiserated with Ed and me for our two monks' cells overlooking the garage. Actually I don't like the 'view', which consists of smooth English lawns edged by a precipice and beyond it scratchy grey mountains, mostly pine-covered. We stopped on the way up to look at some tall orchids, irises and thalictrum growing in a damp armpit.

6 July

This parador stands at four thousand feet, but in the full heat of morning we climbed another two thousand feet in search of a 'rare violet' which the porter said might still be in flower, but only just. We found some bunches of violet leaves and I rushed into a thicket in search of flowers, found none and tore my legs to ribbons. I grew stronger as we climbed, perhaps from the excitement of seeing so many strange new plants – pink with grey leaves, clear blue, yellow or white, scrambling over the rocks like lichen or coral, all bathed in brilliant light and brooded over by the scent of pines and maquis. No sooner had we got down and I had crammed my flowers in water than we were off again, winding through the network of roads. Lunch at a *venta* under its flowery trellis, off fried eggs, salad and wine. Our table was set among pots of geraniums and two red-legged partridges in tiny cages. Afterwards, drowsy beyond everything, we all wanted to go home and subside on our beds.

At about seven, we set off by another route to the 'nacimiento del Guadalquivir', which Jaime was anxious to see. Following a wild damp valley beside the infant river (Ed and I got out and rushed whooping after some giant orchids) we came to the source itself – a still pool of dark water enclosed in a smooth barrel of rock. Mysterious and awe-inspiring, and all round was freshness and greenery, a surfeit of plants, including a lovely red-brown foxglove. 'There's a wolf!' cried Jaime, and only he and I saw it – a greyish creature slinking along, with a rather bushy tail. Uncertain of the way home, dusk falling, we took a rough track that bore us aloft through sensational Gustav Doré peaks, to the charming little town of Cazorla terraced on the lower slopes of the mountains. It was full of Sunday evening gaiety; even ado-lescent boys wore spotless shirts and trousers, and the little girls had been lovingly arrayed in freshly ironed frocks, bows in their hair and white sandals. We sat in the square, making our dinner off whisky tapas while we watched this lively pageant: grand-parents with the littlest children on their knees, bigger ones racing each other with prams full of sleeping babies, abandoned moenads flying round the square or circling in ritual and obsessional isolation, or running with their arms round each other's waists. Hardly any were quarrelling. Behind in the dark-ness stood magnolias and oleanders in flower, the handsome tall façades of the houses and the indigo sky with a thumbnail moon. It seemed a perfectly happy existence. Really, I reflected, perhaps it wasn't so bad being a human being here. I thought of Oxford Street and people futilely struggling for enjoyment from telly, cinema, etc. In the mountains we had asked the way of a forester's wife, whose contented face seemed to show that she missed none of those so-called civilised things, but was busy and happy with her isolated lot. Home through the darkness smelling of pines.

7 July, Tramores
Wakened by the telephone. Janetta drove me to Gerald's house at Alhaurin el Grande. Gerald, brown and well in his stringy way, and Lynda, stately in a pink trouser suit, came out to greet me. The new house is charming.

13 July, Alhaurin el Grande
It's always an effort to adjust to a new life that is not one's own, though I do it so often that I'm becoming almost an adept. We breakfast, dine and go to bed much earlier here than at Tramores. The heat is if anything greater, lacking the breezes from the sea. Lynda is smiling, beautiful and serene, but there's an under-current of nervous tension about her, repression, monkishness; she has even become more flat-chested. If we are alone for a moment Gerald tells me of his love for her and boasts of his good fortune. He doesn't fail, either, to emphasise that it is wonderful for her to have a house, a car, freedom to 'work' (but what *is* this work?). And can this attractive girl continue to abjure sex? The heat drives everyone to their beds in the afternoon. In the cool of the evening we drove into the vega and had a walk. Literally only when the sun is sinking is it possible to do so. At dinner, it needs only two glasses of wine to make Gerald argumentative and coat-trailing. Perhaps I irritate him; perhaps I remind him of the agitating past; perhaps I have slipped into the skin of their last visitor. At any rate there was an abrasive note in his conversation last night. I tried to brake for all I was worth – but perhaps not sufficiently.

14 July

I sit outside under the shade of the large balcony and listen to the deafening noise of the crickets. In the bank opposite my bedroom some beautiful blue birds called bee-eaters have their nests. Their swooping erratic flight is as exotic as their kingfisher colour and they utter whooping cries. I have just walked with Gerald to see a rare and very poisonous wild delphinium; not far but the sweat rolled down my face. Today I shall be back at Halkers, impossible thought.

Yesterday passed as before. After tea a drive up the hillside to Coín. All the images I connect with Spain were there – the mountains, velvet-folded in the evening light, men riding loaded mules, a smell of burning aromatic wood; the hour of the *paseo* with the girls in crisp clean frocks and the whitewashed houses greenish under a sky shading from pink to lavender, piercing purity of sounds which find no obstruction in the clear air. Nostalgic smell of rue on fingers that have picked it. Lynda is a little hypochondriacal and neurotic or just easily tired. Gerald is loving and supporting and admiring, but it must be like living with a hedgehog and I wonder that she puts up with him so well. She always speaks quietly to him, never a cross word, but I do feel there's something nun-like and unhealthy about her very restraint.

We dined out of doors by candlelight and he boasted about women who had been in love with him – Helen Anrep, Angela Culme-Seymour – and then returned to the perennial analysis of Carrington's character and behaviour. It's very peaceful here, very beautiful, but I'm glad not to be staying longer. I haven't Lynda's dedication, nor motive for it.

16 July, West Halkin Street

Back two days, but my toes have hardly touched bottom yet. I have seen Eardley and Joan and Cochemé,[1] and talked to many others on the telephone.

Julia has been staying at the Savernake Hotel. At first the food was 'delicious'; after a week it was 'quite impossible'. She is too isolated and thinks of going to the Three Swans at Hungerford. Mary asked her to lunch, but when she said would she come over again when I was there for a weekend she replied, 'I wouldn't dream of it. Frances and I have fallen out.' M: 'Whatever about?' J: 'I'd rather not discuss it. I know you think she's marvellous, but I don't.' M: 'So you mean you really don't want to be asked while she's here?' J: 'Most certainly not.'

What is my reaction? A sigh of relief principally. But sadness too, and a sense of waste.

I am trying not to be submerged by London fever.

19 July

Robert and Cynthia have been here. He seems jubilant at having finished his book, and I think it has had a good effect on his relations with Cynthia.

I went to see little Tam in her Hospital for Nervous Diseases – the word 'nervous' is ambiguous, but she has had a most alarming time, with loss of the use of her legs, and shaking hands. Julian, who came and spent an evening that was delightful for me, was quite exhausted and suffering from delayed shock. He says the trouble is not organic.

---

1 Wife and husband; she a painter, he a biologist.

22 July

Back from two days at Glyndebourne, staying on my own in an Alfriston Hotel, full of noisy children and middle-aged parents who had not a single thing to say to each other at breakfast but splashed boisterously in the swimming pool after dark. Solitude in a crowd is always rather an eerie experience, though I was not much alone, going to Maw's new opera with Desmond on Sunday night and visiting Quentin and family and Duncan next day before *Eugene Onegin*. No sooner back than the telephone begins ringing and I have someone coming to every meal until next weekend. Yesterday Nicko for a drink and Joan for supper. Nicko and I talked of Robert's book – agreeing mainly – and he also told me that about eighteen months ago Janetta had consulted him about the legal aspects of her marrying Jaime, saying that 'they might as well', for 'conventional reasons', etc. This surprised me as I suppose conventionality in those I love and respect always does, yet I have a ghostly feeling I've heard it from Nicko before. When we were in Warsaw he asked her about the marriage project and she said, 'Oh, no, Jaime doesn't want to.' This must have been when I left them alone in the hotel at Cracow.

Maud Russell has rung up explicitly saying she would like me to write some impressions of Boris.[1] I have to decide within a fortnight. Meanwhile Robert has left me two large further dollops of his book, so I am in no sense unemployed.

I have to face two friends in dire trouble – Margaret today and Celia[2] tomorrow.

---

1 Maud Russell, hostess; Boris Anrep, 'consort'.
2 Goodman.

29 July

Raymond said last night that he 'thought well of Mr Heath, without any special reason'. I was prepared to think well of him too but I *do require a reason* and he has given none. With a stroke of genius Frances Phipps says, 'I can't bear him! He's just like Pigling Bland!' I visited Frances from Stowell, and found her sighing and chattering over some mauve crochet-work. Mary and the Tycoon get on better now or so it appears, and this makes it much pleasanter being with them. Philip no longer trails his coat, but comes to meet me halfway, even declaring that Sir Alec Douglas-Home is 'past it'. They took me for a drink to a grand mansion at Ascot, owned by Heinz Beans, where I sat next to the large, smooth bulk of George Weidenfeld. He has opened a possibility of further translation; so has James McGibbon. So I no longer feel that door is completely shut. But oh, how I long for a few thoughts!

4 August

Not exactly thoughts, but confused emotions, were aroused by being given the proofs of the Carrington letters to read by Noel at the weekend. They are amazingly evocative of her personality and that included an element which was near-genius, or so it seems to me, original, inventive particularly when combining melancholy moods with high comedy.

Far the best were written at Tidmarsh, when all her feelings were concentrated on Lytton and painting. This was also the best period of her painting. By the time I knew her a certain disintegration had begun, partly from her different love affairs, with Ralph, Gerald, Henrietta Bingham, Beakus [Penrose], and her social life. There was also her strange guilt about what she often refers to as her 'inside' – her more intimate feelings, her painting, being a female – and this made her secretive about her work and produced the tendency to lie which so maddened anyone who was in love with her. But the result is still a very fascinating book.

Margaret has been here, bringing a touching letter from Julia, analysing her own state, and begging Margaret to visit her in affectionate terms which I couldn't but contrast with things she has said to me about poor Margaret ('inharmonious', 'really *too* lacking in aesthetic sensibility', etc.).

From Julia's letter: 'I'm still suffering from my melancholy madness just as badly here as in London. The sunlight and the beautiful trees here make me if anything sadder. I remember only with anguish all the happiness such scenes used to give me . . . I think I really am suffering clinical madness, because it's all of three years now since Lawrence left me – and I still can think of absolutely *nothing else*. So of course I can't "write". I can't enjoy or even stand a single thing in the "real" world . . . The advantage of being down here is simply and solely that I am *forced* to eat. This is what keeps me physically alive . . .' Naturally Margaret was moved by this tragic and unusually affectionate letter and rang up to say should she come on Tuesday or Thursday? A cold voice replied: 'Oh, don't bother. I shall be back in London in a fortnight and can see you then.'

9 *August, Thorington*

I'm here in the tight embrace of as awkward a situation as I remember, yet such a familiar one: wife, husband, mistress – and two friends of the couple, Kathleen Hale and me. The only person who is enjoying it is Lionel, who manages to blinker himself against Margaret's anguish. Margaret is *desperate*, and her desperation brings out all that's strident and obstinate in her character; she becomes the 'stumping', 'inharmonious' person Julia described. I've had more of a look at Dunyusha and find her an uncertain, unhappy creature who, if one shows her the least friendliness, is friendly and pleasant back. No sooner was I in my shiny double bed (part of Bessie and Freddie's' 'suite') and in a room so impersonal and empty that there is nothing left in it but their smell, than I began to toss and turn and palpitate over the various problems. Everyone always eagerly administers blame; but as usual I see three people in a knot that none of them has deliberately tied. Kathleen is furious with Dunyusha. If anyone is to blame it is Lionel – who has every reason to consider Margaret (but doesn't) and who is enjoying himself on his Sunset Boulevard like anything. I believe Dunyusha really has rather a fixation on him, as daughter to father, or pupil to master.

How should these three civilised people behave? Practical morality usually amounts to making the best of a bad job. No need to sympathise with Lionel, who's having a whale of a time, but I do enormously with Margaret, who is always so kind to others in trouble. I think I'm coming round to the view that it – or anyway Dunyusha – might be much worse; that an old man can't be expected to abandon his last fling, and that Margaret must try and make the best of it. In Kathleen I notice a retributive desire to punish Lionel and Dunyusha, or for Margaret to leave Lionel, or frighten him by disappearing for the night. Part of the behaviour of old friends and *confidants* in this sort of triangular situation is, I believe, simply a craving for something exciting to happen – for drama.

The Sunday paper produced a new focus for Margaret's fears. A homosexual has admitted to marrying a Pole, also called Dun-yusha by a strange chance, for a hundred pounds, to give her British nationality. So, Margaret concluded, *that* was why Lionel showed such a strange desire to take Dunyusha to visit Dicky and Denis (leaving Kathleen and me behind, though we are both old friends of theirs). She is to find a homosexual to marry her and put an end to her nationality problem. Rather a good thing, I thought, as it would prevent her trying to marry Lionel; but Margaret was appalled, as it would mean her staying in this country indefinitely.

11 August

Dunyusha and Lionel set off early, and later on we three females drove to Hadleigh, where Kathleen was due to pay a visit to Cedric Morris[1] and Lett Haynes. Cedric, at eighty, is charming. His friend Lett Haynes, a tall, quite bald, rather 'creepy' man, paints eerie pictures and makes little Hieronymous Bosch figures out of bones and human glass eyes.

Margaret and I then started on the long drive home to London. As soon as the dreaded Dunyusha disappears she calms down and becomes a rational, intelligent and kindly human being.

I sent Julia my usual cheque with a short, friendly note in a lightish tone, begging her not to acknowledge it, as she had done so long ago. I wasn't at all sure how she would respond, and when I saw her writing on an envelope by return of post I guessed she had returned it. So she had; with a nice letter, though carefully substituting 'My dear' for 'Dearest'.

The gist of it is that she 'sincerely did feel all too inharmoniously at our last meeting that we are *not* suited to each other as companions – for quite some time I have realised that we did not, basically, get on together . . . Well – all that being so, you can surely picture that I honestly feel unhappy, and undesirous of

---

1 Painter and baronet.

receiving gifts from you . . . Personally I feel we could still be friends *on paper* – in other words your letters are really too wonderful and I'd greatly like to hear from time to time what you have been doing and how getting along . . . I *do* really feel we should do better not to meet in person – it's almost always so very upsetting in the event isn't it, nowadays. Anyhow – thousands of thanks for your generous gesture after I've been so tiger-like of late. Any time you *might* feel like writing me a line, I'll be glad to reciprocate.'

My reactions? None, really. Total blank. Some sort of anaesthesia has settled in that particular nerve. I suppose she has genuinely forgotten that during my frequent visits to her in her 'bin', we got on very well. It's rather a good solution, take it all in all, for I think Julia has had some satisfaction in rejecting my present and repeating in writing that she doesn't want to see me.

18 August

Julia is said by Margaret to be in 'wonderful form', so said with a relish that gave me to think. Was Margaret wanting to rub in the fact that Julia could get on very well, or better, without my friendship? Maybe. Unnecessarily, because, I have now fully digested the fact that she doesn't want it, and I have no further desire to press it on her.

Back in London after a very nice visit to Eardley with Dadie (whom I drove there and back in my Mini). We all got on extremely well, without so much as stepping back to see if and how we were doing so. I really love Dadie's company. The mesh of his enjoyment has become, it seems to me, much wider – Julia would disapprove, but I like it. On the way home he told me that Roger Senhouse is dying. And full of life, energy and enjoyment as he is, he declares that he 'looks forward to dying himself'.

I returned to find two boosts to my ego in my post – a nice letter and cheque from John Murray for my last translation, and the offer of a new one for Knopf, via Hilary Rubinstein. These two items people a silent and lonely day, with hardly a tinkle on the telephone, but lots to do. Wrote to Bunny, read *Julius Caesar*.

Last week I had two delightful meetings with Duncan. He came to *Carmen* with me at the Coliseum, arriving with wild hair and somewhat tremuloso, having walked all the way in haste from the Embankment underground. (He belongs to the generation that almost never takes a taxi.) He was thereafter absolutely alert and interested, and remained the best possible companion, eating cold supper in my flat until midnight. Next day I went to have a drink with him in the basement of Pat Trevor-Roper's house where he is now lodged. He has made it very attractive, with lovely pictures, painted screens and books. Beside Pat, we only had the unprepossessing 'Don' (poet Paul Roche) and 'my new friend, David Pape', a young Canadian. I asked Eardley what was supposed to be the point of Don? 'He has the most beautiful figure in the world.'

Georgia took me to Ken Tynan's pornographic revue *Oh, Calcutta!* at the Round House. I got there early and stood watching the mixed crowds coming in – self-conscious, demure, hearty and 'beat'. The show presented no surprise except perhaps that beautiful naked bodies are more beautiful when fully displayed, and the bush is an adornment. There were some lovely girls, particularly a negress; two muscular Michael-Angelesque young men and two others that were flabby and unattractive. There was something inevitably phoney in the assumed lustfulness of their movement and dancing, when no male had the ghost of an erection. And the little sketches were despicably feeble, their prep-school humour sprinkled with defiantly uttered four-letter words. Could anything have been made of such a performance? Yes, if it had been (a) really funny and (b) really pornographic.

I got a fearful tickle in my throat and nearly expired of trying to stop coughing. Georgia thought I was upset by the performance, and said she was, and 'had no idea it would be all about SEX'. I'm not sure if I managed to convince her that I was not in the faintest degree embarrassed, but I've had a brute of a summer cold for a fortnight and can't get rid of it.

20 August

Julian's voice on the telephone made me realise how much I have missed him and worried about him. 'Not without reason,' he replied, and came later in the afternoon to tell me the pathetic story of Tam in Italy. As I suspected, he took time off and went with her to Richard King's Tuscan house, taking in a couple of operas and a motor drive from Verona on the way. Though far from well, Tam was set on this part of the holiday. But she couldn't unwind.

Julian is the last person who can stand such a strain, and he was worried by her inability to keep a face up to the rest of the world, and only reveal her tremendous anxiety to him. With her earlier symptoms of paralysis, the picture looks like hysteria, as described by Freud.[1] Julian is going to report on her state to the Hospital for Nervous Diseases, where she was before. But Margaret tells me there is a complete schism between the doctors there and the psychiatrists. The nerve doctors refuse to bow to

---

1 November 1994. Poor Tam, now the wife of Andrew Murray-Thripland, the mother of two children and a qualified lawyer, is in a wheelchair with multiple sclerosis.

the Unconscious. It is as if all the wind instruments in an orchestra refused to pay attention to the conductor.

The load on Julian's back at present is piteous to contemplate. Tam has no money and no job; there's no one else to take responsibility. I urged him not to try living together as soon as she comes back, on the grounds that two drowning people are worse than one. He always says she has lots of friends and I hope he can find one to shelter her for a while; meanwhile she clearly needs psychiatric treatment.

Gerald has arrived, and comes to dinner tonight.

21 August

Gerald and Georgia gave a dazzling star performance, shooting off rockets that broke into many-coloured stars, each responding to the other without allowing their personal egotism to falter. It was a delightful evening, even though at the start it seemed that Gerald might get stuck on sex as usual. Towards the end Julian and I sat back and listened, looked and laughed, and we didn't break up till after one.

27 August

Last night provided what was meant to be a treat for Gerald and Lynda, though I'm not sure how much it was one for Gerald. I took them to *The Magic Flute*. They liked the idea of it, had neither of them ever seen it, and hardly knew the music. I'm afraid the only number that drew spontaneous applause from Lynda and broad smiles from Gerald was Papageno's 'Pa-pa-pa-pa'. And Gerald looked rather frantically at his watch several times during the second act. He moves through life like a blind man, whose scales fall occasionally without warning from his eyes. Afterwards to dinner in an Italian restaurant close by. Lynda had been making contact with old friends and it had been rather a shock to find most of them are now deeply soaked in the drug world. One had recently even died of drugs, she told us. Gerald made no comment. I was interested and wanted to draw her out, but Gerald obsessionally wanted to talk about his bogus clergyman friend Charles Sinnickson, the 'Vicarette', a futile Firbank figure who is only drawn to religion by its choirboys. Lynda saying she couldn't bear him and my saying nor could I and I didn't want to hear about him, only made him keep on about him even more relentlessly.

Not really a very successful evening.

28 August

Some groping in my thoughts as a result of confronting two views of sexual morality, neither of them exactly mine. Kathleen McClean[1] at lunch was one – promiscuous in youth, she now clings desperately to certain rules. 'Hands off married men' was Mary's simple axiom. Kathleen's seems to be that 'if you are the mistress of a married man, you should never let his wife be your hostess, feed and look after you' à propos of the Penroses, of course. I had been trying to say that I didn't think any of these three were 'monsters', even Dunyusha, but that genuine feelings were involved on every side. Kathleen now agrees that Dunyusha has a real affection for (or fixation on) Lionel, but insists she *must be* 'a monster' because she stays at Thorington – it seems to me an extraordinarily trivial, hard-and-fast ruling. I think of legal marriage as a convenience, and human relations – especially love – as supreme. But what sort of love persists between the

---

1 Under her name of Hale, authoress of successful children's books: *Orlando, the Marmalade Cat*, etc.

Penroses who have been squabbling for years? Even Kathleen had to admit that Lionel finds Margaret's thumping, rough, noisy way of life exacerbating. Even Margaret says she's unable to deal with him when he's ill, and would like to have Dunyusha then. So the balance cannot be adjusted by these inelastic rules.

My other visitor was Robert, who talked allusively rather than explicitly about sex. Was he reverting to a Puritan view?

Bank Holiday, The Lakes, The Old Farm

Here I am again. Physical surroundings perfect: the grey and the green, the shimmer on distant hilltops, smell of fern crushed in my hand; one exquisite white Grass of Parnassus flower in a bog; thunderous gurgle of streams bursting out between stones; rich royal purple second thoughts of foxglove plants; mild smell of rotting vegetation – and all the rest. Marjorie Durbin is here but leaves tomorrow.

Dolly Hamburg[1] also goes tomorrow, and though she is nearly ninety, she's the most distinguished and original human being in the company.

1 September

They have all gone off – Tom and Nadine escorting Dolly and Marjorie to the station. I have 'free time' as Nadine says, and goodness, how I revel in it.

As for Dolly Hamburg – it is just that one grieves so for her, and admires the stoicism with which she takes her decline, and wonders what in her clear brain she thinks about it. I heard Nadine sweetly telling her in the kitchen that she was 'lion-hearted', and so she is. Nadine and Tom are both as unfailingly

---

1 Widow of Mark (pianist) and Nadine's mother.

kind to her as Marjorie is bossy and patronising. It was agonising to watch her white face and folded gnarled hands, clutching 'Wotan' her walking stick, as she sat patiently composed for departure, crowned by her white wavy cap of hair.

7 September, London

Back for two nights in the warm south, I reflect on my stay in the cold beautiful north. God, how cold it was, and often wet and windy too. Yet the glistening brilliance near and far, and the flying patches of blue sky above were well worth going for. Yes, I did enjoy being there, though the once-ambitious mountain excursions have dwindled to two-hour walks. One, on the day I left, started by rounding Longhrigg Farm, and then by way of Grasmere and Rydal, to end up visiting Wordsworth's house, Rydal Mount. Another day we drove across into Yorkshire, to the wild and lovely dale at the top of which stands William and Linda's[1] little grey stone cottage, backed by a group of tall dark trees. Linda came out to meet us, radiant and sunburnt and immensely, proudly pregnant. (Her baby is due this week.) Both of them seemed intoxicated with happiness, each other and their incredible surroundings. William took us what he called 'a walk' after lunch while Linda rested. Having wellingtons on himself, he made light of ploughing through a bog, which soaked our feet to the bone. The cottage is hardly furnished at all, except with wedding presents (very nice china and glass, stacked on orange boxes); no easy chairs, two hard kitchen chairs bought at a sale for five shillings each and a measly rug 'which Linda bought in a lot for a shilling. We had to throw the other things away.' But why worry in the face of such blazing happiness?

---

1 Garnett.

We had various other social occasions – a visit to an eccentric Cambridge don who thought *The Three Sisters* 'the worst play that had been written in the last hundred years'. I got fairly cross with him, and was able to point to this when Nadine suddenly asked me on a walk 'if I ever got cross?' But it was comforting to be asked such a question because I often feel I'm too inclined to blaze up. Julia-guilt again, perhaps. I think about her almost every night before I go to sleep. There's something eerie about cutting off a lifelong friendship which neither death nor physical separation has interrupted. The only person I have news of her from is Julian, who went for 'a bite' with her last week. He described her as 'fairly all right – but she hadn't a good word for anyone or anything. We had a laugh or two, and she admitted she hated the world.'

11 September

A delightful evening with Desmond, driving to Abingdon, to see Handel's *Sosarme*, and back. Bed after one. I found the music even more substantially satisfying than I expected, and the performance adequate, if a little homespun, taking place in the old-world setting of the ruined abbey with cool draughts blowing through the rafters and an exhibition of arts and crafts upstairs. Talking of an aria in *Jepthah* which particularly moved him, Desmond, quite literally, though briefly, broke down while we were dining at the Abingdon pub. Perhaps it is old-fashioned for men to shed tears; I don't remember any of my young friends doing it, but a letter from Bunny this morning says that on receiving a telegram announcing the birth of William and Linda's son Merlin, he 'unexpectedly (to myself) burst into tears'. He added that he always found 'births very emotional events'.

Well, I have made my start, raised my pickaxe and brought it down on my new translation yesterday afternoon. At it again today, and for some odd reason it does have a steadying effect.

15 September

What is the point of memorial services for the dead? I went yesterday afternoon to one for 'Coney' Jarvis[1] – someone I greatly admired and liked, even though not knowing her very well. The large, conventional-looking congregation and the humdrum hymns and drawling clergyman (who tried without success by long pauses to put significance into words which had long since lost any for him), the rebuilt Wren church, the backs of the bereaved Ralph and obviously shattered Caroline[2] – all this somehow added up to something which had no bearing whatever on Coney, or how she was missed, or even on the deeply moving fact of death itself.

Last night I had some young guests – Amaryllis, Jonathan Cecil, Ed (very much on his best behaviour) and Vivien John, looking so reminiscent at fifty of her sweet fourteen-year-old self that she touched me greatly. Quite a nice evening.

24 September

Yesterday afternoon I went to a preview of Tristram's telly film of David Cecil talking about his friends. Walking among the macaws and other exotic plumed and feathered birds of Wardour Street, I suddenly met three birds of more sober appearance, but distinction and confidence, peering and stalking slowly; visitors from another world. 'Cecils', I thought at once, and so they turned out to be – the Duchess of Devonshire and Lady Harlech

1 Antonia, *née* Meade, wife of Ralph Jarvis.
2 Her daughter, later Countess of Cranbrook.

('Mina' and 'Mowcher'). We herded into a tiny theatre. Rachel, in a really comically hideous hat, suddenly said urgently to Tristram: 'Would we let you down if we *ate a sandwich*?' (It was five o'clock.) She took one out of her case and began munching avidly, reminding me of Molly (MacCarthy) in her sudden abandon to the physical. David was much at home on the screen, easy, witty, and sometimes plumbing depths beneath the relaxed talk; confidently presenting his values – his hedonism, Christianity, enjoyment, and worldliness. Yes, that last I suppose on reflection was the sediment that was antipathetic to me. The famous people he had known included Lytton, but he spoke of him with a certain condescension.

30 September

Weekend at the Cecils with the glorious Bayleys,[1] Hugh and Laura. No more congenial company could be found, and conversation raged like a forest fire. Beautiful Indian summer weather.

Sebastian[2] has just paid me a long lunch-time visit. He wrote that his 'dear friend Charles, who looked after me for forty years has died. I am in a distressed condition.' Well, so he was I'm sure, though he looked pink, plump and well. The garrulity of mourning. I've long since learned my lesson, and I at once began asking about Charles. I had only to open my ears and listen, and out poured a stream of symptoms, nurses, decline, funeral arrangements, wills. After which he moved to Morgan[3] and began all over again. I think he thoroughly enjoyed telling me it all, and

---

1 John and Iris (Murdoch).
2 W. H. J. Sprott, Professor of Sociology, and fringe Bloomsbury.
3 E. M. Forster.

so did I hearing it, not being emotionally engaged. Morgan's 'policeman' Bob and his wife May told Sebastian that only after he had become ill did Morgan confess his homosexuality, and they were amazed and appalled. What puzzles Sebastian is that Morgan met Bob years ago through another policeman who was a 'roaring Queer', and as Bob's only charm was his looks he simply doesn't believe that the relation was platonic. Also he (Sebastian) has been left all Morgan's 'chattels'. These include books and diaries which he has been reading, in which (though there was much about lust – it figured largely in Morgan's life) the only likely reference to Bob was 'Bob and I ⌣⌣ ' [1]. Conclusive, I should say. I didn't realise how important a figure Sebastian was to Morgan, perhaps the most important in his life. He has left him also a life interest in all his royalties, capital, etc., so he has done pretty well. Talking – or rather listening to it – about Morgan, it struck me he had been something of a leprechaun in the MacCarthy sense, and I asked Sebastian whether he thought he had warmth of character, deep affections. From his rather uncertain reply I deduced that he didn't. Responsive to the warmth of others, preoccupied with lust, but not a man of outgoing feelings. The thing that struck Sebastian most had been the *misery* expressed in the diary. All diaries got that balance wrong, I said. One rushes to them in moments of gloom, not to confide triumph or optimism. But what was he unhappy about? About himself, his idleness and ineffectiveness. Simon Raven's picture was not far off the mark, Sebastian thought. Beside the homosexual novel there are a number of pornographic stories and the diaries, and all will some day probably see the light.

---

[1] Presumably a code sign that sex had taken place.

5 October

A newspaper strike over the last fortnight has in a way sheltered everybody from surrounding horrors. This morning here is *The Times* once more and I take a shying horse's glance at other strikers – dustmen again, sewage and ambulance men – as well as disagreeable pile-ups further afield. One has only to walk up Sloane Street these last few days to see the revolting heaps of uncleared rubbish which are being blown about by a high wind. Worse, more grotesque and macabre, sewage is being discharged 'untreated' into rivers; corpses are remaining unburied; old people are not getting their hot meals; sick people not getting to hospital. 'You see how important we are,' say the council workers involved. Of course, but so are doctors, butchers, bakers, nurses. We are threatened with 'possibly undrinkable water supply', and something like that beastly wartime fog is returning to cloud our skies.

6 October

A succession of peaceful working days, with a lot of reading. Yesterday Rose came to tea and talked about her working life, about Georgie and Jean-Pierre, and America. She has cool judgement, a sweet and affectionate character. But there is a feeling of reserve and of deliberately affixing a mute to her strings which worries some of the many people who fall a slave to her. I don't think it is more than having a very sensitive nature is bound to be. She looks at one from her little pointed face flanked by pink, wing-like ears, and out of clear grey eyes, and quietly makes one feel one would gladly do almost anything to further her happiness. I deeply respect her honesty.

Janetta is with us again, and received her usual royal welcome. Magouche, in her magnificent hospitality, produced dinner for about seventeen of us last night, Jaime, Julian, Patrick[1], the Campbells and all the houseful.

23 October

Bunny has just been to see me fresh from America. To my utter amazement he said his publisher there had talked admiringly of my translations, saying that I wrote such excellent prose.

Last night Raymond came here to talk about the Carrington Letters which he is reviewing. I gave him as good a tutorial on her character and life as I possibly could, interesting myself a good deal in my task. I feel I know her emotional construction through and through – but had to think hard when trying to analyse some of her mental processes. I was relieved because Raymond had been moved by the exchange of letters between Carrington and me over my going to live with Ralph, for it cost me quite an inner wrench to agree to Bunny's publishing them. Raymond thinks the book as a whole fascinating, the end profoundly moving, and likes least the whimsical letters, as I do.

He and I went on to a party at Jock Murray's in honour of Iris Origo's new book. The company was dwindling, but we dined afterwards with those two and Mrs Murray. It mystified me that Iris, whom I've met but a few times and briefly, once again singled me out, insisted on sitting opposite me at dinner and carried on a high-powered, rather intimate, electrically charged conversation with me. But I was flattered, and still more so when she said to me, 'You've always been a life-giver.'

At the party I was introduced to Jack Lambert, Literary Editor of the *Sunday Times*, and little Kelly Clark, Kenneth Clark's pretty and intelligent daughter. Lambert at once greeted me with an

1 Kinross.

exaggerated deference in which I smelt a rat. He had 'long heard about me', etc., etc., etc. Then, with hardly a pause, he launched on an attack on Bloomsbury. 'I'm proud to say I'm Raymond's BOSS,' he said aggressively. 'And Cyril's and Desmond's. Of course I've always found Bloomsbury infuriating. They were so supercilious, they *despised* everyone; I simply hate it.' Kelly Clark intervened and said Raymond was the kindest of men, not supercilious at all. And look what a charming man Duncan was. JL: 'Oh yes, Raymond *is* supercilious. They all were and are. What I feel about them' (warming to his work and talking louder, shouting almost) 'is that they're just *dolls*.' (He repeated this more than once.) 'There's nothing to them at all. No one cares now about anything they did.' F: (mildly, I hope) 'You mean Maynard and Virginia's achievements are worthless?' He brushed this aside with a hasty 'Yes', and returned to his dolls. I can't remember responding except that Kelly and I looked at each other with exaggerated gestures of dismay and I said, I think: 'Well, you *are* going it.' And then, 'You know, I think a lot of people a good deal *younger* than you don't agree with you,' which was, I daresay, below the belt. I felt appalled that Raymond and Desmond should work for such a master, who was evidently seething with violent hatred and frustration, and seemed to me a thoroughly nasty man.

My life has been over-full lately – a night in Nuffield College with Paul Levy as host, to *Semele* with Desmond, Janetta here most of today, proofs to correct. On and on it goes, and away in hot haste goes what is left of my life . . .

24 October

On the eve of setting of for Wexford, with Margaret and Kathleen McClean.

26 October, Wexford

We three make an odd little party and perhaps one that is a trifle out of the general jollity here. We have two magnificent rooms with bathrooms, and the endless and apparently simultaneous prattle I hear through the connecting door makes me thankful for my own solitude and silence. Janetta saw me off most sweetly and I found my companions at the airport. A Mini was awaiting us at Dublin, in which we trundled south by the beautiful Vale of Avoca, and Glendalough, mostly in rain, through which, however, we saw the deeply saturated orange of the dying trees and purple of the mountains. *Albert Herring* last night perplexed some of the Irish audience, who have hardly heard of Britten.

We have had an unexpected jewel of a day, softly brilliant, mild and sweet, no wind to speak of, a sense that the water and air are remarkably pure after London's current filth. All goes very well and I have no difficulty in keeping my vows, even though Margaret is a bit inclined to be fussily bossy. She likes to drive most of the time; I plan our outings and map-read. Kathleen cannot do either, nor does she want to. Drove to the southeastern tip of Wexford down empty green lanes to the seawater lagoon of Lady's Lake Island, where we got out and strolled and stood and gazed at white dead trees against bright blue sky and indigo clouds, birds in hundreds on the water, ruined abbeys, and heard the extraordinarily loud umbrella-flapping of innumerable swans suddenly taking off with outstretched necks. On a long spit of shingle between the lake and the sea we at once found the extremely rare cottonweed (the only site now left in the British Isles) and still in flower. Cows looked pensively over hedges, a donkey pulled a low sidecar, a horse gazed at us with its gentle face.

Margaret makes heavy weather, in the strictest sense, of stumping *heavily* about to no purpose with a quite extraordinarily frustrated and blank expression on her face. 'I'll be ready to start in five minutes' turns into an hour while she looks for her spectacles and at length finds them carefully zipped into her sponge-bag. 'Paranoid', she calls it, but it is a tragic measure of her unhappiness.

27 October

Desmond and his family are in the hotel – I talked to him briefly after last night's two Italian operas, Donizetti and Rossini.

Rather a long outing today, to New Ross, and lunch in a bar (off 'Paddy' and sandwiches) at a dear little place called Inistioge. On to Jerpoint Abbey with its magnificent carvings and back by Waterford. Coming in I found the Shawe-Taylors and sat talking to them.

Finally *Lakhmé* – enter the Moynes with attendant sprites and invited us to a party tomorrow. I'm glad to be able to hand on this social event to my companions, as they have had no benefit from my contacts with Desmond.

1 November, London again

''Bye now,' as the natives all say, to sweet-soft, soothing-syrup Ireland. We none of us much liked *Lakhmé*, the music too flimsy to grip the attention. Another marvellous day of soft bright sun and two more whacking great abbeys, Tintern and Dunbrody. Moyne party and Abbey Theatre play in the evening. Drove back to Dublin next day, and so home. Yes, a success, I think. We saw really everything within convenient reach and filled our days full.

Today Henrietta and Sophie visited me, charming both, joined later by Georgie, Jean-Pierre and Chloe.

2 November

This week sees the combined explosion of the exhibition of Carrington's pictures and the publication of her Letters edited by Bunny – they are sure to arouse in some that hostile anti-Bloomsburyism that appeared after Holroyd. I have read the book and returned to it, and the past has been ruffled up and revived with all its conflicting and violent feelings. How strange that the sex life of a living person – Gerald – should be so openly revealed to the world. Discussing what the dead 'would have felt' has never seemed to me what Freddie Ayer calls 'meaningful', but had Carrington known when alive that her letters and diaries would be published, she 'would have been' amazed and horrified, I imagine. But the activation of this emotional area makes me feel tense and as it were pregnant and that I shall be quite glad when Thursday is over.

Before I went to Ireland, Julian rang me and talked in considerable distress, for almost an hour. How I wish I could console him! He comes to dinner tonight and I do hope I can get him to unwind and unload a little of his sorrows, which seem chiefly to be *desperate* anxiety for Tam and guilt because he feels he can't bear the burden for her without cracking himself.

4 November

Julian kept up a bold front, particularly about his work, which has presented some worrying developments. But when at dinner I asked him about Tam he couldn't restrain his tears, to which I added mine. It was heartbreaking to hear him say, 'One *mustn't* abandon people,' and he repeated how much he loved her, yet on the evening that she came to London and he told her that living together was impossible, I was amazed to hear him say that he had told her she 'was a bad wife, not to ask him about his work', surely unnecessarily cruel when he was sacking her? Small wonder she quietly departed, taking most of her things, before he was awake. Oh, the pathos of it all. If good, kind, sensitive people can torture each other so, what must it be like to be mixed up with real brutes?

The Carrington pregnancy ends tomorrow; the 'waters break' with a review by Holroyd in *The Times*, I believe.

6 November

Holroyd's review was immensely long and very favourable to the Letters. Now I sit up in bed pondering over the opening ceremony to the show at the Upper Grosvenor. The crush was inconceivable – quite a large room was continuously wedged with young and old, for hours on end. No fear of being face-to-face with Julia, whom I glimpsed in the distance, but every soul I knew seemed to be there. The pictures were invisible and not many people looked at them; those who did, commented appreciatively.

Among disquieting encounters – I had one with a bearded man who turned out to be Raisley Moorsom.[1] Having exchanged a few words with him I thought I had finished – but no, he returned later and, fixing me with a gimlet gaze, insisted on talking about the remote past in the very centre of the throng where our words were drowned in the surrounding hubbub. Finally he shouted softly, 'You made me more unhappy than I've ever been in my life.' What could I reply?

The show was to be opened by Lord Eccles, and Bunny brought him to introduce him to me. His face was familiar. I dimly remember hearing that long ago, when I was a young bookseller's assistant, he had taken a sort of distant shine to me. His speech

---

1 He had been in love with me in my twenties.

in fact began in the most ludicrous and insignificant way by saying that he had opened a book out of which fell a piece of paper saying, 'Bought from Frances Marshall'. Uncomprehending amazement from the vast majority present who had never heard of the creature. Next day, he went on, he was asked to open the Carrington show, so 'of course he agreed'. He then proceeded to make my blood boil by saying that Carrington was not a professional painter and only painted to assert herself and because she didn't want to have a child. He ended on a note similar to Jack Lambert's — about what a rotten lot the Bloomsburies were.

9 November

The re-turning of the field of my deeply ploughed emotions by the publishing of Carrington's Letters has been more agitating than perhaps I expected.

On Waterloo Station, on my way to stay with Kitty, I met the jet-black Osé and Caroline West.[1] Osé politely and with snowy smiles offered to carry my suitcase and I felt apologetic for having got myself a first-class ticket for fear of the crowds on this late Friday train. In my comfortable carriage I was suddenly accosted by a nicely dressed old lady about the 'blacks' and how everyone hated them. (I'm sure she hadn't seen me with Osé, but I rather hoped she would on our arrival at Salisbury.) 'In Australia,' she said proudly, 'where I've lived for a long time, we manage things better; they travel in trains like other people, but *they go back to their reserves at night.*' The gap between us was too big to begin to bridge, so I hummed and hawed and waited for her to shut up.

Osé is indeed very, very black, a shiny black lined with pink, with little eyes and very thick lips. When I had got over the slight

---

1 Kitty's daughter and her African husband.

shock of his appearance head-on, as it were, I saw that he was rather beautiful, and admired his domed forehead and delicate gesturing hands. He is also intelligent and thoughtful, though his obsessional Marxism leads him to take every problem back rather boringly to that first principle so that what might be an interesting conversation subsides in muffled sand.

Before leaving London I wrote a short, sharp letter to Lord Eccles, encouraged by Janetta.

The Sunday papers produced their right and left about the Carrington Letters – Raymond so tenderly flattering and consoling that I feel he has almost overdone it.

Little Joan (Cochemé) rang up this morning to say with characteristic deflation that she had been to the Carrington exhibition and there was no one there but Quentin and she thought she 'had a slight, decorative gift, not really good'. She has told me at least three times that Virginia Powell has 'a *tiny* gift, of which she has made the most'. Eardley, of course, has none. Ralph used to tease her and tell her to her face the fact that she couldn't bear to hear any other painter praised; and got her to laugh and admit that it was torture to her.

Margaret spent the evening after Carrington's show with Julia, who apparently pitched in to me, hot and strong, and has worked up a lot of things I never said into never-to-be-forgiven insults.

10 November

In my letter to Lord Eccles I said that it was quite untrue to say Carrington wasn't a professional and that if he felt so antagonistic to her and her circle I couldn't think why he consented to open the show. He replied that it had been 'silly to ask him, and sillier to accept' and 'he only did it for the frivolous reason you know' – i.e. my name in the book.

I went to see the Carrington pictures this morning, viewed them at leisure and pondered over her gifts, her character and my feelings about her. In championing her cause, as I did to Lord Eccles for instance, I have to some extent suppressed my own criticisms, such as they are. Looking dispassionately at the pictures (which are shockingly hung), I thought they showed an immense natural talent, which perhaps never fully matured. Looking round, I felt the colour glowed, but there was something static, rather than productive of that heart-leap of excitement. The public response has led to what was saleable – her drawings – being very quickly snapped up, but I think her letters have aroused even more interest.

14 November, Snape

Rain sloshing down all the time and rheumatic pains in shoulder and back combine to destroy my mobility and slightly damp my spirits. But I'm happy to be with Heywood and Anne, and we talk and talk, darning every aspect of their American tour and visit to Italy and the lives and current situations of their daughters. Anne obviously reacted more vividly to America, and is inclined to champion it when attacked. Heywood's response, and also the expression on his face (when asked about it) are blurred. I heard about Lucy's marriage to her Scotch, working-class Muslim in the Signoria at Florence. On politics and the horror of the Conservative Government we agreed and didn't argue. Except for side dashes to Julia, Julian and Janetta, family was the great subject and Anne relates every irrelevant judgement to it.

Julia (at the Carrington exhibition, looking at a portrait of herself): 'What a *beastly* face!'

Julian: 'Why?'

Julia (briskly): 'Hard. Cruel. Frigid.'

Julian: 'But wasn't Carrington in love with you? Perhaps she made you unattainable.'

Julia (delighted): 'Yes, I think that's quite true. How clever you are! What a clever boy!'

I heard from Isobel that she invited Julia to have drinks and meet John Strachey. She arrived rather drunk, saying, 'Come to my arms, my cousin!' Thereafter she was so rude to young Mr Liddell-Hart because his father was a military expert that he rushed from the house in a high huff.

19 November

Last night in a hellish downpour, wading through puddles to the Festival Hall with Desmond for a concert of Janáček, Dvořák, etc. How much did I enjoy it? *Quite* a lot I think, for there's always some intoxication derived from being confronted by this huge complex organism of wood and metal and human beings and catgut all so admirably devoted to the pure pleasure of one sense. Desmond came back, coughing and sneezing, and sighing over his own coughs and sneezes, and bleeding at the nose, to have supper here. I asked him about his new black friend from Zanzibar; he looked pleased to be asked, rosy and with an endearingly absurd and watchful look in his eyes.

20 November

How it still rains – great sticks of grey rain, falling perpendicularly from the sky . . .

Last night I togged up in my best and went to a party for Pat Trevor-Roper far away in Highgate. A large, noisy, smartish crowd gathered and drank and shouted at each other till hearing became impossible. After bellowing at John Hill, Sebastian Walker, Adrian Daintrey, and Cynthia Gladwyn, I found myself trying to guess from the rat-trap opening and shutting of Bob Gathorne-Hardy's[1] mouth what he was saying – something about Julian Vinogradoff[2] having gone quite mad on the subject of her mother whom she didn't care for when alive, and refusing to let him, Bob (Ottoline's only surviving literary executor), publish the second volume of her memoirs. Whether Bertie Russell was or was not her lover somehow came into it. I joined Raymond with plates of food, felt an immense wave of fondness for him, and as I have now quite decided not to go on a Hellenic cruise with Eardley, Mattei[3] and Dadie, I suggested that he might meet me in north Italy after I had (perhaps) spent a short while with Jaime and Janetta in Corfu next spring, a plan very much more to my taste.

5 December

I am belatedly reading *Cancer Ward* with enjoyment and admiration. So much of it is moving without being hopeless, yet through the hospital it infolds the whole human situation, not only that of old age, and rams home the fact that one must pick one's way through the sharp spears of Roman centurions gradually closing in.

Yesterday I saw no one except Mrs Murphy and shop assistants, devoting the day to work and the evening to wireless and reading. So this morning, before driving off to Alix and the Carringtons, damned if I didn't feel lonely, and queer, until I'd spoken to Mary Dunn on the telephone.

---

1 Brother of Anne Hill.
2 Daughter of Lady Ottoline Morrell.
3 A Bulgarian refugee and great friend of Eardley Knollys.

7 December

The load of other people's unhappiness that landed on me yesterday nearly sank my ship. It reduced me to loathed palpitations and a feeling of desperation because I can never be sure of getting time for work, dull slog though it may sometimes be.

The drive home from Lambourn ended stickily, as most of the traffic lights weren't working (the Government and the electricians' union standing up to each other like two bristling dogs). Nor was my wireless. It seems likely I shall have no heat, light and nothing to cook on. Must buy some candles and a torch.

I rang Janetta and she came to lunch and I loved seeing her. Then Bunny rang up and gave a huge sigh over the telephone. 'What does that mean, Bunny?' 'Oh, I'm LOW!' – in a shaking voice. 'Not physically – emotionally.' I have asked him to dinner.

Bunny arrived in a great state about his current love. Did she really love him as she seemed to when they had an evening together, or not at all, he asked, and I tried my best to console him without falsifying the facts as I believed them to be – which always seems to me too disrespectful of the confiding friend. It's difficult, though, and not always successful. I said I thought she certainly loved him, but probably not as much as he did her. That her life was very full of lovers of various sorts, concerns, pure sociality, restlessness, and that the *only* thing he could do was make the most of what he'd got. To try and 'clear the air by a row, so that she would realise how insensitive she'd been' was quite fatal. One couldn't enforce love, and a sense of guilt didn't increase it, quite the reverse.

He took me out to dinner, and I hope I cheered him up a little. Did I reconcile him to his position *at all*? I doubt it. Once or twice he said, 'I'm perfectly crazy.' Or, 'Why won't she come away from it all and live with me and be my love?' He was at times very close to tears.

4.30 p.m. Today was supposed to be the great day of 'political strikes', but blackouts held off here until the coffee stage, when the electricity suddenly went completely. I sat down then to my work table, but darkness is beginning to fall and my flat has got gradually colder. No fires, of course, and no possibility of cooking anything or boiling a kettle. Well, I thought, I'll sit near the radiator. And found to my dismay that that, too, was going cold. So, no hot water either! If it doesn't come on before evening and there are no street and traffic lights I don't intend going to the orchestra; it will be too frightening, and probably cold when there. All I can do, and I've done it, is get into bed and light two long orange candles fixed in bottles. Really, what a go! I wonder how Julia is managing?

All I have for company is my little transistor wireless. Doorbells don't ring, lifts don't work, and I'm doubtful even about the telephone.

What can possibly come out of this stand-up confrontation? 'Civil war', I've thought once or twice, and I almost feel I may have been right.

9 December

We are in CRISIS. Yesterday, as I lay in bed at 5 p.m., Magouche rang up and suggested my going round. She 'had a fire'. I did, most gladly, and found Rose, Mary and later Janetta and Tristram Powell.[1] Mary is treating it like the war, and frankly adoring it. I find it hard not to bristle at this a little, although I know it is partly that she enjoys helping people in distress. Perhaps, also, a

---

1 Son of Anthony Powell.

background of boredom. This morning we have wintry sun, and so far no absolute cuts, merely great reductions. The shops operate on few lights, 'patriotically', people compare their sufferings, ladies whisper over the counter, 'Any candles?' as if asking for dildoes. There are none anywhere. What happens if and when my five, long, peach-coloured ones expire?

11 December

When the lights suddenly go out I very soon grow aware of being a primitive jungle animal, and ever-increasing cold and darkness brings a surge of brute fear. Worse, deep gloom and loneliness. One expects to die silently and unobserved, since here already is the coffin all around.

Yesterday's blackout, from two-thirty to five-thirty slowly undermined me, and as evening drew on I gave up the struggle to work by three candles and clambered into bed. Lying there, I rang Margaret for company. Had she any news of Julia? She telephoned later to say Julia said she hadn't had a single cut, but was enjoying the television with all fires blazing. Later I heard on my transistor that Tottenham Court Road would be blacked out from seven to ten.

More Julia-blackout-news this morning; Margaret rang up last night, suggesting calling on her with Shirley and her boyfriend. 'Not on any account,' said Julia. 'I'm in bed, and I'm simply furious. They announced a cut here, and there *hasn't been one*. I've been ringing up all the authorities to complain!' Heywood took her out to lunch two days ago. He says she ate well but seemed a little wild. She also had a front tooth missing. He thought he'd better make no comment but as they were leaving she referred to it herself: 'A shower of saucepans fell on me.'

16 December

Electricity cuts over, Christmas bearing down on us, people vanish. Magouche is off in a day or two; the thread of life dwindles. For that reason perhaps I've put more concentration into my relations with those few people I have seen. Margaret and I went to the theatre last night, and I longed to cheer her up by some special attentions for the bleak time she's been having (Lionel off with Dunyusha all the time, evasive, untruthful, and – when he is there – saying everything is 'her fault').

Lord Snow booms away on the wireless that we're 'all done for'. A sympathetic Russo-Germanic growl from Professor Karl Popper says that there's no such thing as certainty, only degrees of belief. This is something I've long had a high degree of belief for. 'What is truth?' he was asked. 'Correspondence with facts,' he rapped back. 'We know what that *means* even if we are unable to be sure what it *is*.' I find this sympathetic and reassuring. He reckons induction is out as a valid means of acquiring scientific information – it only reduces the field of error.

21 December

A Sunday in London yesterday. Strange, and in its way eventful. Got up slowly after a good go with the Sunday papers in bed then, after an early lunch, I went off to see a show of Morandi at the Royal Academy; not one of those pictures had I ever seen before, but a postcard Lawrence used to keep on the dining-room mantelpiece at Lambourn quite bowled me over and had remained in my mind. Rightly so. He is a superb artist, splendidly sure and subtle. A long time since I looked at pictures by a comparative modern so satisfying, and I would have adored to possess one.

Back at my work table I suddenly heard far-off but unmistakable sounds of revolution; organised shouts, pulsating to a regular beat like a dog's bark, gradually getting nearer. I put on my fur coat, went out on the balcony and saw a procession coming up West Halkin Street, carrying banners, shouting and walking sluggishly. A police car headed the long cavalcade (nearly as long as the street), two police buses followed and there were lines of policemen hedging it in on each side. They were shouting 'FRANCO OUT!' and other things in favour of freeing the Basque prisoners; of course they were heading towards the Spanish Embassy. But though to me a crowd is always frightening, and crowd emotion more so, I felt more pathos than menace in this one. They seemed to be wearily and hopelessly performing a ritual act of drudgery. They seemed like a faecal mass relentlessly and slowly pursuing its way down an intestine. And I wasn't interested enough to follow them into the anus of Belgrave Square.

Next came the arrival of Robert to fetch me to see a live television performance by Noel Annan[1] in the series 'An Evening With'. Perhaps because I didn't try to make him confide, he suddenly and apparently effortlessly began. Sitting on my sofa, looking rather desperate but not embarrassed, his hair very long and now sprinkled with silver, his face deeply grooved, he began suddenly: 'Things have been very bad in the home lately.' And went on with what seemed like detachment to say that he thought both he and Cynthia would be glad to end their marriage tomorrow, except for the children. We discussed how much their bad relations upset the children. He said: 'The normal thing in such cases is for one to find someone else, and neither of us has.' That he did 'look around, but couldn't seem to find anyone attractive'. At the time I was relieved because he was so detached and

1 Historian and Provost of King's College, Cambridge.

realistic; now I'm rather worried, as one must be when someone is so low, and then I suggested, as I have before, his finding a temporary place separately 'for working in', to see what it was like. 'But I don't know if you much like being on your own?' 'No, the trouble is I hate it.'

The telly performance was amusing for me, as I'd not seen one before – the religious formalities, staring light, silently revolving cameras in the back of which I could just see a tiny picture of what they were looking at. Noel Annan was amusing and lively, we all thought, but the producer irritatingly commented that we were a 'dead audience'. Drinks afterwards and dinner with the Kees, who gave a convincing performance as a secure and happy couple.

23 December

The eve of Christmas Eve. Tomorrow I go to the Cecils. Mary has been lunching here with her two little dogs trotting upstairs in front of her; she was looking very pretty in a coster cap.

I am wondering whether or not to attack the translations of my Spanish interviews. Better not, I think, till after Christmas.

I keep on worrying about *finishing*, or not finishing tasks. But behind all this lies the inescapable fact that what I'm really busy finishing is my life.

Christmas morning, Cranborne

I've woken in peaceful comfort in David and Rachel's[1] spare room, a crisp, still morning, very faint sunshine and snow lying (and also falling) thinly. My room has big windows on each side, and pale light streams in, revealing this understated vision. On

---

1 Cecil.

the mantelpiece an elegant clock ticks away and gives a silvery chime, harmonising with the rest of my surroundings, but rather disturbing in the small hours.

David and Rachel have hurried off to early church. David's Christianity, I deduce from various signs, gains on him, though this doesn't alter the lively, debonair front he presents. I wonder how it affects his attitude to the inevitably increasing pre-occupation with death, and what and how precise a fairytale his intelligent mind envisages. I really would like to know, but this sort of thing can't be asked, bother it.

Hugh and I arrived in time for lunch yesterday; Laura is in bed with a cold. Rachel is solicitous for everyone's comfort, as aware of one's material needs (and others too) as David is of the drift of one's thought. Perfectly delightful, easy conversation. Hugh's style of talk makes him odd man out from the rest of the family – somewhat ponderously pursuing a subject in a way that is enthralling when one has him alone, as I did over Scientology and the Process. A little walk with Rachel, looking like a robin in a dear little brown knitted cap ending in a scarf. Perfunctory references to Christmas decorations – with wild, uncoordinated gestures David tore the most unsuitable greenery, such as privet, from the hedges and then left his gatherings in a basket in the hall.

I have a delicious sense of there being *heaps of time* – I don't worry about getting up, but lie snug in bed where (breakfast over, with its coffee mysteriously full of large black grounds) I've been trying to bring my mind to bear on an article about Wittgenstein. The desire to keep philosophical muscles active that are long since, I fear, atrophied, is probably futile, like the desire to keep physically nippy or able to read the notes of music. But I wouldn't, I think, try if the trying didn't produce a few exciting gleams among such murky darkness.

Boxing Day

More snow, inclement, and a whirling wind. I was traumatised by Warsaw and Russia last February, and now really fear wintry weather. Yesterday David and I walked through the deserted precincts of the Manor, looking tragically beautiful in its thin white carpet, and picked up a little pile of discarded holly with berries on it. Today looks far less tempting.

The chiming clock on my mantelpiece has mercifully stopped; in fact I believe I made it do so by turning it round. So now there is peace, and that extra silence given by the snow and lack of posts and newspapers. And very welcome isolation, though I know I shall be quite ready when the time comes to re-enter my own life.

Presents were exchanged in Laura's room, bottles of bath essence hastily smuggled to Hugh by Rachel for him to give to me; exclamations of 'Just what I wanted! Telepathy!' My Indian silk scarves seemed to go down well with all.

I spend a good deal of time in my bedroom, reading. Galloped through *Vile Bodies* – pretty good rubbish, really. I was hardly amused at all. Laura is still mainly absent, a pity because her astringency is a valuable ingredient. She came down to dinner last night, and we were discussing some young people having displeased their parents by refusing to get married with a huge fuss. David suddenly got emotional and excited, and said they might at least do this one thing to please their parents. Everyone at the dinner table was against him, and thought that their form of marriage was their own affair. 'Yes, of course,' said David, pink and angry, 'but I should think *less well* of them, if they were so selfish as not to consider their parents' feelings.' Someone said wasn't it equally selfish of the parents not to consider their children's feelings? And David actually replied, 'After all they'd done for their child!' A few minutes later, when we were talking on quite another theme, about paying or not to go into museums (and here we *all* agreed), David took Laura up sharply and she showed, by look and word, that she had become aloof. David said, in a rather insensitive way I've heard him use before with Jonathan, and a little condescendingly: 'Oh, I don't want to be *snubbing*.' Whereas it was plain to me that, for a moment, Laura was acutely critical of David. I think he overestimates the influence he has over his children, and of course the steam from the marriage question came from his uneasiness over Laura's possible marriage to Angelo.[1] But he was admirable in one thing – that after consideration he withdrew what he had said about the need to marry as your parents like, a very hard thing to do gracefully, when his feelings were engaged. For of course he has a very sharp and tender awareness of other people, especially his children, underneath the smooth, even smug enamel surface that came out in his telly interview for Tristram.

He and I had a discussion in the passage, moving from foot to foot on the stairs, about Hamlet's religious beliefs. He thought his excuse for not killing Claudius when praying (that in that case he would send him to heaven) was genuine and didn't see that if so, it was much beastlier, or even less Christian I would say, than one can conceive of Hamlet ever being. Nor would he hear of Hamlet having been tormented by speculative doubt. So he seemed to me to miss the whole point of his character, turning him into a bigoted fanatic and doing so with a somewhat fanatical gleam in his own eye.

Reynolds, Janet and Emma Stone to tea. How Janet suffers to be beautiful! She wore a puff-sleeved crimson blouse and a long

1 Hornak.

tight pink skirt with an agonisingly wide tight belt, pink stockings and purple suede boots. (Someone told me she was at a Royal Command concert the other day in a long white dress with a white bandeau round her head, and a white rose sticking straight out in front 'like a miner's lamp'.) It's all rather gallant, but what happens next? Emma has bloomed suddenly, as girls do, and softened, and was all in sage-green velvet, carefully copied from Kate Greenaway. Reynolds crooning compulsively, and a little too gushingly. They do overdo it a bit. Both were enthusiastic about the Carrington Letters, which they're reading, but when Janet said to me, 'Your sister seems to come alive to me for the first time,' and I remembered that all that is said is that she was 'remarkably ugly' and what savage things in other letters (not printed and I believe suppressed by Noel) about the death of poor Ray's[1] malformed baby, I unthinkingly blurted out, 'But Carrington didn't like Ray at all.' This, of course, put Janet in an awkward spot, caught her out gushing to no purpose, but I tried to retrieve the situation by saying how she did emerge from the White–Garnett letters, and assuming she had confused the two.

I must get up, from my soft warm boat between two windows filled with falling snow. It's nearly eleven.

27 December

Probably I wasn't fair to David, he's an exceptionally loving and sensitive father with very few lapses, and I noticed that he slipped off after dinner to Laura's room after his tiny brush with her and talked to her for a long time. Family communication is at its usual high standard. Last night Hugh was following a train of thought aloud to David, and as it came out, almost painfully, in jerks

---

1 My second sister and first wife of David Garnett.

between 'sort ofs', 'you knows', 'I means', I was most deeply impressed by the kind and ingenious way David acted as midwife, anticipating what he wanted to say but not too actively, and reining in his own impatient thoughts in the interests of Hugh's safe delivery of his. It was such a moving display that I couldn't read my book for listening. After we had all gone up there was the usual burst of happy excited talk from Laura's bedroom; I could distinctly make out that all four were talking at once, and '*on dirait*' a cocktail party.

How the time spins away! It began snowing big, claustrophobic flakes at lunch-time, and we walked out masochistically wrapped up as in Russia, Rachel and I together, David and Hugh striding on ahead. Doubts about going to Cecil Beaton's cocktail party, but we crawled off in the dark along slippery white roads. Cecil Beaton very white-haired now, and looking rather ill; his room densely packed with a hopeless hubbub in which surely I saw no faces I knew? But, oh yes, Lettice Ashley-Cooper, Billy Henderson and Frank Tait, Vivien John, Reine Pitman and her daughter Jemima, the Baths and Georgia.[1] Jemima had shrunk from a once-handsome, blooming young woman to a plain schoolgirl. When I asked her if she still ran concerts, a fixed mad stare suddenly came into her eyes and she said, 'Have you heard of the Maharishi? Well, I work for HIM.' Reine told me she had seen Julia last week; she'd told Reine she thought of going to the country again, and looked ill and thin and unhappy. But as usual what is said, or shouted, on these occasions, is very small beer indeed.

I read *Hamlet* all yesterday afternoon and talked to David again, finding a meeting-point about Claudius. Now I've gone on to

1 Daughter of Virginia Bath.

Othello. Woke in the night and read more. It seems insane to read anything else, when there is always inexhaustible Shakespeare.

28 December
Snow and Shakespeare combine to freeze and preserve my existence here in a way that is marvellously soothing. Last night David read us the prologue to his next book on the Cecil family in the fiery heat of the drawing-room. His writing has become quite illegible, like shorthand – he has therefore to dictate his books. It was a description of Hatfield, patient and loving, vivid and skilful, and he took any small criticisms we made very well, much better than I thought he would. I looked across the room at Hugh and Laura and wondered what they were thinking. Hugh has burgeoned and become his own man, and only needs a little more articulacy; he admires and loves David.

II

3 JANUARY TO 30 DECEMBER 1971

3 January, West Halkin Street

Here we go *again* – it's a weary thought. On 1 January I had a bad go of New Year melancholia, with its dreaded undercurrent of near-madness, tottering reason. But Julian came to dinner and the pleasure of his company and conversation restored me, or set me up at a higher elevation anyway than where he had found it. This London Sunday has swathed itself in freezing butter-muslin, and the futile pleasure of reading the Sunday papers turned to pain. *Horrible* things – with their tales of squashed bodies at football matches, and gradual self-strangulation of each other by cigarette smoke, poison in fish, noise, marijuana. I pushed them aside and hurried to get up and drive off through the pale mist to buy some bread and meat to give Faith,[1] invited for supper tonight.

Yesterday, piano quartets with Margaret, Shirley and Anne Ottaway. We all played badly, as if thinking of other things. I lingered and talked a little to Margaret, who had rung up, desperate, a morning or two ago when I couldn't talk to her. She had been lectured through the night by Lionel telling her they had nothing in common whatever and never had had throughout the forty years of their marriage. It is too cruel. The two swaying trees making up a marriage, unless they intertwine and prop each other up, do seem to set up a grizzly form of mutual abrasion. And I feel Margaret has little love left now for Lionel – yet she is obsessed by him; meanwhile she gets fatter and fatter week by

---

1 Henderson (mother of 'Nicko').

week, stuffing herself to compensate for lack of love. Oh, how sad!

4 January

Blood is returning to the constricted arteries of London life, with tingling, anxious pins and needles. Foreseen, but still surprising, sense of being in a community of a sort. The telephone woke me, and Eardley and Isobel (both back from Spain) and Mary (just off there) followed in rapid succession. Under this outer pressure, getting on with my own activities somehow became easier.

7 January

Children and dogs, on the way to Harrods: a dog left alone in a parked car sits very erect with a proud yet anxious expression just as children sometimes do, responsible, in charge, yet longing for its owner's return. A little boy holding Mum by one hand and Dad in the other, hops along with an air of carefree happiness which rather seems to support the head-shrinkers' theory that it is important to possess two parents.

These have been anxious days expecting Sophie's return from France. First a French strike, then fog. (People have had appalling journeys, diverted to Manchester, fighting for trains, or not getting off at all.) But after holding my breath for several days, I can now relax. She is safely back, thank God, under Jane's[1] wing and I'm taking her to treats of various sorts tomorrow and the next day. I asked if she seemed tired. 'No, absolutely *fizzing*, and she's had a wonderful holiday.'

---

1 Wife of Richard Garnett, with whom she was staying in term time.

13 January

Skimming along, as if on roller-skates, I have lately had several sources of quiet happiness. Two outings with Sophie at the weekend. She has become such a dear little girl, and so thoughtful you can talk to her about anything; every moment I had with her was a delight. At the play she wished that 'books had a button you could press and all the people come alive and move about'. At the film of *The Railway Children*, which was very soppy and had caused me several spurious lumps in my throat, she told me 'Sometimes when I'm happy I cry.' She has suddenly grown up, and showed me some excellently written, spelt and expressed holiday work she'd done for her school. That, then, was all golden good, though the thought of her advancing into the frightful world agitates me deeply.

On Sunday afternoon to the National Gallery, a brilliantly warm and pretty afternoon. Happy children and cheerful young parents were feeding pigeons among the fountains.

Next day to *Lucia di Lammermoor* with Julian, who was looking and feeling desperately tired but the best of companions. The performance was uninspiring, the American prima donna trilled away in her bloodstained nightdress in the mad scene and moved me not at all, nor was she moved herself, judging by the perky little visage that took her call afterwards.

London is very very pretty just now; a huge pale moon like a Cheshire cheese rolls along in the bluish-mauve sky; still, with a faint haze.

Today, going to a bookshop off the King's Road to buy Iris Murdoch's lectures on Ethics, I looked in and saw David inside with a wave of affection. I wish I had masses more book space; buying books is so enjoyable.

I grow more and more intolerant of the rich and their passionate clinging to their privileges, even including Mary, when she tells me with delight how the friend who took her to the cinema bribed the commissionaire to get them seats ahead of the queue. 'I love that sort of thing,' she said with her cream-licking expression.

18 January

Weekend at Crichel – all three denizens and Dadie – was immensely enjoyable, though the dust of etymology grows thicker at times. One hardly dare open one's mouth, and the conversation is disrupted while Raymond, burning-eyed, takes a ferret run to the O.E.D. next door. 'Never mind – it's the only exercise the dear fellow gets,' says Dadie with his sweetest smile, behind which (enhancing it) remote savagery lurks. Raymond returns triumphantly: 'It's not "de-suétude" but "dé-suetude", and a coda follows: 'I like to get things right.' He is a little febrile, but says he feels well, and this is borne out (on past observations of mine) by this schoolmaster's mood being in the ascendant. When Raymond is at his sweetest it's a sign he's not feeling well. He does look extremely thin, especially in his touching new pair of 'off the peg' bell-bottoms which reveal that his own bottom is quite unpadded, the usual folds and pockets not being there to conceal this fact. Desmond is suffering from toothache, poor fellow. Pat, just off to Borneo, suddenly looks older. But it has all been delightful in spite of the breath of powdered chalk and blackboards. A lot of my pleasure came from Dadie's immensely life-enhancing presence, and – on the whole – good nature. He did 'rib' Raymond once rather fiercely and I don't think Raymond enjoyed it, though he 'asked for it' by saying, 'I always *nod* to our postman when he brings the letters in the morning.' Dadie: 'Oh, REALLY, Ray? How *extremely* kind and condescending of you!

You mean you *actually* say "Good morning" or something of the sort?'

Dadie read a lot from Wordsworth's *Prelude* to us – and other things – and very greatly did we enjoy it. I wish poetry could be more often read aloud, and so well. It doubles the pleasure.

On a walk, Dadie and I talked of nothing but Shakespeare.

21 January

To Duncan's[1] eighty-sixth birthday party last night – eighteen people to dinner in his basement, and a lavish meal of soup, garlic bread, cold meats and salad, lots of wine. I crawled home at midnight with fearful indigestion, not the least of the things I couldn't digest being close contact with Julia, whom I hadn't expected to see. Close only in the sense of proximity; we greeted each other – no more. I had a momentary brave urge to talk to her, but the occasion didn't offer and I don't think she wanted me to. Butting in when not wanted is not what I like. Otherwise there were many old friends – some had become impressively large: Ros,[2] Olivier Bell appear to be draped monuments. Quentin looked much older than Duncan. He's let his beard grow wild, long and grey and seems to have come straight out of a book of Mrs Cameron's photos. Angus Davidson wailed distressfully about his tiny personal worries and said rather smugly, with his eyebrows going up to his hair, that it was wonderful the way Duncan never worried, but *he* did 'and if one's the worrying sort there's *nothing* one can do about it', with a grimace that was somehow ladylike. I talked to Freda Berkeley about anorexia; her son has a girlfriend who's got it.

---

1 Grant.
2 Rosamond Lehmann.

As Duncan's party wore on and people left, the survivors grew slightly tipsy, inclined together, threw their arms around each other. Freda and Pat were openly making the most of their last time together (emphasised by a drunken squeeze, him to me) before he goes to Borneo tomorrow. Amaryllis and Nerissa were both peering out of clouds of hair. Fanny has returned to being a male impersonator. A cloistered world, but very lively.

I've just finished reading Iris Murdoch on the Good. She illuminates, but never really gets to grips with the philosophical concept. In other words, she states her credo but hardly tries to justify it, and this I miss.

22 January

Wet and grey Friday morning, and I'm off on my jaunt to the Isle of Wight with Julian and Georgia, to be joined tomorrow by Janetta and Rose.

25 January

Got back last night from our island trip which was packed with heterogeneous impressions which I wish I'd made notes of at the time. On our return all five of us piled in to have soup and cold meats with Magouche, and I think I wasn't the only one who was overcome with exhaustion – Janetta and Julian both declared they were 'whacked'. Bunny was there, and the *extreme* slowness of his tempo (something had pushed it to the lowest notch) seemed to increase my fatigue. While waiting for the meal I sat upstairs, along with extremely pregnant Bimba MacNeice and her pleasant but spotty husband, listening while poor Bunny beamingly and with snail-slowness told us the story of Puss in Boots. I had the feeling we were all children in our nightgowns and his wording was adjusted to our embryo brains. He went on to recount in similar detail a sequel to the story, which he had thought of, but never finished. A great sadness overwhelmed me at the running-out of the sands of time, the slowing-up of the clock's tick.

As for our journey to the lighthouse (the Isle of Wight), in all sorts of ways it was refreshing and stimulating. Georgia had literally burst into tears over the telephone when she heard we had booked rooms there. 'The Isle of *Wight*!!!' in tones of horror. (We might have suggested going to Peking.) 'Oh, but the sea will be so rough! And I've never been there!' In the event I think she enjoyed it as much as anyone. Our hotel was extremely nice and we were each given a large room looking straight onto the sea just beneath us, and flooded with sunlight when we arrived; the rushing roar of the waves breaking on the clean sandy beach was with us all night. During the time before Janetta and Rose arrived (on Saturday afternoon) we had some splendid, three-cornered ideological conversations. The rain of Friday morning gave way while we were crossing the sea in our solid, old-fashioned boat, to gentle sunlight which illuminated the fields and strokable hedges (wintry but already pregnant with spring), the pale blue sea and white cliffs beyond Shanklin, the small prettily painted houses with Jane Austen balconies. A comforting, non-hysterical landscape, an island for friendly dwarfs to inhabit. Having taken possession (and taken also a fancy to the hotel's proprietor), we started off at once to walk along the shore in the direction of Shanklin, returning to a plentiful tea sitting in the warm sunshine in the glassed-in verandah until dusk.

26 January, London

To *Hamlet* with Magouche – an extraordinary evening. I expected to be dismayed but was not; in fact Alan Bates perhaps came nearer to my view of Hamlet's character than anyone else has; he also said the poetry well and showed that he understood every word. With a good King and Polonius, and not bad Gertrude and Ophelia, the fact that the performance took place inside a large shining biscuit-tin didn't worry me at all (it was meant to concentrate attention on the miraculous words, and in a way it did). One was left to enjoy the amazing text. Was it moving enough? Perhaps not, though I was totally gripped.

Poor Margaret has been dismissed from our orchestra, anyway until after the concert. This has upset her greatly and given me appalling *angst* about my own inadequacy. I dread this evening's rehearsal, which won't make me play any better.

30 January

At the Slade, alone with Eardley and Mattei. On Friday night, Eardley and I had an immense discussion about values, right and wrong. I fear I may have talked too much, or too egotistically. Cold, sopping weather, unattractive. Walking alone along the lanes I thought what a good thing I hadn't tried to make a go of living alone in the country.

We've also talked about politics, which obsess me unusually at present. I'm a little surprised at Eardley's lack of interest. I'd thought he would be able to answer the sort of questions Ralph always so splendidly did. And he went so far as to say £16 a week was 'about right for a postman with a wife and two children to live on'. Really, if he thinks for one second what he spends on himself, how *can* he? But I'm astonished that anyone who assumes, as one must, that the present inflation must be stopped, should be quite happy to make the lowest-paid workers suffer for it. Perhaps they have to, but so should the highest. I'm awash with rather priggish indignation and it's liable at any moment to over-flow.

Another thing we talked about was courage – a quality I perhaps admire more than I used to. Eardley endearingly (and I think truthfully) claimed to have very little.

1 February
Yesterday evening Mattei left us, and Eardley and I spent some time goggling at the television – partly at yet another American moon shot, partly at a film about Anne of Cleves. The moon shots disgust me in some curious way; there seem such wide disparities involved – between the boredom of listening to a flat American voice reciting figures and distances, mixed with 'OKs' and 'ERs', and the horrifying human tensions and anxieties lying behind them – and between the courage and danger of the astro-nauts and the cowardly Eardley's enjoyment of that courage and danger. Perhaps I malign him or exaggerate the nature of his emotion, but I take his feelings as typical of many people's. So what is left but dismay and semi-disbelief as I loll back gazing with a sort of distaste at the infinitely brilliant mastery of space by men's minds.

4 February
I got back to find my flat full of a fierce and penetrating cold. All the central heating was off. When I asked little Mr Sultana [a sort of caretaker, Maltese], mad marmoset that he is, he replied with a crazy chuckle that he'd been able to get no fuel for five weeks and after next Monday there would be no hot water. Gloom and hysteria mixed. I turned on all the electric fires and left them on all night.

The state of the world has not depressed and obsessed me so

much since the war. And I find hardly anyone agrees with me that under Pigling Bland[1] and his catastrophically stupid henchmen we're heading for total disruption – strikes, strikes, strikes, and he does nothing to stop them but grow a few more double chins, go swimming and boating and burble about the 'British people'. Does he really suppose you can or ought to put back the social inequalities of a hundred and fifty years ago?

9 February

Today is the opening of Nicky's[2] first exhibition and also the date of Janetta's return. I drove to Jean-Pierre's little gallery in the morning and bought a picture. The pictures have a lot of Nicky's character in them – her strength, originality and vitality, a bit, too, of her muddle and lack of finish. They raise questions in my mind. What are painters at? Discharging their own emotion whatever its nature – possibly including indignation, fear, disgust? Self-expression, communication? Or in some way, through formal relationships between colours, shapes and representation, creating what we call beauty and which Iris Murdoch in her recent book on ethics describes (more or less, I paraphrase) as one aspect of the same structure to which Good belongs, arrived at through 'patient and loving attention to reality'. Nicky's work usually aims at the first, occasionally the second. Did the great masters – Piero, Rembrandt, Goya – have a message they wanted to communicate? Goya yes, Piero and Rembrandt surely aimed at number three.

Yesterday I started rereading Iris Murdoch with the same patient loving attention that she admires, and got a lot more from it as a result.

---

1 Ted Heath. Frances Phipps' name for him.
2 Sinclair-Loutit, Janetta's eldest daughter.

20 February

Once more at Cranborne with the Cecils, in my same large soft bed, the clock ticking and the electric fire giving off pistol shots. I couldn't get to sleep last night, tired though I was. Perhaps because the evening's conversation had taken a restless turn. At dinner I decided to do all I could to get into rapport with the thoughtful, mysterious Hugh, who sat beside me. I think I succeeded, and our talk went on and much later in the drawing-room it drew in the rest. There's always something going on in his mind, and one has only to take the end of it gently in one's fingers like a piece of wool – the 'end', that is, that he casually lets fall – and it will unwind. I had exactly the feeling of someone moving their hands from side to side during wool-winding. He was talking about his own subjects, his attitude to the work he is doing, and to work in general, and how much it should interfere with living his life. His desire to start again *at once* when his present task is over rather surprised me. Should it be the story of a German general in the jungle in the First War, or the history of certain thinkers who interested him?

F: What did they think about? The nature of the universe?

H: Yes. *Near*-religion, but not quite.

Later we moved on to boys and schools, why prep-school boys could have real friendships, but when you got to Eton the business of keeping afloat in this impressive institution left no room for friendship. Ramifications between forms of school culture, the way a small, ungifted, unathletic boy can employ a group of loutish myrmidons, all this enthrals him, and his face grew animated as he followed the drift of his thoughts. Of course I was horrified to hear of the suffocation and stultification of small boys' friendly feelings to each other. Hugh emphasised how natural *protectiveness* was among schoolboys – which of course became suspect later as homosexuality.

This is a subject that brings out the worst in David, who began his heraldic prancing, turned pink and repeated again and again: 'I don't see how *I* could disapprove of Eton, since *I* was happy there.' We had all been describing people who were wretchedly unhappy at school, and of course it came to my lips and Julian's, and nearly overflowed: 'Yes, you could disapprove of it if you considered the feelings of others.' Well, of course, that's unfair – he often does, but there is a layer of relentless egotism, evidenced in his famous failure ever to pass the biscuits. Again and again he returned to the charge if any of us suggested that schools could be improved, and any criticism of the Eton system made him irritable and on the verge of reminding us 'what he had sacrificed to give Hugh the best education in the world'.

It's lovely having Julian here, but he slightly tends to make everyone's contribution into a performance – perhaps by his very appreciation; I feel tired and want to relax and 'be myself' such as that is. Julian and David were preparing a telly programme, Rachel and I drove over to have a drink with David's cousin Anne Tree. Julian Fane was staying there, and David casually implied that Rachel was 'in love' with the gentle, introverted fellow, and would drive any distance to see him. She certainly talked to him exclusively while two exquisitely pretty little female sprites, one very dark, one fair, dressed up as oriental princesses behind the sofa with shrill cries of 'Don't look! Don't look!' They were our hosts' adopted children.

On the drive I talked to Rachel about Carrington. She has just finished reading the letters. People often ask me what she was like and I try to give an accurate picture. On the whole she's credited with more cruelty and less deviousness than she really possessed. A sort of reserve prevents my reminding people of my own intensely happy thirty years with Ralph, yet in a sense I feel I've betrayed him by not doing so, and long to tell the forgetful and oblivious world about it, and about my daily, ceaseless missing of him.

28 February

Janetta came to dinner last night, I hope she will go back to Spain for a while, to have a rest while Rose is safe in her nursing home leading the life of a happy nun. Janetta says she is perfectly content there, busy from morning till night, but refuses to eat bread, butter, milk or sugar.

Today, a cold, still London Sunday, but a lot has happened. I met Janetta in Belgrave Square Garden and we walked round looking at the fine, huge trees with their roots in London's underground, and the pathetic plots of crocuses and miniature daffodils mashed up by scampering dogs. Then I followed her to Chapel Street, finding there Nicky, Georgie and Jean-Pierre, and the McGibbons' left-wing doctor son Robert, who talked interestingly and at a terrific rate about education, noise, industry, medicine and boredom.

News that Henrietta is in London and may visit me later. Janetta pressed me to stay to lunch but I felt drawn to my blessed privacy, and am now listening to the broadcast of *The Makropolos Case*, which I saw last week.

Yesterday, at Golders Green, Margaret told me Lionel had hit her hard that morning and she had hit him back. She fulminated against Dunyusha, longing for me to throw fuel on the fire of her hatred. This I won't do, after seeing the use that's always made of it; nor have I seen Dunyusha lately, or had reason to review my view of her. Julia has begun ringing Margaret up again, and

Margaret says she 'can hear she is again in a bad way'. My feelings are horribly mixed – anxiety and affection warring with sheer *relief* that I can no longer be called on to haul her out.

1 March

Lamb-like arrival of March with fluffy clouds in a blue sky, but further austerity in a one-day strike that has stopped newspapers. So now there is nothing to read with my breakfast – no letters, no newspaper, but I'm listening to a Dvořák quartet on my new transistor.

Henrietta came to see me, with Fanny.

6 March, Snape

Thin snow was being shovelled into corners by a Russian wind as I arrived here last night. This morning there's a white carpet and, often blowing parallel to the ground, big light flakes with a hole in the middle of each. 'Like corn plasters,' I said, and Heywood muttered, 'God shedding his corn plasters.' I love being at Snape, and would gladly go through three times the physical struggle to get here. As I sat for expensive hours in my taxi to Liverpool Street, I thought about all the *paper* in my life, the respect I treat it with and always have – it's the only thing I'm tidy and organised about. It struck me as sad, and that perhaps it had taken the place of flesh and blood, becomes too important, and that may be why I've minded the postal strike so much. Has my life become too much 'on paper'?

Before leaving I had a rather hysterical call from Margaret. Latest Julia-ism: Margaret invited her to the theatre; she accepted with alacrity; Margaret bought expensive seats. On the morning of the performance Julia rang Margaret and said she had discovered there was something on the telly about Bernard Berenson and she'd like to see it, so would Margaret mind if she came and 'settled her comfortably in her seat and then left her?' Even Margaret's great good nature was shaken. Anne, Heywood and I watched the programme in question – it took seven minutes and was quite pointless.

In my room is a bowl of primroses, deep purple violets and sugar-tong snowdrops. I finished reading Lytton's 'auto-biographical pieces', started in the train. What a dear little boy, appreciative and eager for life and impressions. Sex as usual disrupted the perfection of his early balance. The best are an excellent description of Lancaster Gate, the detailed account of a day with the Bells. In the diary of his last journey to France quite alone a few weeks before his death, a certain selfishness emerged. Even when thinking of those he loved or was attracted to, Roger, or Le Mooncalf, he was entirely egocentric, not trying to interpret *their* thoughts and desires.

7 March

With Heywood in his jaunty little cap to Aldeburgh to shop. The bitter weather brought everyone out in frisky defiant gear, wool caps with pompoms, and sailing clothes. We called on Ruth Gathorne-Hardy (wife of Anthony and mother of Jonny) in her suburban villa, its drawing-room newly papered in really hideous orange check. I like her, her broad swarthy face, her self-dep-recation. She asked about Carrington and I gave my stock (but I believe accurate) account.

I've felt frivolous, reckless and inconsequential – a nice change from what I fear may be my sometimes tedious solemnity. It might be quite enjoyable to throw my cap over the windmill and become a wholly farcical old lady – but no good, my seriousness is, I think, deep rooted. I remember Julian telling me that Gerald had said the great thing about me was I was *gay*. Good heavens!

Resisted Heywood's suggestion of a walk in the afternoon and happily read by the fire.

8 March

So the strike *is* over, and my life must return to its paper consistency. A flat feeling, a perversely sinking heart, as if going back to school. Where is my ruler and pencil? What is today's timetable?

I'm fast approaching it all in a snug railway carriage, at the other end of which a young poetic man with a beautiful profile gazes out at the swans drifting on the grey river, and (later) with equal detachment at the hideous glum warehouses in London's suburbs, and scribbles in his notebook – verse, perhaps? His young spectacled wife, huddled and speechless, appears not to appreciate him.

Better day yesterday, and I was able to walk round and admire all Heywood's improvements, which I know he likes, followed by a drink with Jock and Fidelity[1] and lunch with the Medways[2] in the big house. They are all likeably untidy, scruffy and humorous, and involved in natural history in one way or another. The 'pocket Napoleon'[3] parked his car at a distance, so that we could walk up to Great Glemham through 'the Dell' where snowdrops and snow made equally white patches. Caroline Medway's two-year-old boy is a picture of health and energy, with scarlet cheeks patching his white skin, bright blue eyes and yellow curls. I thought again of the balanced all-rightness of children before they

---

1 Cranbrook, eldest of the Gathorne-Hardys, and wife.
2 His son and heir, and daughter-in-law.
3 Julia's name for Heywood.

have been corrupted by education and civilisation. Gathorne [Medway] is a tall, thin, impersonal fellow, equable but less interested in human beings, I would imagine, than in rats and earthworms.

Ranged the garden for twigs and buds and then retired indoors with Sunday papers.

Poor Heywood, wanting terribly to win at Scrabble, blew up violently and was then dreadfully ashamed: I felt involved and sad for him. Sometimes I fear Anne irritates him a little, for all his loyal admiration.

10 March, London

Went with Margaret to a lunch-time showing of Visconti's *Death in Venice* – a marvellously beautiful, but shapelessly overflowing and sometimes crude affair. Margaret has been in an intensified stew about Lionel. She is now afraid Dunyusha may leave England by the end of the month, and dreads what it may do to Lionel's health; thinks he may actually die of her departure; thinks also that this is what he thinks. So that, ironically, she now almost wants Dunyusha to stay. She gets through two bottles of whisky a week, but says sturdily that she can 'manage'.

She and Cynthia both give bad accounts of Julia, who sounds as if she is going to pieces as she did a year ago. She told Cynthia she was 'disintegrating completely' and she dined with them last night, getting lost on the way and arriving at nine-fifteen. The story of her muddled sadness has wrung my heart once more and given me an impotent craving to do something to help her. But what *can* I now do?

15 March

'Of all the men I am, we are' (as a Spanish poem I'm trying to translate goes) . . . Of all the women I am, one is a peculiarly sharp-tongued schoolmistress, who could – all the same – bite off her tongue as soon as she's uttered her sharpnesses.

I'm thinking, I suppose, of a telly programme of Julian's I witnessed last week with Jonny. It took place in the steep amphitheatre of the Royal Institute, and was a lecture by Mary McCarthy,[1] followed by discussion. We were deeply impressed to see our dear friend Julian controlling with apparent ease enormous vans full of equipment, technicians and the audience. Jonny and I were handed slips of paper bearing possible questions to ask her. But we didn't take a fancy to any of them. The lady was handsome, clever but somehow a dull speaker. Her subject was a non-subject – writers in exile – and I didn't think she drew any interesting or provocative conclusions, and alas I grew bored and inattentive, and showed it in what I said to Julian – as I shouldn't have.

Dinner later with Jonny and Georgia at the French Club. Anxiety about the young, and how the old can avoid offending or disgusting them.

Weekend at Kitty's, picking her wild daffodils, dining with Cecils, lunching at Crichel. Spring's glorious twitteration had begun and Sunday remained still and fine till evening, with tits swinging ecstatically on the lumps of fat outside the glass door. On such days there's nowhere like England.

Many thoughts of Julia. Might she in her distress even be glad of my help? May she have forgotten 'giving me the sack', so confused is she? I don't think so, however. Should I write (as she

---

1 The American writer.

136

did in fact ask me), simply saying I am *here* still, full of friendly feelings and concern?

16 March
This morning two calls from Cynthia about Julia, after one evening when she was confused and drunk or doped, fell asleep in the theatre and dropped her knickers on the floor. She's hurt her leg by a fall in her flat. I pass messages between Margaret and Cynthia, and Margaret is going to see her tomorrow.

17 March
Meanwhile I hear that Julia's wicked old doctor has been rung up by Barbara and says that Julia blackmails him into giving her drugs, saying she'll throw herself out of the window if he doesn't. He proposes recommending her to go to some convalescent establishment in Oxford. So the impotent wires buzz and revolve, trying to rescue human beings from ghastly torments that nobody is deliberately inflicting on them.

19 March
Janetta has just rung up and said characteristically: 'Jaime and I are going to do that *marrying thing* tomorrow.'

My reaction was a warm glow. I don't feel there's anything else to say about it. As I was striding up Sloane Street this afternoon, I ran into Jaime, who looked brown, happy and young. I'm dining with them and Magouche tonight. Is my pleasure rational or not? For *very* great pleasure it undoubtedly is, not perhaps quite unmixed with fear, but the fear that's involved whenever happiness launches its boat.

We were talking (Kees, Powells and me) last night about 'soft' or sympathetic feelings. Robert rather defiantly laid claim to great hardness and toughness, said he felt nothing really for people in distress – like Cynthia's mother or Julia. I believe this to be perfectly untrue, but wonder why he says so. I realise I've got softer, more soppy maybe, about small children, the sight of whose hopefulness and helplessness moves me easily to tears. Virginia Powell was near me in that, and in hating tough films. A photograph in the *Listener* of the head of a premature baby wearing a crown of electrical apparatus and an expression of deep gloom undid me utterly.

20 March

I slept soundly but woke in a frenzy of agitation difficult to analyse. At the thought of the fast impending marriage: – *deep* emotion, in which happiness and anxiety were mixed. There's something to my mind especially touching about people who have been lovers for so long, suddenly making this outward and symbolical gesture. Last night I met Janetta, Jaime and Magouche at Pruniers after their film, full of welcoming things to say to Jaime (I had already conveyed my pleasure to Janetta on the telephone). We talked about the coming wedding. 'I do wish I could come and be bridesmaid,' I said, and was told Magouche and Julian were doing this. I couldn't make out how they wanted the news of their marriage taken. I still don't know; but woke this morning into one of my full *bungling*-neuroses, a sense of having done the wrong thing, been clumsy, failed.

I dashed round packing, distractedly wondering what to do, and thank heaven had the idea (and was able by some freak at eight-thirty to carry it out) of ordering a very large bunch of flowers from Pulbrook's to greet them after the ceremony.

My fluster remained though I'm well aware of the insignificance that 'what I said or did or didn't do' has in their landscape.

The thing is that I'm so deeply moved by anything nearly concerned with Janetta's happiness. I reflected that when Magouche asked me to dine with them, yesterday on the telephone, she didn't 'tell' me they were getting married. If *only* she had – I could have adjusted and responded better to them. But what use are 'if only's'?

24 March, Job's Mill[1]

I felt I was rather a strange elderly guest as friend to the daughter of the house – but there was an even 'older mousie', Lady Katharine Stanley, Henry Bath's sister, a splendidly handsome woman in full possession of her considerable wits and more than considerable confidence. Oh, the confidence of these aristocrats! I can never get over it, and in a sense it makes my revolutionary blood boil; also it makes them more boring than they need be or really are, with all that talk about their relations and who someone 'was'. However, Henry is a true English eccentric and I find his stylishness delightful and funny. Virginia can be very funny too and her sweetness of character is charming. The situation of the house is romantically lovely – the broad river flowing down the valley and gushing under the house, the plantations of spring flowers. I liked the animal life (huge dog, happy white cat, guinea pigs, and a kestrel with a broken wing that has sat on the same stump for three years on end). Every creature is sleek with stroking, including the Spanish manservant.

On Saturday afternoon Georgia took me to Longleat, an outing I enormously enjoyed. Better weather, yet the house looked sombre and grim. But the quantities of elegant giraffes propelling themselves about the park with outstretched necks in slow

---

1 House of Henry and Virginia Bath.

motion, the stout zebras and spotted cheetahs, were a joy to behold. One giraffe bent benignly over our stationary car and licked the windscreen with its huge tongue. I didn't much care for the mouldy old lions with their hopelessly cross expressions. Inside the house, we penetrated certain rooms not opened to the public – one, a huge library, was lined with splendid books in super bindings; all had been recently greased and polished and glowed with health and beauty. They made my mouth water and my normal feeling that 'books ought to be read' slipped into the background.

'You won't mind if we go out to dinner?' I was asked, and of course said, 'No. Who with?' The reply was vague – a bachelor who often had some girlfriends about and kept horses. There were seventeen to dinner, many of them very pretty girls in 'hot pants', a queer actor and his boyfriend (who laughed incessantly, loudly and witlessly and must have been 'stoned'), Suna Portman's handsome silly mother, Gerard Campbell.[1] The house contained no pictures or books and almost no furniture; a roaring log fire with several huge labradors lying dazed in front of it in one room, a long table with two long benches in another. A procession of servants brought in a not very good dinner and worse wine. I was unfortunately put next to my host, 'Dandy Kim' (a well-known crook) with Georgia on my other side. He had no conversation whatever and kept jumping up and leaving the room. It was strange, but not quite strange enough to be interesting, and I longed to be gone as of course Georgia realised. Still, this was the only flaw in the weekend. On Sunday night the Baths left for London. Georgia and I talked hard that evening and all the way up in the train – about love and how to live. Golly! How she talks, cascades and fountains of it.

Now I'm back to work and enjoying it. An extremely attractive

---

1 Eldest son of Robin.

young woman from Knopf brought me more to do yesterday, and I have been quietly busy all day.

Then Janetta lunched with me on Monday, wearing her new ring, arranging about putting the announcement in *The Times*.

5 April

Now the giant's elbow has given another horrid nudge. Just back from a weekend at Crichel, the telephone rang. 'Italy wants you.' I hadn't time to wonder who or why, when Joan's voice came through, saying she had something 'very sad' to say. Cochemé had had an appalling heart attack and died in her arms. Elizabeth and Brian[1] are with her. I asked if she would like me to go out at once. She said no, but she would let me know if she would later. I could sense the realistic, brave, wound-up way she was taking it, and even as we were talking I heard her say: 'Oh, here are the undertakers,' and to someone else, 'They'll want to measure the body.' That enormously vital, clever, seemingly indestructible little man suddenly reduced to 'the body' – it's amazing, horrifying and dreadfully sad. Shaken and shaking, I passed on the news to those friends she mentioned.

My Crichel weekend was true to type but more so – Desmond's hair longer and greyer behind and balder on top, his pink face slightly more anxious than usual. Even more facts, grammar and pronunciation exchanged, but two very good evenings of more general conversation. One about myths – Pat thought we needed them. We all admitted we were nourished on and had sprouted from the manure of those we had absorbed with our education; but I said I could see no need to foster new ones, life was not as ashy as all that. Before this my pacifism had

---

1 Cochemé's adopted daughter and her husband.

come out at the dinner table. They all attacked me for thinking it would have been better not to have fought the last war and as usual it was put on a personal basis – '*You*,' said Raymond, 'would probably have been murdered.' Which is utterly beside the point, if true. All of them pointed triumphantly to twenty-five years of peace in western Europe. Do they forget that the last war engendered the atom bomb and do they really not believe that the next twenty-five years will probably see another and worse war and perhaps the end of the world? And also that war in the rest of the world – Korea, Vietnam, Israel – has never stopped?

7 April

I dined with the Penroses last night, my first sight of them since Dunyusha returned to Warsaw. There was an elderly botanist with bobbed white hair staying with them; he described himself as 'the groundsel king' and told 'funny stories' with beaming self-confidence. I liked him better than his Chinese wife, who listed the fruits that grow in Peru in a level, humourless tone. Lionel said he had enjoyed his daughter's wedding. He said he found Carrington's Letters almost unbearably moving and had read them twice. After dinner the telly was turned on, and Margaret and both the Harlands went to sleep in front of it. Lionel vanished upstairs, and when I was just beginning to find the 'go' a bit too 'rum' it was switched off, and conversation resumed, till I took myself off rather early.

The muddle of my plans – Campbells for Easter, Bunny next week and always the possibility of an SOS from Joan – has made me feel a little mad.

Lunched with Janetta and Magouche. Janetta looks happier and quite a lot younger. Were it not for Rose's trouble, her horizon would be sunnier than for years, and it gives me a curious pleasure to see the gold band on her finger.

Magouche, Janetta and I talked of how modern life put too anxious a strain on the mind, and how we should all return to being more manual, which would profit our serenity.

13 April

The afternoon was interrupted by the unexpected arrival of Nicky, whom I was enormously pleased to see. I gave her tea, access to a bath, and a drink, and she told me with a look of beaming jubilation that she had a new 'friend', that it was simply marvellous, the 'best thing that had ever happened to her', she 'had never dreamed you could be so close to anyone. I mean, it's not just an affair.' She had just been to Wales with the 'friend' and his friend, and vividly described her amazement at the beauty of the country (never seen before), the 'little black-faced cottage' they had been lent, with currant bushes just coming into flower. I listened in delight.

Now today I get an enthusiastic letter from Knopf, who seem delighted with my translation. This is a good send-off for my little holiday in France, which starts tomorrow. And after a wobbly beginning to the day I quite begin to look forward to it.

14 April, in the train from Paris to Cahors

I was wafted almost unconsciously to Paris, but as I breakfasted at 6 a.m. I'm going to take the monster train lunch. I'm glad to be in this uncompromising, realistic country.

15 April, Le Verger de Charry, chez Bunny

France seemed an enormous country, as my stopping train crawled across its dull central plain. Then suddenly I was looking out at Souillac, and thinking back to my visits with Ralph and Raymond, then with Ralph, Burgo and Vicky Strachey, and finding its image deeply imprinted (though full of holes) on my mind. Very hot in the train, my all-male companions sprawled in shirt sleeves. I saw blackthorn in flower, cowslips under the fruit trees and a faint powdering of green on branches, solid farms and châteaux, grey shutters and brown roofs.

Cahors at last, and Bunny[1] flapping penguin arms. After shopping he had driven his car into a field to read the newspaper, and it wouldn't start again. A passer-by came to his help, and he'd finally got a taxi which drove us out to this sweet little stone house on the hillside in the dusk. 'Ah *mais*, vous êtes bien dans la campagne!' said the driver. We passed the splendid château where Angela Penrose[2] lives, and see its round pointed towers from our windows.

The cottage looks out over the valley through the mossy trunks of several elms and an oak. Bunny sleeps in the sitting-room, where there's a huge open fireplace, a long table. The furniture is all solid, old, walnut, French. My room leads off on one side, on the other a nice kitchen and bathroom. Bunny looks quite a lot thinner, younger and less red in the face: it suits him here.

Now (10.30 a.m.) after breakfast of coffee, croissants and honey, he has gone off to see about his car and will return the Lord knows when. I'm savouring the all-pervading peace – a velvety, solid peace of muted colours. Outside my window is a quite large rough grass plot edged with box and backed by a grey cliff. I slept long and deep and feel soused in calm, as if I had

---

1 David Garnett (after separating from Angelica) had taken a cottage in a village near Montcuq.
2 Daughter of Alec, married to a Frenchman.

*Nicko Henderson
in the British
Embassy, Warsaw*

*Janetta and Magouche
beside the frozen Neva*

Dadie Rylands and Eardley Knollys in Alderney

Sophie, nearly 7, in West Halkin Street

Bunny Garnett writing in his garden at Le Verger de Charry in the Lot

Janetta in Corfu, making ink drawings of olives which marked her return to art

Jaime, Janetta and Ed at the Parador, Jaen

Gerald Brenan and Lynda in Spain

Rose and Jaime on a fossil beach near Agios Gordis

Jonny Gathorne-Hardy, Heywood Hill and Lucy

At the Aldeburgh Festival in Suffolk: Anthony Gathorne-Hardy and John Nash

Dadie Rylands and Raymond Mortimer in Bergamo

Picnic in Belgrave Square gardens with William, Linda and Merlin Garnett, Matthew, Maro and Saskia Spender, Magouche

been suddenly steeped in it, and it was streaming through me.

Last night we supped off soup and omelette and Bunny read me a letter from Angelica. He says Henrietta had a narrow escape from death in the Sahara, as they were without petrol, water or food for two days and had no compass.

The pearly mist shrouding the valley is beginning to lift.

16 April

The sun came through and the valley emerged in full beauty, fruit blossom and luscious spring grass. I am enchanted by my surroundings. A tunnel-like path between the trees drew me down to a tiny hamlet and a church below. Bunny returned for lunch out of doors at a round table under a tree. Outbreaks of surprisingly interesting talk; Bunny had been ruminating some general ideas – such as that it's very important to have general ideas – rather than 'collect pebbles' like Raymond. We talked about truth and whether ethical and aesthetic values were absolute or relative to culture. He reminded me that we had had a fierce argument long ago, because he wouldn't accept that Shakespeare *was* less good during the seventeenth century just because he was less appreciated – but seemed prepared now to agree that if beauty and good are relations between beholder and object, that question doesn't even arise. Then he went on to say how much more important individuals were than communities, with an analogy of trees that are planted too closely being unable to develop as individual trees. More conversation in the evening, after supper of avocado pear, porridge, cheese and red wine.

18 April

I've had a glimpse inside the château where I found the Dervilles breakfasting in their huge kitchen.

Our days are full of gentle, peaceful activity. I hear every sound from Bunny's room, and the first in the morning are deep sighs as he forces himself to get up and start the day, surprising in such a euphoric person. He makes our breakfast of coffee and warms up the croissants, while I have my bath.

Then, for me, walks and flower-hunting, letter-writing and reading, a little reluctant work, while Bunny writes his novel. The limestone hill behind us is covered in junipers, grape hyacinths, potentillas and two kinds of orchids.

Bunny has given me a chunk of his book to read. It's so extraordinarily unlike anything else that I can't judge it, and describes the Caucasus in 1840. The horrifying central incident in which a terrible old father kills his little son in order to smuggle a treasured icon inside his dead body, appears to be true and happened to an ancestor of Frankie Birrell's friend Basil Koutchichachvili. Talk of books led to W. H. Hudson and the block that prevents my reading him. I took *The Purple Land* to bed and was surprised by the quality of the writing and at the effortless ear (which few writers now possess). But found it too romantic and picaresque, with its flawlessly beautiful Pre-Raphaelite heroines. I'm giving up the attempt and trying *Far Away and Long Ago*.

Yesterday morning we drove to Cahors in Angela's car, and I drove Bunny's now mended one home after shopping. A crowded market day, with stalls selling monster cauliflowers, little cream cheeses wrapped in chestnut leaves, espadrilles, écrevisses and trays of live chicks.

Thundery rain in the night has turned everything greener and brought the wheat up by inches and more fruit trees into flower. Star of Bethlehem on the hill. We lunched off fresh sardines, with roast chicken and spinach in the evening. Conversation largely about Magouche – her fierceness in the past and recent 'adorable sweetness'. He described an incident in Corfu some time ago, which she had told me about. B: 'I was enjoying myself playing about in a rough sea, with waves probably twice as high as this room. You know? Magouche seems to have told me to come out, but I couldn't hear what she said and anyway refused to take orders.' This septuagenarian boasting of manly toughness was not to my taste and I remembered that she described him as being almost in a state of collapse. I told him my sympathy was entirely with Magouche – one shouldn't be so inconsiderate as to show off by courting danger. Going too far? He didn't seem to mind.

19 April

Another perfect morning. I'm absorbed in the rapidly unfolding spring, half horrified by its speed and wanting to say, 'Stop! Hold that!' to the poplars which have just covered themselves like conjurors with leaves of pale toasted yellow. Everything is shooting up and outward, the cuckoo goes off into intoxicated roulades, dogs bark, the farm turkeys gobble comfortably and Bunny's typewriter taps. We both wrote a number of letters in the morning and after lunch I walked down to the hamlet in the valley, where I'd noticed a faded letter box against the church walls, to post them.

Angela Derville and her husband Jo came to have a drink with us. They are rather a touching pair – she tiny and lamed by an accident, but with a rosy happy face; he a square, kindly, beaky fellow, who understands virtually no English. Angela talked about other Penroses, Ralph Wright (whom she was fond of), Barbie also, but Frances' dubiously.

Talked about the increasing speed with which time passes;

---

1 Her stepmother, Alec's second wife.

Bunny is the first person who has ever accepted my theory (that one's own life feels like eternity, and if you divide eternity into three years, each one seems much longer than when there are seventy). More talk of Magouche. Of Janetta, he said she must be baffling to her men, and I remember her describing her horror at his climbing into bed with her on the morning she slept there. I suppose he believed he'd had some sort of invitation.

20 April, 2.30 p.m.

Morning in Montcuq. Now, after lunch out of doors, I'm lying sprawled under the prehistoric cliff in dappled sun and shade, as well as in *lassitude et mollesse*.

Yesterday's nature notes: two very pretty red squirrels, quite unaware of me, capering among high branches. An *enormous* snake – a snake a yard long – rustling away from under my feet in quick coils, with a large lump in its middle, either from greed or pregnancy. A nightingale singing its heart out in full daylight. Two swallowtail butterflies darting after each other on our grass terrace. I walked across the valley to a field where melons are being grown under curious zebra stripes of plastic.

A letter from Joan Cochemé pouring out her feelings of bereavement, whose familiarity moved me. I wrote an answer about nothing else.

I've finished reading the first part of Bunny's novel and we discussed it last night. It is remarkable, but what else I'm not sure.

21 April

On the limestone hill I found two more orchids yesterday, *purpurea* and *lutes*. The ground was purple with *morio* and further on the 'spider' was common as buttercups. A white rockrose just opening. Sun very hot. I tried to fix my handkerchief into my botanising spectacles as a veil. Picked branches of cherry blossom to decorate our sitting-room. Bunny looks on at my floral activities with kindly amusement.

Evening conversation largely about Shakespeare. Bunny surprises me by liking the comedies best, I the tragedies and histories, and I suppose most of all the sonnets.

22 April

A nagging, rushing wind is blowing and the sky has turned pale grey.

Yesterday I walked in the pinewoods under the château, and collected fircones for our fire. Bunny has suggested excursions, and we may go to Moissac tomorrow but he's in the toils of creation and I tried to convince him that I love this peaceful life. I do. Evening talk about the Marshall family and also the strange case of Noel Olivier.[1]

23 April

Wild wind and a threat of rain yesterday, so we put off our trip to Moissac, and shopped in Montcuq instead. I settled to solider work, from which my rapture in our natural surroundings has distracted me but the rain beating against this solid little house made it seem a mere walnut-shell. Bunny said he was feeling gloomy, and loud sighs and later loud snores came from his room.

About four it cleared a little and I set out in a mac and thick shoes, walking briskly in the cooler air down to the valley and along beneath the château. Then I climbed the next hill and found several fine deserted-looking farmhouses and sheets of orchids,

---

1 With whom Rupert Brooke had been in love.

including a new one, *Burnt Stick*, and lilac trees in flower. Deviously home by the château to find Bunny still depressed. Whisky, followed by porridge and the usual talk in two armchairs.

24 April

Yesterday was atrociously wet, and kept it up till dark. Moissac had to be abandoned again, and we ran into Montcuq instead. We went to the château for drinks, where were a Canadian painter Cronyn and his wife. Jo Derville took me over part of the château, his eyes sparkling with love and delight as he explained his restorations and improvements. The splendidly simple, vast kitchen was as it must have been for hundreds of years, with a tiled charcoal stove, well-worn paving stones and a silent, beautifully oiled roasting spit. A noble spiral staircase led upstairs and we crossed narrow wooden outside galleries with a superb view to a small round room in the tower. The library was lined with books to the high ceiling and had a roaring fire. Cronyn was reading Gertler's letters and interested himself in the world of which Bunny and I must have seemed relics. Coming home we opened our post. Bunny read me a splendid letter from Magouche and I read aloud a ludicrous one he had received from an American admirer of his, which sent us both into fits of laughter.

25 April

Yesterday, amazingly, it cleared, and though sopping wet underfoot the sky turned blue with some cauliflower clouds. We set off for Moissac, following tiny roads that wound through villages and past desirable old farms bowered in lilac. But while we were marketing in Moissac, inky black clouds gathered and disgorged a cold deluge on us. Lunched in a simple restaurant frequented by people who had come to market, and then went to look at the superb church doorway, cloisters and the musée. Bunny talked at lunch about various episodes of his past. I'm sure his successes with women aren't just boasting – Minna, Indian Sushila, Italian Giovanna, Magouche, and he handed me a letter from Diana Gunn (the mother of Henrietta's Nicholas) to decipher a word, and I caught the concluding words 'my darling love'.

We talked of loneliness, partly. Bunny doesn't often ask personal questions but he did enquire if I felt it. 'Often,' I said. I asked if he thought he'd ever return to Hilton, and in a tremulous voice he said: 'The truth is I don't want to. I love the house, but it's too full of ghosts.' I stated my belief in the arch-importance of friendship, and he rather characteristically dived at once into an account of his own lifelong friendship with Harold Hobson.

26 April
I'm heading home in 'Le Capitole', the grand all-first-class express to Paris. It's more like a *soucoupe volante*: doors open as you approach, the voice of Big Brother announces stops and meals. It is smooth, silent and spotlessly clean. Yesterday – my last day – was divinely beautiful, and quite still, ending in a perfect evening with the long shadows as clear as in water, and voices heard distinctly across the valley. I took two walks, but have exhausted all the flowers; in the afternoon I took Bunny up to my limestone hill to see the orchids.

29 April, West Halkers
No sooner home on Monday night than I rang Chapel Street and was asked round to supper. I found there Magouche, Julian, and Janetta and Rose (both off to Corfu next day). I like to think of them there.

Now, Thursday, I've had three days to sort myself out, and

suppose I have more or less done so. But there are outstanding confusions which I can't make sense of. My future for one: (1) more work has come. (2) Raymond expects me to go abroad with him, and I don't know quite when but fear sooner than suits me. (3) I'm half expected in Corfu. (4) Joan will return in May or June and definitely expect me here, where I must be. I'm unkeen about the Raymond trip and have decided to use (4) as an excuse. But I dare say I shall end up at a loose end.

Borges and his translator are to be in London next week. I'm putting the last touches to my translation of his interview, and have been at the Hispanic Institute trying to clear up some points. Nearly every morning as I set forth into the streets I feel that I'm one of two things – a fake, someone pretending to be a translator and almost pretending to be a human being, and, secondly, a ball of paper rolling down a moving staircase in the underground . . .

Two letters from reviewers of the Carrington Letters in America awaited me here. Gerald writes that he's doing it for the *New York Review of Books*; 'I have written it very impersonally, without mentioning the fact that I knew her'! Anthony West is doing it for the *New Yorker*: 'I hadn't realised what a devil she was . . . unconscious devilry, but it's amazing how lethal her proceedings were . . . a terrifying picture of somebody hell-bent on destroying themselves and doing in as many people as possible on the way . . . The combination of egotism and insensitivity which Gerald brought to his collaboration with Carrington in her Ralph-wrecking operation seems to me almost to justify the use of the word *wicked*.'

30 April

That feeling of helplessness or fake is always best dealt with by practical activity. The trouble is I feel more in danger of bungling than I used. So it was some satisfaction that I produced for Magouche and the Hendersons a delicious dinner with very little effort – gulls' eggs, poulet à l'estragon, braised chicory and potatoes in milk. Nicko and Mary arrived in euphoric high spirits, and looking years younger, because his surgeon had let him off the operation he thought might be hanging over him. An exceedingly lively evening resulted and they stayed quite late.

Now I've been steadily tidying up my Borges article, which goes to the typist on Monday.

5 May

Magouche has stuck an icicle into my heart by telling me in strictest confidence that Robert had had some attack of depression during Easter when staying with friends in Holland. I've not seen him, but during a long talk on the telephone he said that the Dutch holiday 'had been quite a success'. If only one could break down this deadly reserve of his. I may hear more from Magouche; she has sent me an article by him in the *Listener*, on death, in which he says that 'the fact that we are all going to die is the most important single one in our lives'. But is it? It's like saying a full stop is the most important thing in a sentence. Or talking of memorial services, etc., as 'secret ways of dismissing the dead. And this is the last thing one wants to do . . . I still find it an insufferable affront to them personally and to humanity in general.'

Death. I write about it to Joan, and await her arrival and her desire to talk about it with a slight inner quaking. I think often about it. We all do, after sixty or so. I believe a lot of one's activities are some form of reaction to it – pretending it's not there or playing at eternal youth, which one doesn't even in a ghostly way believe in.

7 May

Straightening out, I feel, but I wonder if I really am. I've managed to make contact with Borges' translator, di Giovanni, and will go to Borges' lecture and meet him next week. A certain sorting out of plans. My fear that Raymond wanted me to dash off to Italy almost at once proved groundless; we are temporarily pledged to go there – plus Dadie, an excellent scheme – in September and today I have a letter from Janetta which looks as if I might combine it with a late summer visit to Corfu.

11 May

Last night I went to one of the 'Evenings with Borges' at the Central Hall, Westminster. Di Giovanni read his translations of the poems and Borges commented – but, alas, the poet only read one himself in Spanish, a sonnet about Spinoza. His appearance and personality seemed extremely familiar and also quite delightful. His blind face stared out over the audience with a look of vulnerable sensitivity, of desire to pick up with his ears what he couldn't with his eyes, that I found deeply moving. The eyes themselves, destroyed though not entirely lifeless; the long Spanish upper lip and the mouth moving silently in time with the English translations which he obviously knew as well as the originals, the very quick, and ironical crescent moon of a smile that crossed his face and disappeared in a flash as soon as it had come, the occasional appearance of being moved to tears by his own words. 'That is a very *in*timate poem,' he would say. He is an impressive and charming man, his English fluent and idiosyncratic; his knowledge of all literatures – particularly English – was dazzling. And he has been unable to read for the last sixteen years.

I gave di Giovanni my translation. He was a friendly, clever,

Italian-looking fellow, and he at once said with what he called 'brutal frankness' that in Borges' case it would be necessary to read him my transcript and alter anything that was not as he (Borges) *would say it in English*. 'Of course,' I said.

In the poems there were several references to his not believing in immortality – not *wanting* to – which I found sympathetic. To old age, to his blindness, and to being 'rejected by a woman'. I gather from di Giovanni that his wife has done this recently. He married her at seventy, a year ago, and spoke in his interview about 'belated happiness'. It's seldom that one is confronted by a personality so entirely charming and admirable: impossible in a sense not to fall in love with that little grey man, moving along slowly with his stick.

Another such was Duncan, my fellow guest at Crichel last weekend, a gloriously summery one. He began badly by stumbling on the stairs at Waterloo and falling full length. I didn't see it, mercifully. He looked a little white, and more than usually windblown, but made light of it. 'I'm quite all right. It's nothing. I'm quite used to it. You see, I do it the whole time – and I've learnt that the great thing is not to put out your hand to save yourself.' How he touches one merely by being so splendidly himself, and also so funny, courageous and eager for experience. He was pleased, I think, by Desmond's sensitive and affectionate consideration. He sat drawing us as we played croquet, enjoyed records of *The Magic Flute* in its entirety and visiting the Cecils. (Pat whirled us there and back in an open car at quite terrifying speed, but Duncan didn't quail.)

12 May

I'm back from dining with the Kees. There were Brian Inglis and his wife, and Terry Kilmartin.[1] It was 'in-talk' about 'in-groups' — in-telly, in-journalism, and somehow as pointless and gossipy, uninspired and unprovocative as conversations about whether you believe in ghosts, or 'Where have you been?' or 'Have you seen so-and-so lately?' My fault very likely, but all of a sudden it became ashy for me. Cynthia was looking pretty and friendly, Robert handsome but haggard, and when he came out to see me off he said something about 'all human relationships being meaningless', and the street lamps shone on his face with its dreadfully sad expression. What can one do about it? What could *I*, one of those 'meaningless relationships', do? Yet I can't bear to do nothing, and lay wondering what.

Then returning through the long, dark, unfriendly streets inside the frail tin box of my Mini, I was horribly aware of the viciousness of other drivers — rogue elephants, or jousting knights in armour rather than people trying to get somewhere, and the eeriness of it all struck me, and the sense of being lost in a wilderness of bricks and concrete, so that it would seem easy to charge off the road and crash into a building or hoarding.

14 May

Irritability — how to keep it under? I fear it when I go to the Penroses as I do tonight. Yesterday we were playing quartets, and Margaret took my precious bound volume of Mozart quartets and violently broke its back *twice*, though I'd screamed the first time.

It's quite a problem though, when one feels fond of someone who tramples so on one's nerves. And what shall I find the position between Lionel and her is like, now that Dunyusha has

---

1 Proust scholar and Literary Editor of the *Observer*.

returned to Poland? Margaret says Lionel is in a very bad temper all the time. I believe quite a lot of it is due to her simply not hearing (because she's so deaf) the noise she makes. But as she's highly intelligent one is tempted to try and persuade her – to wear her deaf aid, to lose some weight, and so on.

I liked a phrase from Henry James' notebooks: 'the immense mild summer rustle, the softened hum of London'. It's not applicable any more, alas, and I'm almost shocked to find myself able to tolerate the increased noise in West Halkin Street.

19 May

Well, it went off all right on the whole, though it was as I'd foretold. Margaret says complacently, 'I'm greedy' or 'I love food' and crashes, bangs and stumps about as usual. I'm certain that this irritates Lionel, who looked dwindled and grey. I had some delightful conversations with him, asking him about his own subject (which he likes) whereupon Margaret immediately fell asleep. Apart from her unconscious personal violence, largely due to her deafness (she has broken her hearing aid and no wonder) Margaret is kind and considerate to Lionel. We came back by train in time to see *Owen Wingrave*[1] on telly, a success with us all.

My days are tranquil, but full of work and social engagements. Bunny – returned from France – has just lunched here, looking spry, cheerful, and young. A long letter had come to him from Mary Jelley (one of our country neighbours), about Ralph, me and Burgo at Ham Spray, full of lots of little remembered details.

I've had some surprising contacts – a visit from Carol Hubbard, a person I particularly like, lunch with Frankie Donaldson,[2] who

1 Benjamin Britten opera on TV.
2 She was writing a biography of Edward VIII.

asked my advice at great length, and yesterday Georgia, who comes, I think, for an injection of self-confidence.

My bereavement correspondence with Joan goes on, and quite soon she will be here – depending on me, I think, to some extent, but certainly surrounded by other friends. When I think that it is ten and a half years since Ralph died and how much I miss him still, and how I seem only *just* to have started learning to live alone, I'm terrified about how much I can help her . . . I think of him though now really with more pleasure than pain, whereas thoughts of Burgo are like an agonising pressure on a scar.

21 May

Margaret has just told me on the telephone that, having strained her back, she was forced to let Lionel drive her Mini back to London, which he did 'appallingly, and hitting me all the way'. Also that Julia had rung up from her Sussex hotel-nursing-home to say it was 'hell down here' and Margaret mustn't come till she was back in London – quite soon now. Poor Phyllis Nichols, I suddenly hear, has had two awful operations for cancer. No wonder we all feel hemmed in.

Oh, poor human beings, how they are put through hoops!

I listened to a broadcast record of G. E. Moore[1] and another philosopher talking about memory. Fascinating, like watching a masterly game of chess. Moore advanced a bishop; memory was (or could be, I forget which) *direct perception*, not as Russell so wrongly said a deduction. Longish pause. Then another piece was moved by a very gentle voice: 'Then would you say, etc. . . .?' Pause. Quietly but weightily, Moore brought up yet another: 'a

---

1 Cambridge philosopher.

perception, but of course one that was subject to possible error'. It was an impressive and amusing display.

23 May

Sunday morning at Litton Cheney. Enter Janet with breakfast tray (I am just awake), her orange hair adrift, sits down and streams forth — what shall I call them? — comments, statements, complaints of Reynolds (their sting carefully removed) because of his conservatism, religion and dislike of going abroad. I relax, open half an ear, then begin tucking in to toast and honey. Next comes Janet's broadside of flattery: 'Two things I want to ask you – how is Sophie? And what does it feel like to have more friends than anyone in the world?' It's really *too much*, the whole scene is *déjà vu*, but it gives me neither pain nor pleasure. Nothing.

William Plomer, professional raconteur, was there on Friday evening. We visited the delightful Hubbards, a pleasant conventional couple came to lunch next day. I decided that it would be welcomed if I took the Sunday evening train home with Edward,[1] and I think it was. A strange, graceless, but sweet-natured young man, he interests me a good deal. He's very direct, asked me what I felt about Burgo's death in a way that gave no offence at all. I could not but ask him in for a drink when we arrived, belated though our arrival was, and his appreciation and depreciation of what he saw delighted me. He at once commented on Carrington's portrait of Lytton, on my hall wallpaper, on Boris's mosaic, the Duncans, Dicky's flower drawings, all of which he liked. He disliked the Vanessa and I thought at the time he was right. Is mad about Proust. With this directness he combines a youthful lack of self-doubts.

---

1 The Stones' eldest son.

26 May

What is the cause of my underlying disquiet? I couldn't sleep last night, in spite of pills, woke at two with painful thoughts bristling like porcupines in all directions. Yet the evening had been pleasant. A small party for Caroline West's wedding to her West African Osé. They were both jolly and friendly – but there were no blacks present except the bridegroom. Rebecca West made a gracious appearance.

I dare say it is the approach of Joan with her sorrow. Tonight comes widower Ralph Jarvis, whose own health is extremely precarious so I understand.

28 May

Contacts with the afflicted: 'Poor Old'[1] looked and seemed really dreadfully ill, and I can't think he will be with us long. But he was pleasant company. He has to put his feet up on account of swelling of the legs, can't walk upstairs, was thin and white, and spoke obsessionally about his symptoms. He also described going to faith healers and homeopaths, the last resort of the despairing.

In that department, too, comes a letter from Phyllis this morning, which 'took her three days to write'. She has had cancer of both lungs and fifty-seven stitches and 'is rather breathless in the evenings'. 'My only consolation was to tell the surgeon that my mother is still smoking aged ninety.' Dauntless as ever, but in her way pig-headed.

Joan arrived yesterday, came to dinner last night, came again tonight and on Sunday we go to Kitty's for two nights together. All that's best in her is brought out by adversity, as I imagined from her letters. She is, mercifully for her and everyone, a realist.

---

1 Nickname for Ralph Jarvis.

And while speaking of the '*terrible* pain she had suffered', much worse than she could have believed possible, she was simple and realistic and moving about that pain, and at the same time, could laugh at the fact that she had had Cochemé's trousers cut down but that the flies work the wrong way, and tell me that he used to say that if he died she would marry Eardley. She looked at me enquiringly, and I thought to myself she'd better think again. Then she said – she is sixty-eight – 'Of course I don't want to marry again, it's unthinkable. But it's awful having no one to love.' Indeed it is. I was reminded of the need to talk about the loss of the loved one, and the extraordinary way Julia and Lawrence never mentioned Ralph to me, once, and looked embarrassed when I did, when I took refuge with them.

29 May

Joan here for another evening. I am full of admiration for the courage by which she has – all alone – lived with her grief, accepted it, hugged it to her bosom one might almost say. She has deliberately thought about nothing but Cochemé, death, her life with Cochemé and now wants to 'get back to life'. Listening to her, I feel she is braver than I ever was, leaving no corner of the agony unexplored – as a bad tooth with the tongue whereas I know I poured drugged sleep and books in on mine to stifle it. Her recovery will be all the more effective for this, and there's always the ironic fact that one is in a way strengthened, unified by the sheer horrifying *simplicity* of the situation that has to be met in terrible grief.

She arrived last night, gasping out that Elspeth[1] (with whom she is staying) 'won't leave me alone – follows me into my

1 Wife of Craig Macfarlane, my solicitor.

bedroom, lies on my bed, follows me into the lavatory, even'. I was indignant when I heard that she had told Joan she should never have told Elizabeth she was Cochemé's bastard. What falsity, and how criminal to deprive Elizabeth of an important feeling of a human link with the man in whose house she was living, and who was someone as remarkable, as intelligent, and as Joan said (with one of her occasional flashes of brilliance) as 'oaken' as Cochemé. Anyhow, it has been proved that adopted children brood and brood as to how their real parents could have been so cruel as to abandon them. So this at least she was spared. My relations with Joan have been particularly easy.

But whatever the cause – probably the revival of past feelings, some of them undischarged – she leaves me restless, tense and unable to sleep.

3 June

Magouche and Arshile's daughter Natasha Gorky held a party last night for her wedding to her Chinaman Ed. It was the most visually glamorous affair (mainly young people blended together by Magouche's great warmth – she's the best 'hostess' I know). There was a certain punctilious grave ritualism ('ancestor-worship') on the part of the married pair. Natasha looked ravishing – for once the word is no exaggeration – in a long off-white dress, low-cut, of some cottony texture, pleated, and of most distinguished cut, her beautiful oval face set off by her smooth raven hair, which was drawn back and fastened with a red peony behind. There were lots and lots of glamorous girls and young men, and among their legs little Saskia Spender romped recklessly to and fro, obviously intoxicated by the fumes of other people's champagne. I met and talked to Nicky's Patrick, and liked him; Georgie and Jean-Pierre looked elegant and happy; I talked to Jonny, Nell, Tom Matthews, Ian Watson, and Antonia's Trevor. Mary seemed oddly out of place, and badly dressed. But in the course of a long reel of coloured impressions, the strangest and most disagreeable was that made by the Connollys.

Cyril was to me as he always is: an amiable kiss, a perfectly meaningless invitation to visit them at Eastbourne, a proud father's production of an equally meaningless snap of his little son in a push-chair. He had come with one purpose alone – to get an invitation for Stephen and Natasha's daughter Liz Spender's coming-out ball tonight, and he brought it off. Apparently he and Natasha Spender have not met since an occasion when Cyril wheedled some pre-cious first edition out of Stephen, and Natasha begged him to return it (as it had been a special present to her from Stephen) and he declined absolutely. Hearing of the ball, and determined to go, he stood Stephen a good lunch at his club, but got no invitation. Magouche says he was wild with rage over this, and towards the end of the party he cornered Liz Spender, sat down beside her, and after ten minutes' intensive talk came away carrying a huge invi-tation card like the rabbit in *Alice*, a perfectly shut smug expression on his face. Then made for the door, without a word to Magouche (whom I was talking to) except, 'Goodbye. Come on, Deirdre, if you're coming, unless you want to catch the next train,' in a voice as flat as a tin tray. And out he marched. Magouche says there will be hell to pay. Natasha will be furious, and poor Liz get into trouble.

But how extraordinary to want to go where you don't wonder but *know* you're not wanted.

4 June
Feeling a little like over-stretched elastic as a result of social life and work, both speeded up, and the tug of the unhappy world near and far, from little Joan's personal misery (she has just rung

me up and cried like a child down the telephone: 'I don't *want* to go on. I hate my *tiny* life!').

I had hoped to keep most of today free for work, but Margaret proposes to come to lunch and I can't say no.

8 June (now 12th)

And I don't really want to write anything down – any of these complete trivia that make up my day, different elements in the stream rising to the surface by turns, mainly work and rain. I have been hard at it finishing off number 4 of my Latin American interviews,[1] and on the whole liked working hard a good part of each day. This last fellow, Cabrera Infante, is an exile from Castro's Cuba now living in London, and yesterday I went to see him, to check a few points. One of the Natural History episodes I enjoy – zoology in this case. Already knowing quite a lot about him from his interview – such as that he was married to an actress and liked making love to her, and that he owned a Siamese cat, I was not surprised to see a large, almost empty room with elegant cat and trousered wife (shrouded in a mane of dark hair) crouched on a mattress in one corner. The writer was a swarthy, stocky man in his forties, his rather negroid appearance relieved by a sweet and intelligent smile, and very delicate small hands. We despatched our business, I think with mutual respect and understanding.

Julia is back in London, finding everything marvellous, especially because Lawrence was in the flat to greet her and has made friendly moves. Margaret took her to Suffolk for the weekend. Though tortured by pain from her own 'bad back' she carried up Julia's tray each morning and Julia didn't appear till lunch-time except one day when she came down in a furious

---

1 A book I had translated from Spanish.

rage, saying the milk was cold. (Very likely; it usually is.) Margaret confined herself to saying, 'Don't shout at me!' and later on Julia apologised, saying she 'was too ill to go on visits'. Sequel: a telephone call from Julia, wanting to continue the quarrel, always a difficult thing to do with Margaret, by suggesting that she should be psychoanalysed as she was 'evidently totally unaware of her surroundings'. Margaret said she had been visiting an analyst. J (surprised): 'Did it do any good?' M: 'Well, anyway I enjoyed seeing you, and you were very useful as a buffer between me and Lionel.' J: 'Lionel? He never addressed a word to me!' Not a word then or at any other time, of thanks. Margaret said she crouched over the fire the whole time and never went out at all.

14 June, Snape
I've been here two nights. It is the Aldeburgh Festival and rain deluges steadily from a grey sky, except that Heywood and I snatched a brief walk yesterday morning, through warm, still air with a hint of sun and the cat-smell of flowering broom. The immense sociability of the festival means that people walk in and out at all hours — meals and drinks are nobly provided, and the kitchen is a wilderness of used saucepans, bottles, etc. The way that both Anne and Heywood deal with these incursions, kindly, ironically, unfussed, compels my admiration. Also here is the little bird-gnome John Nash,[1] limping, rather older, his eyes no longer starting out of his head with brightness, but alert and interested in everything, and quick to come out with his opinions. Yesterday afternoon Anne, he and I sat 'listening' to the Maltings concert — deep snores from them both, and he is a great music lover so that it seemed somehow sad to see his little knob of a

---

1 A painter at the Slade with Carrington who he was in love with.

head polished and brown like the handle of a walking stick, forlornly thrown back on his chair and his mouth wide open. Jock and Fidelity fresh from lunching with the Queen Mum (everyone here is interested, respectful and a little proud of her coming to the festival in her red helicopter), Celia Goodman, and a whole gang of Humphrey Brooke's all came after the concert. I like talking to John Nash and think we get on rather well. But I've not mentioned the little family – Lucy, Scotch soft-spoken Geordie and baby Justin, who is usually somewhere in the room in his pram. Next to John Nash, I've of course enjoyed talking to Heywood and then Geordie, whom I've taken a liking to. A tall, very dark, handsome man with several days' bristle of beard, marvellous teeth and almost black eyes. He is gentle, helpful, loving and attentive to his little son. I'm more surprised that he's intelligent and ready to talk – about India for instance. He answered my questions about the Pakistan horror (cholera epidemic, ejection of refugees, starvation), and how it came about, in a thoughtful, well-informed way.

15 June
Rain all day, appalling nightmare rain. I didn't go out until the evening concert – Janet Baker singing marvellously – and ended with a migraine. Worked fairly hard at tidying up my manuscript, while little John Nash groaned over his arthritis in a chair, was ready for talk, at one time nostalgically romantic and *almost* boring (he's never quite that) about being an army artist in the war. Odd that someone who has become distinguished as an artist, eminent even, should be proud to tell you stories about what amounts to prep school life, being hauled over the coals by commanding officers. But he's delightful. His wife Christine came to pick him up; an old Slade friend of Carrington's (John

told Heywood that when he asked Carrington to marry him she said, 'No, I can't. You'd much better marry Christine.') She has a round, face like a stuffed pincushion, uncritically enthusiastic, friendly and dull.

Geordie has gone off to London. I'm sorry – would have liked to talk to him more. So we are left with Lucy and her baby. He has Indian bells strung across his pram-bed, so that when he moves in his sleep a tiny jingle makes one aware of his tiny thread of life.

16 June

The tiny thread was almost snapped yesterday when Anne Heywood, Rose Gathorne-Hardy and I were eating dressed crab after the Purcell opera. A terrified call came from Lucy next door: 'Mummy! Come quickly!' My mind instantly rushed to the truth – the poor little creature had choked on his own sick. How do they ever get reared? The crisis was past before Anne got there, but Lucy sat shaken to the core, and most vividly described what she felt – 'everything seems quite unreal'. I could hardly bear it for her – nor the touching sight of Heywood sitting over the fire later with the homunculus cuddled on his lap – Justin's dark eyes gazing reflectively and contentedly into the flames. Whether it was the agitation of this near-catastrophe, or what, I couldn't sleep, and am now whirling back to London dazed and done for.

I brought Anne and Heywood Gerald's review of the Carrington Letters and Anthony West's letter about them to read. They were enormously interested and Anne came out in fiery indignation against Gerald, exploding about his treachery, hypocrisy, monstrous behaviour to Ralph and constant denigration of him since his death. No one can take up the cudgels more vigorously than Anne, and she was on the point of writing to Gerald, arranging in some way for Ralph to be rehabilitated and the world told what a remarkable, impressive, lovable person he was. 'Well do, go ahead,' I said. It's not much good my saying so, though I think it.

The skies cleared yesterday morning, enough for Heywood and me to drive to a botanical site John Nash had told us about and walk through long damp grass beside a narrow 'cut' reflecting the blue sky for miles in both directions, set off by a number of swans and yellow waterlilies – and growing right in the stream, hurray, a never-before-seen and pretty plant, *Hottonia palustris*.

22 June

An enormous pink poppy, brought back in a tight bud from Snape, has just dropped its petals with a plop in the ashtray like the weeks of this curious summer.

I drove down to Eardley's on Friday afternoon in rain so thunderous and cataclysmic that I felt the world was ending. It collected in rivers at the edges of the roads, rose in dense mists to cloud the air, and was sent by other cars in great waves against my windscreen. A hell of wetness. Yet with surprising fortitude, the fields, the roses in Eardley's garden, the birds, all perked up next day in a warm, blustery, drying wind, as though nothing had happened. Joan was there – just the three of us. Mattei didn't come, perhaps finding the atmosphere too feminine. For in spite of the trousers she wears, Joan does spread an intensely feminine radiation around her. She and I went two walks; she needs to be talked to incessantly (and I remember finding this tiring when she was a guest at Ham Spray). I left her and Eardley to it, and did some translating in 'Mattei's little French sitting-room'. I hope she doesn't demand too much of Eardley. I don't *think* she will. If she doesn't, he could be a very great support and comfort to her. Her desire to talk about Cochemé all the time, and now and again emotionally and tearfully, is salutary for her, but sometimes embarrassing for others.

Very nice evening with Julian at the new Pinter play *Old Times*, which we both found gripping and stimulating. He is the perfect companion to analyse such impressions with, but though we spent some time on it, some clots were left undissolved. Georgia appeared after dinner and gave a marvellous account of her new job at the College of Heralds. She went to the annual Garter ceremony in pouring rain and was moved to tears by 'the star quality' of the whole Royal Family, who drove past her at close quarters. 'Film stars are simply *nowhere* with them.' It was 'something to do with the way they carried their heads on their necks', 'were so beautifully groomed': she 'got a terrific buzz from them all, *even Princess Anne, perhaps most of all Princess Anne*'. I listened in surprised delight, quite positive that none of them had as much 'star quality' as she, Georgia, has.

24 June

Bloomsbury-hounds yesterday. Catherine Dupré, who is doing the broadcast about Carrington, rang me up. She said she wanted to write a book about Bloomsbury. I thought her a nice person when she came here before, but naive and a little stupid. Everything is 'super'. She is a Catholic – that rules her out in my view from writing about these rationalists. Much more interesting was a young man called Stanley Olsen, who had written me such an obsequious letter, 'Most Respectfully Yours', that I nearly put him off. He turned out to be a plumpish fellow with dark, bobbed hair and highly intelligent grey eyes looking out through specs. He is writing about the beginning of the Hogarth Press and was particularly interested in Ralph. So I eventually gave him my opinion, inspired by Clare Shepherd and Anne. I also gave him my last copy of Ralph's book. We had a delightful conversation and he looked at my Hogarth Press first editions with exclamations of astonishment. 'This is *very* valuable! This is worth about £800 and it's a superb copy.'

I can't quite get over the oddness of the interest of the young in the people who made up my life. I have a great desire to tell them the truth, but that isn't always easy.

I often remember Julia's phrase 'the eeriness of the universe'. What weapon has one to defeat it with? Literally the *only* one I feel I have is a reasonably good mind, and I'm so afraid that may crumble with the years, and my God, what then?

1 July

Catherine Dupré came today. She's a GOOSE I fear. Gentle, well-meaning, but stubborn. Her vision of Carrington *must* be the right one, regardless. She sees her as a fiercely loving character, with 'terrifying vitality' and a 'north wind' blowing around her.

What's more, she has the entirely unsuitable idea of after the broadcast writing a history of Bloomsbury, although she admits to total unfamiliarity with their works. 'Don't you, as a Catholic,' I asked her, 'find their atheism and rationalism antipathetic?' She looked bewildered.

Last night I got into bed after a pleasant evening and long chatter with Dicky, in a curious state of intense visualisation. Faces of friends leapt into my mind's eye, one after the other, in vivid, coloured detail. Duncan – the flower-like blue of his eyes, and his crumpled rose-leaf complexion, combined with his look of tousled age, and (in profile) of an old Jew. The freshness of his response to music, opera, people. A pang seized me at the thought that all this, here now but only just, might vanish at any moment, like the beauty of an Iceland poppy or the spring green of trees every year. I saw it as agonisingly under threat. Next appeared the face of Eddie Gathorne-Hardy, convulsed with amusement at some obscene joke just about to gurgle up from the depths. I not only *saw* it, but heard the gurgle. Soon after, his mother, Dorothy Cranbrooke, as she was some years ago, with her fine candid brow and excited talk about the Aldeburgh Festival, coming in little rushes.

6 July

Early and somewhat anxious awakening. I'm getting tired of my own company – tired of being *married to myself* for so long, and that's what a solitary life is after happy marriage, apart from the longing for support, the warmth of ever-present love.

I got, however, a certain feeling of warmth from a beautifully fine weekend at Crichel. That is I went to bed supported by the sense that those dear fellows had affectionate feelings for me as I for them. I hope it's not a delusion. When entirely surrounded by homosexual males it's impossible not to be conscious of being odd woman out. But this left me very soon and a feeling of perfect ease and comfort followed.

One painful situation developed, though. Desmond approached me with the suggestion that he should join Raymond, Dadie and me in Italy in September. Would I suggest it to Raymond? I felt very dubious how Raymond would react and he did with immediate and violent shakings of the head. 'Dadie would chuck, and I couldn't face it.' What was I to do? Desmond had, in my view, broken an unwritten law by his suggestion, but I hated the thought of his feeling rejected and unwanted. It's plain he has no conception that his violent excitability makes him an 'impossible' (so everyone says) travelling companion. Insensitiveness? I suppose, in a way. I was left in the awkward position of dreading being alone with either Raymond or Desmond because of the inevitable clarifications. At breakfast on Sunday I found Raymond alone and said, 'We must have a word about this painful matter.' He then took a quiet but masterful line, said he'd thought it over and decided it was quite impossible and would tell Desmond so, as unbrutally as possible. He did so after breakfast, and of course poor Desmond *was* hurt and spoke to me later about it. I tried to pour unguents on the wound as far as possible, including a suggestion that he and I took a trip some time, to show that by me at least he wasn't unwanted.

Margaret on the telephone this morning in great distress. I found it rather shocking that this wasn't so much because 'Lionel is in a poor way. I don't think he'll live long', as that she had to 'take that tart's (or 'bitch's' alternately) letters to him every day in hospital, and then he reads them.' Also that Barry, the doctor who seems to be a rival – or so Margaret thinks – for Dunyusha's affections is 'trying to get her over here, and it'll be simply *awful*. I don't know what to do about it.'

The threat of Lionel's death, to me such a preponderantly terrible fact, hardly seemed so to her. But I may malign her. She was more or less in tears, saying, 'I don't see why I should be supposed to be the only person not to have feelings.'

7 July
Quiet working day and visits from Henrietta and Raymond. I was delighted by Henrietta, her gaiety and sense, and the story she told me of her travels in the desert was quite incredible. A day of rest is really a blessing now and again.

17 July, weekend in London

After a patch of scratched chicken-pen life, dry, aimless and shapeless, I suddenly today came alive to some experiences describable as *joy*. Playing trios with Margaret and her friend Anne – for some reason we all played better than usual, exploring unfamiliar works and not entirely at sea. Then talking to Lionel, convalescent after his spell in hospital and sitting in his large garden with a rug over his knees. At tea, I questioned him about a telly programme he's just done with Eysenck (on race and IQ). Listening to the definitively explicit expertise of his answers, and being aware of the power and accuracy of his mind was joy, and I felt a wave of real love for him which was joy too, although there is the dread that he won't be with us for long. Now, listening to Caballé singing *Traviata*, alone in my flat and not at all minding being alone – that too is joy. Not only excitement, but joy.

19 July

And there was more to follow – the pure delight of hearing two superb singers, Monserrat Caballé again and Shirley Verrett, singing in the Festival Hall – perhaps Verrett was the better musician, Caballé with an extraordinary ineffably floating quality of voice which I've never heard equalled. Robert and Cynthia came too, and were as enthusiastic as I was. We brought back Des and Julian to supper. I reflected again that Robert is the 'man of men' as Julia calls it (this was something Ralph and I always agreed about) and that if he had chosen to become a film star he would have been a wild success.

The current is beginning to flow away from London and also into it. The invading crowd is multifarious, garish, highly coloured, and drags about the streets with the dazed, cross expressions of all sightseers, poor things.

24 July

A delightful evening with Julian. I like best of all being alone with him but the quick swish and whirr of thought removes nearly all recollection of what has been said. Some talk of his work, of films ('You *must* go to *Claire's Knee*; I'm longing to talk to you about it, but you must notice everything very carefully, especially in the last twenty minutes. Nobody agrees about what's happening. It's like a Henry James novel.') I shall go, of course.

Yesterday I saw first Joan and then Isobel. Isobel had asked Joan's advice about her painting and got a slap in the face. 'It's putting a pistol to your friends' heads to ask them to see them in your house. I'd rather scrub floors.' Isobel doesn't easily take offence, but she had a little. I pointed out to Joan – as one wounded bird and I thought she would realise it – that Isobel was another and needed every support. Joan looked fierce and rather conventional with her neat blued hair, little suit and intractable expression. I can note that I found her unkind to Isobel because I've felt in great sympathy with *her* lately.

27 July

With Raymond I penetrated the world of the Lees-Milnes. Neither of us felt entirely at ease. Raymond, hunched and miserable in the queues at Paddington, said he would have turned tail had it not been for me. As we ate breakfast together on the Monday morning train home he asked touchingly, 'Did I disgrace myself? I really dislike staying with people who hate me . . .' 'But they don't!!' I protested in all honesty. 'Oh, yes, Alvilde does. You see, we committed the unforgivable sin and invited Jim to Crichel with his boyfriend, and Alvilde got in her car and drove across country and made a scene. She wouldn't come in.' She is a bristly Aberdeen terrier, someone *hors la loi*, one is never at ease with her . . . and yet and yet, I feel a sneaking sympathy for this poor little rich girl. She and Jim are outwardly loving, 'darlings' fly back and forth, yet according to Raymond the affair with the boyfriend is still paramount. So Alvilde buries her spiky heart in the garden, which is a glorious success, proliferating up walls, cascading, abundant, making blue pools round the feet of trees. Surely some sort of feeling emerges in all this beauty? Yet any other gardener would have given me some flowers to take to London and I would have asked any other hostess to let me pick some.

We were given delicious food, driven round to look at churches, and introduced to several strangers. One family interested me greatly. Charles Tomlinson, a poet, an original and accomplished artist, a don in English literature. A tall man, whose thin, sensitive, ascetic features corresponded with his sensitive, delicate and exact poems and designs. Sitting next him at dinner, I learned that he was a great friend of Octavio Paz (whose interview I'm now translating – and I've since come across references to Tomlinson in it). It's odd. He's not a charming man, but the delicacy and precision of what he does moves me quite a lot. His plump pigeon of a wife and two brilliantly clever, musical little girls, who never look at the telly but read George Eliot and play Schubert, might have been too good to be true, living in their pretty cottage at the end of a deep valley, taking no newspaper, having no wireless – yet they interest me. I mean not to lose sight of them altogether if I can help it.

Yesterday I whirled reluctantly up to Hampstead Garden Suburb to have tea on the lawn with a young couple of American academics – she is the Bunny specialist, and I had given her my letters from Bunny to read and said I would try to answer questions. She was impressed by the letters, said they were 'the finest collection she had seen', and seemed to feel that Bunny and I had a delightful and happy relation. Yes, I think we do. Some of her questions were obscure to me. 'Why hadn't he written any novels during such long periods?' Why should he? I tried to convey that his life was always full, always enjoyed.

A grey roof has returned over London. There's a greyness in my head. The combination of that greyness with the gaudy crowds of foreigners swinging plastic bags through Trafalgar Square struck me today as inexpressibly sad and ugly. I only found comfort when I was back with my dictionaries.

Truth to tell my spirits are low, and I don't feel very well. Last night I lay in my nightgown on the sofa in the box of my sitting-room, lights out, tall oblongs of white-painted stucco opposite, listening to Christoff singing *Boris Godunov*. This box, I thought, has contained me for over ten years, like a solitary sardine in its tin. When the opera was over I tumbled sadly into bed.

28 July

Eardley and Duncan have been painting Rosamond in Eardley's studio, but Eardley quailed into impotence before this mountainous figure draped in a robe of bright green silk. He said the best times were when she talked. She described how the daughter of Peter Morris's 'girlfriend' had been so fixed on Peter himself that when she married she could have no children and the marriage broke up. Then Peter died, she married again and produced several 'strapping children'. Rosamond said musingly, 'I'm sure Peter was responsible.' After she'd left, Eardley said to Duncan, 'Does she really think Peter begat the children from the next world?' Duncan: 'I don't know; but I'm sure she was up to some mischief.'

Alvilde told me that Ros slept in the room I had at Alderley, and in the morning said, 'You know that room is haunted. I think it's a nun under the floorboards.' (The pipes give off gentle reports now and again.) When I told Raymond this, he said, 'Well really, a *nun*! She might have been more original and said a greengrocer.'

30 July
The husbands of absent friends left alone during the hols came to dinner. Robin last night, Robert next week. Robin, who came half an hour before he was expected, stayed till twenty to one, quite a long stretch of tête-à-tête, easy enough, though I began to long for my bed towards the end of it. The chief impression he left was of a tired horse longing to sink down between the shafts, not enjoying its daily trot with a burden. I think his relations with Susan are particularly good – he rang her up long and lovingly. But he longs for retirement and is bewildered by feeling so tired. No doctor seems to be keeping an eye on him, and he said he felt in some sort of decline. I said we all were, and he surprised me by saying, 'You're the only person who doesn't change. You haven't changed *at all* ever since I first knew you.' This must be rated a compliment (I knew of course he meant mentally and characterologically) and one shouldn't record it. But naturally I was pleased.

2 August
My jaunt to King's Lynn Festival with Desmond is successfully over, though I feel flat as a pancake today after a non-stop drive of about four hours from Blickling Hall (near Cromer) to London. Desmond drives much better than people say, but he had set himself a time to arrive and was straining every nerve to do so. While going posthaste ahead he asked me at times to help him out of the sleeves of his shirt, because the sun was shining, or in

again because it wasn't, or to fix a funny little peaked cotton cap on top of his bald head. I enjoyed myself very much and he didn't once 'go off with a bang' and was delightful company. All the same, there was the slight strain of anxious adjustment to another person, anticipating their desires, with the added knowledge that Desmond doesn't like too much compliance.

Our hotel at King's Lynn was comfortable and gave us delicious food. First night of performance of a new 'Dialogue for Cello and Orchestra' by Lennox Berkeley, and another work by Elizabeth Maconchy. Enter the Queen Mum, tittupping along on pig's-trotter shoes with, I must say, a very gracious and pleasing expression, radiating charm – even if consciously – and even if it struck me her face was a little like Harold Wilson's. Being in a church, our seats were incredibly hard, and I find it a distraction being in the house of God, my mind going off onto the subject of religion.

Next day, Saturday, we pelted round Lynn, looking at exhibitions and fine houses and down onto the great grey-green estuary of the Great Ouse. Then drove out to lunch with Lady Cholmondeley at Houghton Hall, where we found the Stones and Berkeleys all staying. Everyone had told me it was 'the most splendid house in England', so perhaps it disappointed me a little. *Too* splendid, too pompous, too lacking in grace and charm or lightness of touch. The same for its furnishings and, apart from a fine Holbein and some Gainsboroughs, the pictures weren't 'all that delightful'. Lady Cholmondeley (out when we arrived) returned with a coarse-looking MP whose nose sprouted black hair and who was once Billa Harrod's lover, perhaps still is; I disliked him. Lady Cholmondeley was extremely chummy, and seemed to single me out, heaven knows why, for her attentions; she sat me next to her at lunch, 'Otherwise I shan't see you and

I've heard so much about you from mutual friends.' I trust she will drop me after this. It's not a world I like, and too much of a strain pretending it is.

Desmond and I drove off to another concert, of baroque music, after lunch and the evening ended with a firework display across the Ouse.

3 August

Flat and working flat out all yesterday. The Bunny specialist came to see me again in the afternoon; she stayed some time talking and returning Bunny's letters, which I'd lent her. They are, I do think, awfully good. I spent the evening rereading them and laughed aloud several times. Another Bloomsbury-hound comes tomorrow. This morning the rain is clattering down on shining roofs.

4 August

A splendid conversation with Robert last night, the best sort. We went first to *Claire's Knee*, a film recommended by Julian, and agreed in our estimation of it as on the whole pretentious and failing to tap the emotions or any real profundities.

Both these our conversation *did*; as for the first, I felt a tear trickling down my cheek. Robert did that infinitely flattering thing of talking with apparent openness about himself and his feelings, his life, his relations with Cynthia, and assuaged my undercurrent of anxiety about his suicidal tendencies. He is taking a new form of treatment by pills, not psychoanalysis, from a Jewish doctor who has 'the attitude of a mechanic' and describes his trouble as 'variable depression'. Whether as a result of the pills or from relief at his family being away for about ten days, he seemed more 'all right' than usual. This doctor asked him point blank if he and Cynthia would have parted except for the children. It's clear they would, and that Robert thinks they still will when the children are older. 'It's been so really *ghastly* for such a long time. The trouble is we're neither of us able to get along on our own. We prop each other up, at least I suppose we do.' He said he thought it was worse for Cynthia than him, that she was permanently scarred and embittered, her not eating is 'aimed at him'. The doctor had them both to a joint session and said to Cynthia, 'You're afraid of this man, aren't you?' Well, no doubt with reason, and I noticed that Robert betrayed no shame over this fact. Also that he was pleased that, though Cynthia had told the doctor that 'it was getting worse all the time', she had 'given herself away' and 'been caught out' saying something else which proved it wasn't. I begged him to hang on like mad to his marvellous, unequalled sense of reality, also to all the pleasures he's so good at extracting – from music, places, books, and above all his interest in everything that happens to him, including misery.

There was lots more on another level, about the cinema and Mr Wilson, the Labour politician whom he has seen a lot of lately and got to like better. 'He's a little man, a cheekie chappie, who happens to have an excellent brain which almost overbalances him.' He said he was fundamentally simple, adored the whole business of politics, and sincerely felt the most important thing was that the Labour Party should be back in power. Otherwise, *principles* or real sympathy for the Clydesiders thrown out of work – none. Nor did he have bad principles, he hastened to add. Merely none at all.

6 August, Cranborne

I don't like the feeling of being witlessly, mindlessly pushed along, 'like a bagatelle ball' as Julian said, so that I find myself out in

West Halkin Street with a basket on my arm, unaware where I'm off to. Also of the skein of the past and its sensations rushing by and *back* through my fingers, of the helpless struggle to fish out some small minnow from it. In the end I do often catch it, but after such an effort it seems worthless. Also in a cowardly way I take less chances, lead a more cautious life, submitting my antennae to less stimuli at once, to save dwindling energies.

Last week was a series of nose-to-nose contacts. Robert far the most stimulating. Then Joan, Faith, Margaret. My fears that Joan and I wouldn't make a go of it were I think unjustified. In the world of nose-to-nose one must be aware of, and face up to, the regions of non-overlap and extract what's possible from the overlap. But it's quite possible to enjoy in a different, detached, even amused way the areas of non-coincidence, and not get frantic with desire to alter them, or irritated as Julia does. There's quite a large, wide contact-bond between Joan and me – her liking for the truth for one thing. Outside it is a certain amount of conventionality, not taking moral judgements back to source, and I mind the way she suddenly switches off and doesn't listen. But we sat talking very easily in her bedroom on the top floor, and then looking out saw the now wonderfully clear sky of London had turned translucent peacock blue, and through the tossing tree tops, the sparkling lights of a skyscraper looked really pretty, with one silently moving aeroplane light seeming to have become detached from them. With Faith I talked politics; she is very clever and on the spot, but becoming what to me seems passionately reactionary like most of my generation, and we disagreed with near-heat.

How glad I felt to see Julian coming up the Waterloo platform. We talked intermittently in our full carriage, and of course ceaselessly since arrival here. I love the way David becomes immobilised by talk in the middle of some practical activity like carrying a suitcase into the house. So much so that when he's driving the car, I feel he might come to a halt suddenly in a stream of traffic. Then Rachel clatters downstairs with a wild, tragicomic gesture of welcome reminding me of Molly.

8 August

Great excitement because Hugh was bringing down a girlfriend, with the bizarre name of Mirabel. They arrived at tea-time. She turned out to be a voluptuous near-beauty, with a generous curly mouth, dimples, low warm voice, a friendly and outgoing nature. In the Mini, driving to have a drink with Cecil Beaton, I pinned Julian down to sit behind with me and discuss two crucial films and their implications, through which I could hear Rachel and David exchanging their impressions of Mirabel in excited *sotto voce*. At Beaton's were Frank Tait and a plain, goggle-glassed daughter of Osbert Lancaster ('an aggressively unmarried mother', so Rachel told me).

This morning, reams and reams of conversation — about selfishness with Rachel and David; when it was fatal and uncurable, when not. The former when it came from the lack of the sort of imagination that wants to enter the minds and feelings of others, the latter when it comes merely from being habitually spoilt, and contact with a tough and more selfish loved one (for one thing) can sometimes cure that. Julian laid himself out on the new 'relaxator' bed, asked me to psychoanalyse him, but answered 'Censored!' to all my questions. Since lunch there emerged from him a hatred of 'being preached at', of 'the eternal schoolmaster' so prevalent in the English character, and a strong resistance to Morgan Forster because of his 'disguised morality'. I was interested, feeling (perhaps wrongly) this to be a temporary obsession. For how, I asked, could one have novels, which deal with human relations, that don't involve moral issues? I should have said *values* – for the word 'moral' made him wince as it does so many. And of course I felt guiltily aware of the 'schoolteacher' within me. But he has one himself!

David's *bête noire* was the 'novelist with the divided mind', e.g. Graham Greene. What was wrong with Aldous Huxley as a novelist? None of us could now read them. And I said I was shocked by the credulity of a man as eager for facts as Raymond yet who fell for palmistry, mescalin, probably flying saucers, which didn't seem to me admirable as it did to Julian. Open-mindedness – I feel minds can be *too* open, the doors can get positively flabby from being allowed to flap about too freely. I felt, as I often feel when in company with people I'm very fond of and in the habit of communicating with freely, that Julian was taking part in a sort of shadow-argument with something he thought I was thinking and very likely wasn't. Or was *I* doing that? But I'm amazed by shrinking from the voicing of values of any sort; they are the breath of life to me. Lack of imagination? Selfishness? *Not* to realise how others feel about them? In this house there is so much repercussion, doubling back, unpicking, restitching, that one runs aground suddenly on a hidden sand-bank, forgetting the side-streams one had been about to follow.

11 *August*
I felt Angelica had drifted out of reach, and (reminded of her uniqueness by rereading Bunny's letters) asked her to dinner. We got onto such an easy footing and there was so much to say, that I wished I'd not asked Eardley to come in with Joan afterwards. With a flick, what had been real communication turned into chitchat. Angelica's metal is so real and rings so true as to turn

Joan's to pinchbeck beside it and, as if realising this, she looked unhappily at her watch and soon left.

I cling to the *simplicity* of depending on the truth. And the truth is, here, that though I recognise Angelica's superior quality and distinction, Joan has something I love and value.

13 August

Julian gave a charming party to which I went with Georgia who dined with me first. Like all really good parties it was bound and blended (sauce-wise) by the love all the guests felt for their host. Also Julian's 'nest' has been redone and glows with prettiness and probably the love of the friend who redid it. Tam and Andrew Murray-Thripland were there, Joan Leigh-Fermor (a nice surprise), Betjeman and his 'Feeble',[1] Diana Cooper, Judy Montague (*very* plain). I most enjoyed talking to another Andrew from the BBC, a colleague of Julian's, and was entranced and magnetised by his wide gaze and slow charming smile and what seemed to flow out from his face and voice – utter integrity, the best sort of curiosity, someone of rare sweetness and loveability. I left about one, still feeling fresh and untired but, as always, determined to go before either sensation stopped.

14 August, Thorington, rain falling

My six weeks as a wandering Jewess began yesterday, when Mrs Murphy went off on holiday. I began very quickly to feel lost without her. I miss her. She supports me.

I meant to drive down here early in the day but Margaret asked me to bring Lionel who was in London for the day. The 'arrangements' had that professorial and ramshackle uncertainty

---

1 His nickname for Lady Elizabeth Cavendish.

typical of Lionel. I had wanted to avoid Friday's grizzly rush-hour, which is a degradation and futility that I try to cut out. Impossible, of course – Lionel when cornered with some difficulty by me, said he'd be ready between six and six-thirty. The traffic was '*er*palling';[1] it took over an hour's slow grind, among furious, vicious, hooting cars to get to Rodborough road at all. Lionel was on the telephone; enter three charming young Spaniards who are living there at present, jabber jabber in two tongues. Lionel appears, coated and hatted, holding his drooping paws up in front in a gesture of professorial helplessness reminiscent of Sir Frederick Pollock[2] and perhaps characteristic of learned men. We start to get in the car and he remembers a hundred and one things he ought to do. At seven-fifteen at last – departure.

Well, of course Lionel is a delightful companion and he talked happily and entertainingly about his own subject. Told me a story of a sex change he had been called in to adjudicate on – a registered male becoming female and marrying a man. Chromosome tests were not – as they usually are – conclusively male or female, I couldn't quite grasp why or how, and he believes it is a case of a genuine hermaphrodite with rather rudimentary womb and testes, who has a legitimate right to choose which to be. The traffic congestion was frightful and by the time we reached a faster road it was dark and I was tired. I really *hate* hurtling along between sky and earth as it seems, amid a wilderness of moving lights. Largely guesswork; and with great relief we turned off into narrower lanes, for the last mile or two. Thank

---

1 One of Janetta's telling locutions.
2 Husband of one of my godmothers, a member of Henry James's circle at Rye.

heaven the 'servants', Freddie and Bessie, aren't here. Though Jane Rendel,[1] her husband Sandy, and two little children are sleeping here they are mostly out at the Hoylands' opposite, leaving Margaret, Lionel and me. And all isn't well, oh dear me, no. When (after a morning's work in the telly room) I went in to the drawing-room at one-fifteen (lunch was announced to be one) Margaret was in tears and a row in progress. She got up and rushed out, banging the door. Oh, *how* she bangs, shouts and stamps. I can't help finding it infuriating at times. Her shouting makes Lionel and me talk softer in the hope of inducing her to do likewise, but that only makes her shout louder. She cooked us some 'fillets of sole', about which there had been much talk. They were burnt to slivers of hard coconut matting; spinach was slopped into a dish, while she wiped her nose on the roller-towel. The banging down of dishes and crashing about and slopping makes one feel one is in an orphanage. Then she contrived to drop her spectacles on a walk so that they were crushed by a car. It is infinitely distressing – I felt her pathos, her goodness and kindness, her insensitivity – all of it acutely. Lionel is in a way much more sensitive but also more selfish. Going a walk with the two of them is agony – Lionel takes well-known (to me) angina walks, slow (especially at the start) and with pauses. Margaret pays no attention, plods ahead, and then suddenly drops behind and stares about her, but is never with us. As I remember *intimately* how aware I was of keeping in time with Ralph, and never hurrying him, making excuses to stop and pick a flower when I sensed he wanted to dally, I simply can't understand it. I feel *great* sympathy for poor Lionel in his plight, walking down his one-way corridor, and also great affection. Margaret must be dreadfully

---

[1] My great-niece.

unhappy, but it makes her behave almost insanely at times. For instance, after lunch she was eager to go for a walk (I would rather have gone alone with her and had her troubles out, but she asked Lionel). I went upstairs to change my shoes and when I got down she was lying on the sofa, fast asleep. She goes often to the cupboard and pours herself out a nip of whisky which (far from having a calming effect) makes her noisier and angrier.

15 August

Yesterday afternoon Margaret announced that Lionel was putting a call through to Warsaw, and took me off to look at her seakale, which was hopeless, about six months too old to eat. I asked her what had upset her so much before lunch. 'We were having the worst row we've ever had in our lives.' It started by Lionel asking Margaret about her possibly going abroad with the Sissons, while he pays a six-week visit to Dunyusha. '*I* don't want to keep travelling about with the Sissons,' she said. But with awful detachment I saw that Lionel had tried to show an interest in her life, some solicitude; had he *not*, she would have had cause for indignation. Then out flew various bottled charges: 'How could Lionel blame her for this and that, when he was all the time committing adultery? Did he want her to divorce him?' 'That couldn't be nice for *you*,' he said (clumsily, but it's certainly what he feels).

I asked Margaret if she would really rather divorce him, and she said anything was better than the present state of things. Dunyusha has made Lionel promise to 'be faithful to her', so Margaret has moved into another room. Of course she is the greater sufferer. He's having the fun; and when he talked to me (he's invariably charming to me) he seemed quite sanguine about his health. So perhaps Margaret's view that he will die soon is (as he thinks or says) partly wish-fulfilment.

Though two good human beings are involved, it's a sordid situation, just as the unkempt house, greasy wash basins, tin spoons and forks, Woolworth glasses and packet non-foods are sordid. No feeling at all for quality.

16 August

A further blow for poor Margaret. She rang the Sissons and they are obviously backing out of their plan. 'I'm afraid we're going to be rather treacherous . . .' They've now become 'the best people in the world to travel with', but I fear the truth may be that they did find her too noisy and bossy before. Feeling the ghost of unhappiness clinging round the house (after Margaret had wildly accused Lionel of locking the garage door and hiding the key, he had suddenly shouted 'SHUT UP!' and the key had been found in the lock), I took off quickly for a healing walk by myself – as I hoped. But first the narrow main road with its procession of possessed, glassy-eyed demons in stinking boxes, and then the Essex cabbage fields, got me down. Finally I crossed a narrow plank bridge and tried to fight my way through shoulder-high weeds and low ones that coiled round my legs till I thought I must surely be dreaming, not awake.

Today, November weather has vanished, and it is cloudless, full summer. I've just driven over to see Phyllis[1] at Lawford, finding her alone with Martin just back from abroad. She looked thin, bright eyed, and handsomer than ever; frail, a little unsteady on her legs. We talked for an hour before lunch, after which I at once left. I thought her extraordinarily brave, realistic, still

---

1 Nichols; she was already ill with cancer.

interested in getting my signature to preserve the life of baby seals, still putting animals before men, perhaps not finding life quite intolerable but clearly not counting on there being much more of it. She was nearly in tears when I left. One braces oneself to meet such encounters and doesn't therefore actually shed tears – but I was terribly harrowed and moved, and still am to think of her fighting her rearguard battle.

The glorious day has mellowed everyone. I've come to the conclusion that there's love and affection and responsibility towards each other still in the Penroses' relation. There's also, of course, abrasive irritability. Margaret complains of Lionel's 'paranoid' way of attributing all ills to her – but she is just as bad, witness the key incident. Yet through it all she can worry and work and contrive how to find a home for a nice, intelligent old lady who has become senile.

18 August
My journey home through the endless East End of London was nearly as bad, and rather like my struggle with the Essex weeds. Monday had been much more serene.

20 August, the Slade
The peace here is greater than anywhere except Bunny's Verger. Concentration on reading and thought is easy. Talked about this to Eardley at lunch, describing the torturous situation at Thorington. He admitted that love was always, if truly love, possessive, but thought that that side shouldn't be indulged in, and was strenuously in favour of independence. What gave independence? Well, it seemed to boil down to living in separate houses, as he and Mattei do. If there was marriage for homosexuals, I asked, would many go in for it? He thought only a few;

I'm not so sure. I asked if he had shared a habitation with Frank Coombs? In theory no, but in practice yes, for months at a time. Whatever Eardley's practical philosophy, it works, and he has been happily spending hours painting in a sandpit near Bedales. But he admits that unless he looks at television he can't endure the evening solitude.

20 August

Polished off my stint of translation and took a lonely, drizzling walk but enjoyed it. Mattei was expected for dinner, for which I cooked a chicken in cider and tarragon and Eardley made peaches in orange juice. The advent of the loved one produced a rather giggly state in him, and I'm sure this waiting happens every weekend. Mattei refused to be met at the station and finally arrived in Robert Wellington's car about nine-thirty, looking bronzed from a Greek holiday, thinner and very handsome.

23 August

Summer and London again, perching briefly before I take off the day after tomorrow. I drove over to the Blakistons to pick up Joan and brought her back to London. She is, I'm afraid, a bit offended that Eardley hasn't asked her to the Slade again since we went there together, and 'wondered whether she ought to suggest it'. When he dined with her, she thought him very rattled and asked him point blank if 'anything was wrong', on which he flared up indignantly at having his privacy infringed on. It's odd after all these years *not* to realise that neither of the above are advisable tactics with Eardley.

24 August

I returned to a glorious batch of letters, fine long ones from Robert, Bunny, Heywood, and poor Margaret's curly script like a row of midget cauliflowers, oblivious as ever (I could hear the tramp and bang of her progress) but deeply cast down because Marjorie Sisson has had a stroke and is lying possibly at death's door.

A postcard from Janetta asking me to bring an 'etching pen' has led to endless telephoning and a journey through the inferno of Oxford Street. The eeriness of the universe is in full crescendo. Julian, who dined with me last night, wore a halo of it, of which I was so sensible that I could hardly find words to encourage him. Instead of travelling out to Australia with his friends, Betjeman and 'Feeble', he has to set off on the frightening journey all alone and be there a fortnight all alone too. His eagerness for the experience has sagged, and I only hope the appetite will revive.

25 August

Packing, sorting, new specs called for. How cumbrous are the arrangements for transporting oneself only a few hours away! It's as if one of my feet was already in the air feeling helplessly for the next rung of the ladder, and the imagination (feeble in my case) gradually plants tiny roots in the scenes to come, and wrenches at those that hold me here. Last night I drove to Canonbury and dined with Raymond; he had gone to a cocktail party and for a while I had to make do with grouchy old Paul Hyslop, bending and grunting over his petit-point, and his absurdly pansified friend Jack Lander. The arrival of Raymond was a blast of fresh air.

28 August, San Stefano, Corfu

My bus to the air terminal was so empty that I thought the aeroplane would be empty too. But not a bit of it. Arrived at Heathrow, we were hurried straight to our exit gate, no time to buy whisky or have a drink, and in the intestine leading to the creature our bags were searched and our persons frisked by a posse of police in shirt sleeves, looking disarmingly defenceless because they had deposited their helmets on the floor. A female bobby searched us women, investigating even the tall boots one girl was wearing. Was it a spot check or had they cause for suspicion? A nice Greek girl sitting beside me in the aeroplane thought the latter. Horrified to find a whole busload had already taken their seats before us, so I had to take the middle seat between my Greek companion and a soporific businessman. Soon after take-off, 'turbulence' was announced and the huge pre-historic monster with its load of over a hundred souls began to pitch, judder and roll, not really disagreeably but it shook me into a passive state. I rang for a drink. A Greek hostess got up as a beautiful blonde but really ugly, dark and cross, said rudely, '*No*, madam. Not while seat-belts are fastened.' Not till midnight by Greek time were we hastily served with whisky and food (the turbulence having stopped) and there was only just time to swallow it. Then I was walking through the darkness, sniffing hard at a resinous waft in the air. It must be what goes into the wine, I thought vaguely. I saw Janetta's dear brown face through the door — how many airports hasn't she welcomed me at!! Behind her, Jaime and Alexandra Henderson.[1] We drove off along the countless bends of the coast for nearly an hour, flashing through Corfu town, with its noble houses shining honey-col-

---

1 Daughter of Nicko and Mary, now Countess of Drogheda.

oured, cream and pink in the headlights; afterwards indistinguishable olive-clad slopes, and the last bit of road down to this hamlet was supremely bumpy and rough.

I've now spent two nights in their rented house close to the edge of what seems more like a lake than the sea, because straight in front, extraordinarily close, is the unattainable shore of Albania, where no one is allowed to land. I am amazed and obsessed by the nearness of this unknown country.

The house is unpretentious but convenient, just built and not even quite finished. We look out on the taverna, one or two fishing boats, and the quay where the steamboat from Corfu puts in and some yachts. Across the water comes the shrill typewriter rattle of Greek voices, and calling of names ('Nico!' usually) and at nights the three-note tune of a bird, over and over, both melancholy and poetic. The morning light is brilliant, still and transparent.

Yesterday Jaime drove us to look at Jacob's[1] house, where a great many workmen were busy. Janetta, Alexandra and I descended into the next bay to bathe, near a two-storeyed farmhouse with striped rugs hanging from the windows, old women hooded in thin white cotton scarves and children on a swing. We went off the rocks into beautifully clear water and then lay in sun or shade.

I remember Julian saying in a small apologetic voice that he was 'bored' here. I'm pretty sure I shan't be and don't at all crave excursions. But I'm still dazed by the shock of transportation. An at-once noticeable change in Janetta is that she has started doing pen and ink drawings, with the same concentration she puts into everything. They are delightful and accomplished, and

---

1 Rothschild. Jaime was at work on his house.

I feel it's an excellent sign of her settled happiness. Rose has gone to Crete. Jaime is tremendously involved in Jacob's house, and apparently happily.

And I shall read, write letters and bathe.

29 August

When Janetta and Jaime went off together to his house I sat down on the terrace to write to Robert, but soon saw that Alexandra was needing attention. She responded at once. The Lycée had been a very bad education; she found it terribly difficult to express herself (this is quite true – it's all 'ackshally, sort-of, you know').

As for the married pair, they seem relaxed and content as never before. Janetta takes very little trouble with her appearance, but Jaime looks at her lovingly and is appreciative of what she does, particularly the new drawing phase. It's certainly the best thing that's happened to her for a long time, and I remember that when a year ago I suggested her going back to painting she said, 'Yes I want to, but I want to do it from a basis of allrightness and not as a sort of drug.' It's certainly her natural form of expression, and writing was not.

30 August

Our plan of life: breakfast downstairs on the back terrace between nine and ten, some dressed, some not, Jaime usually straight from bed with tousled hair; he then goes off to Jacob's house, elegantly stepping up the hill in bathing shorts and espadrilles carrying a briefcase – an odd sort of businessman.

There is a new craze for austerity, for healthy foods like grape-fruit and Ryvita. Jaime is anti-whisky; Alexandra won't eat fish; Janetta won't eat meat.

We've twice sallied forth in a tubby blue rubber boat with an engine to neighbouring bays to bathe, bumping over choppy seas, yesterday to a tiny beach cleft between rocks. The water is perfectly transparent and very warm, no shock at all getting in.

Yesterday we started for Corfu at five-thirty. We drove off and I saw for the first time the winding route we had traversed in the dark, so winding that one was never sure if one was looking at Corfu town or Albania. Corfu is a fine Venetian town, packed with tourists. I followed Janetta through the narrow streets to fish and fruit shops and then sat down with a newspaper in a café, watching the promenade – girls in white Minnie Mouse shoes or with plastic Grecian thongs right up to the knee, sailors and blackamoors, noisy Americans, women in evening dress, remarkably disgusting-looking hippies with pale, bespectacled or bearded faces peering through their lank Jesus hair.

We started home in the dark and stopped to eat halfway in a wayside restaurant. Delicious chicken pie in flaky pastry.

Sunday evening. We've had a dream of a day, bathing in an idyllic place in crystalline water warm as one's own blood and sitting on smooth rocks to eat the most delicious and imaginative picnic. Janetta has been touchingly sweet and affectionate to Jaime and he to her and she's now baking an elaborate cake for Alexandra's birthday, all this interspersed with dedicated hours spent drawing the olive trees.

31 August

My delight in what seems to be the stability and happiness of the relationship between the J.'s grows. Whether the ceremony of marriage was cause or effect I don't know, but their life seems much more of a joint life than it was, and Janetta relieved from that restlessness that has possessed her so long. In fact they appear to delight in each other, and it's joy to see it.

To celebrate Alexandra's birthday an outing was planned to the western coast, via Corfu. I had been buying a sponge as a birthday present and was heading back to the bar where we meet, when I heard a shriek and there was Susu's[1] long brown willowy shape hurtling towards me. There, too, was Magouche, whom I was delighted to see – in her dashing way she had hired a car for her two days with us. In these two cars we reached a little taverna hung with morning glory perched above an unattractive beach with seaweed, and the sea smelling of sulphur. High up on the white face of the opposite hill workmen toiled with yellow bulldozers in clouds of dust, making the foundations of a new hotel. But the taverna produced three very fresh fish, some eggs, tomatoes and retsina, which I've grown to like.

After lunch the party disintegrated – Susu and Alexandra went off in the hired car, Jaime went indoors to snooze, Janetta was lost in her world of drawing, sitting bolt upright on a kitchen chair. Magouche and I sat talking amid clouds of wasps and newspapers, until it was time to drive off to another bay and walk, which one can only do in the cool of evening, along a stony path through the olive groves. The olives of Corfu! They are unlike any others I've ever seen; allowed to grow free, unbranched and fantastically tall, their trunks are full of large 'eyes' or loopholes. We've seen several with fig trees growing out of them. We had started too late on our walk and the monastery was still far ahead when the scarlet football sun began to sink into the sea. Magouche was all for going on, but Janetta – to my relief – said it would be madness. As it was, we got home late and she valiantly at once began cooking tender little chickens in rice, almonds and

---

1 Susanna Phillips, Magouche's youngest daughter.

sultanas. Conversation about Saxon Sydney-Turner[1] for some reason; Janetta and I trying to convey him to the others.

2 September

On Magouche and Susu's last evening (out of two) Jaime went into Corfu and returned with a bright-eyed, excited-looking Rose behind him. She had arrived from Crete unannounced and was in tremendous form, telling us all about her adventures with José and Lucy Durán.[2]

In the evening heavy rain fell suddenly, making spots as big as half-crowns and soon everything was swimming and maquis smells filled the air. Janetta, Rose and I lunched in an open-air restaurant near the Achilleion – now a casino, formerly the house of Elizabeth, Empress of Austria and then of the Kaiser – and afterwards visited it. Its sumptuous garden was full of the smell of jasmine and pines and huge statues of Achilles. One of him trying to pull the arrow from his tendon fascinated Janetta, evoking from her sympathetic groans which greatly amused a gardener. We play Scrabble in the evenings – sometimes in Spanish, very difficult.

3 September

After the Magouche irruption, the four of us are leading a quiet family life. Feeling of change in the air; I have let time flow over me in a very unspeculative, semiconscious way, most of my attention being focused on the life of Charlotte Brontë I'm reading. Rose, Janetta and I walked up the hill behind the village.

---

1 Mystery figure of Bloomsbury.
2 Musicologist friend of Magouche's family and her husband.

Jaime brought a letter to us all from Julian, written in the aeroplane to Australia.

Every night I swathe myself in my loose, striped sheet of Greek handwoven cotton like a soldier on the battlefield, lie down on my platform bed with its hard pillow and fall almost instantly asleep, usually to be woken by the arrival of the Corfu boat at five-thirty, but fall asleep again.

4 September

A quiet private morning with Charlotte Brontë and letter-writing on the terrace; lunch at a taverna by the sea where Lawrence Durrell once lived. Jaime said, 'It would be nice perhaps to drive to the top of our mountain, Pantocrator, where there's a monastery.' We set off just as dusk was falling and turned inland off the Corfu road and began to climb steadily till the pink sun made a second appearance above the horizon. Up and up, through villages where everyone was sitting relaxed and watchful under their vine-covered arbours. Up and up, the huge mountain suddenly towering awfully above us. Excelsior. We left the good road and bumped and rattled and wound higher still, till some sort of wireless station appeared on a col above us. 'Is that the top?' Janetta asked nervously. Jaime said, 'No, I'm afraid we're still a very long way from the top.' And he now told us that he and Ed had tried to reach the top once before and Ed had got frightened because a huge wind was blowing and they turned back.

'Is this Windy Corner?' 'No, not yet,' said Jaime smiling rather sadistically. 'But say, of course, if you find it too frightening.' Frightening it certainly was, and Janetta sometimes softly said, 'Oh, Jaime!' as we wound round lacets so sharp that the car had to take two goes on a skiddy corner with nothing between us and the abyss. Then at last we were at the top. Almost the whole island and a lot of Albania lay mapped out below us in different pale blues, and in the foreground the village and its pitiful attempts at cultivation. The ground fell away so steeply that it must have been easy for the monks to contemplate eternity from there. But was it really a monastery? A small belfry, stalls with tables and seats for pilgrims. One mad-looking monk with a squint and hair growing out in two wild tufts from under his tall black hat was hacking away with a spade beside a wall. Rose boldly pushed open the door and we entered a chapel with a lot of seats of delicious-smelling cypress wood and a barrel roof with faded frescoes glowing dimly. The guidebook says this amazing place was begun in the fourteenth century.

5 September

The present closeness between J. and J. gives me intense pleasure, but inevitably shuts others out. I'm aware of the lack of intimate conversation between Janetta and me, and that she seems to feel no need of it. All is sweetness and light, however. Rose remains in a state of high articulacy and told me she was quite looking forward to London. Saturday is called 'Jaime's Sunday' as he takes time off from Jacob's house; this one was spent on a long excursion to Agios Gordis on the west coast involving a mar-vellous drive through gorges crammed with luscious vegetation – bamboos, apples, pears, cypresses – and small, unspoiled vil-lages, with flocks of sheep, girls riding donkeys, and old women looking really pretty with their brown wrinkled faces and dark burning eyes emerging from scarves of finest white cotton which they wear variously folded, with white blouses under dark bodices and full skirts of faded dark blue. This combines in a marvellous way with the grey olives, blue sea, green cypresses and fruit trees.

7 September

Mid-morning we set off for the Glenconners' house on the west coast. In a huge white barrel-roofed sitting-room, decorated in pale, washed-out blues, greys and greens, we found Elizabeth Glenconner and her daughter Catherine (a plump, handsome girl with alert responsive eyes and a ready smile full of excellent teeth). We were sent to a guest room to put on our bathing things and then embarked in a solid boat in merciful charge of a solid Corfiote boatman, and tossed, pitched and rolled appallingly round several headlands to a bay under a towering cliff, where we bathed in a purest peacock-blue water, while kingfishers swooped from the cliff. I knew that Janetta was dreading the return voyage as much as I was, and was equally appalled when Elizabeth Glenconner asked if we would mind going on further still before we went home to lunch. Janetta bravely said, 'Let's go back,' and back we went, in a considerably rougher sea. A young cousin, Simon Tennant, had also joined us, a member of Constable's publishing firm. I sat next him at lunch on the terrace and we talked about Ivy Compton-Burnett and her novels. Did I talk too much in general? And if so, was it because we have been going easy on talk?

8 September

Up to Jacob's house in the afternoon to photograph it for Jaime. Rose methodically and quietly packing up her belongings, including sheets, carpets, pots and baskets from Crete. Fairly early to bed and now my last morning has dawned. I go to Corfu and spend the night there and to Rome tomorrow. It is bewildering to think that I'm not flying home but to a new country and new companions. I have led a wonderfully happy, restful life here, and have surfaced, free-wheeling on my visual sensations, unconsciously and unanalytically.

Oh, alas! Janetta brought a *Times* from the airport and in it I read of Sebastian [Sprott]'s death. I was to have stayed with him next month. One by one the old friends vanish. After dinner in Corfu, I parted from my two dear friends and retired to my hotel room.

9 September, 7.15 a.m.

Sitting in a small Italian plane waiting to go to Rome. But why don't we start? 'Sixty minutes' delay. We must ask all the passengers to get out.' I got up at five-thirty this morning, and it's cold.

11 September

I flew from Corfu to Rome yesterday evening; a crashing thunderstorm and deluges of rain darkened the skies and came through the glass roof of the Minerva Hotel just as Dadie was due to arrive at the airport. I descended to wait for him about eight, after a peaceable day by myself, and very soon he dashed in, eager and voluble, with his friend John Cambridge, now at the Embassy, who either by nature or infection generated as much noise and excitement as Dadie. This genial fellow drove us off to his huge bachelor flat in the Doria Pamphili palace, where he had four or five grand, large sitting-rooms full of sumptuous furniture and dubious old masters, and opened a bottle of champagne in our honour. A plumpish, clever man, with neat features making spots on the cubical dice of his head. We stared out into the darkness over two of the courtyards of this vast palace, which is a town in itself. Then to a restaurant in the ghetto quarter for dinner of prosciutto and figs followed by little globe artichokes fried whole 'in the Jewish style'. Before bed, Cambridge whisked us up to look at the floodlit Campidoglio and Forum.

We woke this morning to more thunder and drenching rain. Raymond's friends Viv Wanamaker and her lover were sending a car to fetch us to their castello; but first Dadie and I splashed round to the two nearest churches, as well as the Pantheon and Piazza Navona. In teeming traffic and rain we drove out to the astonishing castle rented by Raymond's friends. I liked them both – he is a film producer with heart trouble and she a friendly, grey-haired woman, simple in manner and looking extremely elegant in her bright red stockings. After lunch these kind people sent us on in their car to Orvieto; Raymond very chatty as we sat in the back, he asked me almost nothing about Corfu.

Here at Orvieto – the Signorellis and the mystery of memory. I couldn't have described them before seeing them, for my brief and only previous visit was at least thirteen years ago (more I think) with Ralph and the Lambs. But as I studied them I knew their image had been latent somewhere in my mind. So had the façade of the cathedral, made almost hideous and shocking by its gaudy modern mosaics, but beautiful bas-reliefs. After a clear, warm evening, whisky, thunder again and a good dinner at the star restaurant belonging to our hotel. From my window I look out over roofs and a high terrace full of flowerpots where a woman is busy ironing, sewing or watering.

12 September

There's an unexpected ding-dong going on between Raymond and Dadie. Raymond suspects Dadie of teasing him, but it's done affectionately, almost flirtatiously. Dadie keeps us up to the mark of course, but I don't mind that a bit, and love his enthusiasm and vitality. I've been appointed map-reader and common-purse holder.

Two museums after lunch. Dadie and I walked to the enormously deep double well at the far end of the town and the Etruscan temple.

The more we saw of Orvieto the more we loved it and its brown streets hung with flowerpots. The lack of pavements is, though dangerous, always a pleasure; as in Rome the bare right angle between wall and cobbled street gives a curious pang of delight. Back to the Signorellis, with even greater wonder and admiration. An uncompromising painter, original, modern, inventive, sometimes almost coarse in detail. A jolly dinner at our star restaurant. We're getting on well, I think. There's been talk between the others of Dadie's 'fits of hysteria or rage', but so far no sign of them! They both like to go into *what's happening* in pictures more than I do. This morning I managed to hound down the blue-and-white church of a convent of austere nuns; it was very pretty, not austere and rather feminine.

Then we took the train to Arezzo.

13 September, Arezzo

Our hotel here is impersonal and unsympathetic but perfectly all right – each room with shower and lavatory. Raymond always finds something wrong, however – the light in the wrong place, the room too SMALL, the bed too LARGE, his towel doesn't MOP him properly. In fact he pounces on these defects so eagerly that I think it would disappoint him not to find them, and as Dadie pointed out he even found fault with his friends' luxurious castello ('bed facing the window'). Dadie and I are more adaptable and 'manage' better, I think.

After late lunch yesterday we went straight off to look at the

Pieros – and my God, they are *stunning*. In the presence of such genius one's emotions well up, brim and overflow. One can now put a hundred-lire piece in a machine which lights them up for five minutes – a great improvement. So we put in more and more lire pieces and gazed and gazed. Then to Santa Maria della Pieve, and the great Duomo, with another Piero of Mary Magdalen, holding her cloak in fascinating folds. These buildings, and the streets of tall houses and the Piazza Grande with its enormous loggia are all lavish in space and proportions. So is the long, steep street for walkers only, paved with flagstones set diamond-wise and dipping in the middle to collect the rain. Alas, this had returned to us, but by the hour of the *paseo* it stopped and crowds began their parade – a lot of them young and handsome, few beards, thick curly well-cut hair, girls in sandals with thongs to the knee, all moving well.

14 September

Oh, Italian weather! Woke to grey skies, then wind and cold. Raymond always goes down to breakfast, while Dadie and I delight in our bedroom trays. When I went down yesterday I found Raymond triumphant at having engaged a car to take us to Cortona, and on to Urbino tomorrow. I congratulated him, but Dadie was disapproving. 'You should have asked us first; you must never engage a car before consulting "the tourist office"!' This irritation between Raymond and Dadie puts me in a slightly awkward position, having to balance the issues without favouritism.

I begin to remember how *factual* Raymond's approach is. Apart from what's going on in pictures and his pleasure in recognition of styles and periods, I do wonder how much he *enjoys* works of art. As soon as he enters a church he halts and says quickly, 'Early

Tuscan Romanesque, with sixteenth-century additions, and the dome added later of course.' What can one reply? Is it a sort of game of snap, which he always wins and in any case no one else is playing – or just a form of boasting?

Back to Arezzo, Dadie and I went late in the afternoon for another look at the stupendous Pieros, but long and hungrily as I looked, I felt my inadequacy to grasp and digest them all, and a sort of frustration before the glory emanating from those walls which I shall probably never see again.

Raymond tells me that Dadie is a puritan at heart and always prides himself on doing without what others are enjoying. This is partly based on the fact that at stations he prefers to carry Raymond's appallingly heavy suitcase as well as his own instead of getting a porter, which *is* a trifle self-immolatory, perhaps.

15 September

We've seen no other Signorellis as masterly as those of Orvieto; he makes intricate constructions of shapes, especially with hands and feet, and this combined with all-overish Turkey-carpet colour gives me the impression of a serious and intellectual, rather sombre character who doesn't glorify the universe like Piero.

We have now reached Urbino by car, via Montecchio and San Sepolcro. The *Resurrection* just as tremendous as it can be; each time the eyes leave it and return there's the same authentic thrill. I come nearer to understanding religious emotion when I'm looking at that painting than at any other time. We are lodged in a small hotel in a narrow, cobbled alley, in monks' cells with crucifixes over the bed and a communal bathroom. An ailing, middle-aged man coughs and sneezes as he brings our breakfasts up.

16 September

We saw Urbino very thoroughly yesterday – the splendid Palazzo Ducale, Piero's gentle, unsadistic *Flagellation*, *Hercules and Iole*. Raymond in capricious mood, hunting out 'amusing' oddities to enjoy, showing off his information more compulsively as we become less responsive. I find Dadie's enquiring approach much more sympathetic. But I think we're trying to stuff in too much, and wonder if what refuses to detach itself from the *mêlée* (like the Duomo at Urbino) has left behind anything worth having.

18 September

And thence to Módena – to which Raymond was keen to come apparently because 'forty years ago I spent a miserable night here trying to go to bed with a woman and failing'.

Walked to the Duomo and its museum of sculpture, its crypt and inlaid wooden stalls. Dined in a two-star restaurant, ate too much and felt uncomfortably gorged. Conversation never centres on general subjects; the jokes are of a teasing, donnish sort; Raymond likes to talk about the book he is reading (all right if others have read it) and catalogue facts. I find this dull, and the fact that he never listens to a word one says to him, and the longest reply one gets to a remark is 'Ah', both snubbing and frustrating. *I love him, of course*. But though I tend every time to forget his defects as a travelling companion, they don't decrease with the years.

19 September, Módena to Mantua

We squeezed the last drop from Módena, had a good lunch, and took the train to Mantua – a lovely and lovable town. Our hotel is delightful, right on the Piazza d'Erbe, looking out and down on the roof of the small rotunda of San Lorenzo with its tiles crowded with pigeons as thick as barnacles, and other belfries and towers beyond. Stalls of fruit and flowers go up every morning below us and an extravagantly wide and shallow flight of steps leads down to this small round church. (The strange pleasure to be got from proportions.)

The Ducal Palace is shut both today and tomorrow, so to my delight we stay two nights instead of one; and all have splendid double rooms with proper bathrooms.

20 September

A 'day of rest' ending with a visit to Mantegna's tomb in the Church of St Andrea, shown us by a tiny boy with a piping voice, manipulating a wavering electric torch like a hose. I quite deliberately tried to start a subject of conversation at dinner, about different sorts of selfishness and their relation to insensitivity, and whether it was worse not to be aware what other people were feeling, or to know and still ruthlessly pursue your own ends. Raymond seemed to say 'Ah!' to all this, but in fact, after a few moments' digestion, took it up and it carried us through the meal, along with the infectious fits of laughter of a little boy of about five at another table.

21 September, Mantua to Verona

This last an emendation of our route, which delights me, though I had no part in it. We went to see the Palazzo Ducale at Mantua first thing. It's the only place we've been herded round with other tourists and I hated that, but the Mantegna room, if nothing else, made up for it. Beside these masterpieces the halls of mirrors, and the apartment of the dwarfs, grow dim. Then to the summer palace de Te, architecturally pretty, with frescoes of giants by Giulio Romano, a coarse painter whom I don't care for.

I love Mantua; it has been in no way disappointing.

Dadie again suggested we go by car to Verona; Raymond, patently relieved, said he had resolved not to press us to travel more extravagantly than we wanted to. Nor I suppose has he *exactly*, and yet on the whole he has quietly got his way, and we've travelled in his style rather than ours.

One of Dadie's rare moments of grumpiness when, arrived at Verona, neither Raymond nor I wanted to dash out at once. I like my quiet time, even though I don't sleep during it. When we did follow our scoutmaster leader out into the marvellous centre of the town, he resisted Raymond's desire to sit in a café in the Piazza d'Erbe but, backed by me, we did. Verona's richness and beauty is great compared to Ferrara and Módena. During our whisky session Dadie and I talked unguardedly, unaware how thin was the door between Raymond's room and mine. *What* did he hear? Dadie saying firmly that he meant to divert Raymond from adding Brescia to our itinerary? Or just the jollity that always goes on at these times? I think Dadie was more irritated by 'Ray' at Verona than I was; I've come to terms with the fact that he never listens to a word I say. After dinner he wanted to walk to the Piazza again (Dadie's third visit today). He is excited by the handsome young men with their renaissance hair and elegant clothes and figures, gets carried away and waves and beckons at them embarrassingly, murmuring that they are 'very pretty'.

23 September

Set off in our hired car about ten and found our way with difficulty to the heart of Brescia – a piazza surrounded by disparate buildings which gave Raymond plenty of opportunity to say 'snap'. Arrived rather late at Bergamo in an unsympathetic hotel in the lower town. On the way there Raymond suddenly said, 'I'm so sorry our tour is coming to an end. I've been looking forward to it for months, and now I shall have nothing to look forward to,' touchingly, like a child. I do hope he has enjoyed it, and that we haven't been too disappointing in our lack of response to his information. Part of his looking forward was probably to imparting it, and the other day he said semi-comically that he hoped we 'were making notes of his pearls of wisdom'.

But my worst moment was yet to come. Late, too late, to the picture gallery, to find an astonishing collection: Botticellis, Bellinis, Antonello da Messina, Lorenzo Monaco, Titian, Tintoretto, Velásquez, Guardi, Raphael, Perugino — so overpoweringly exciting to me that I suddenly overboiled with irritation at Raymond's constant interruptions of my all-too inadequate concentration on these masterpieces with his 'pearls of wisdom', or actually getting in between me and the picture I was looking at in the physical sense. This last was what I brutally charged him with, but of course it was the interruption of his whole approach to looking at pictures that I was really protesting against. I'm ashamed and guilty, and the pleasure of being able to go on looking undisturbed and unjogged was small consolation.

We postponed our visit to the High Old Town till dark and dinner-time, and it was a great success, a stupendous experience. Taking a very steep, funicular train up into the blackness of night made it seem like going up to another world. And so it was, a magic one. Though the town is small (and can't spread, enclosed within its walls and on its rock) the buildings are on a gigantic, splendid scale of tallness. It's as if several imaginative geniuses had been set loose building a town for quite a few of Giulio Romano's giants: an octagonal baptistery, a noble, vastly tall portico, the Colleoni tomb richly coated in white marble sculpture. All made more magical by floodlighting. We wandered round corners and gasped at some new wonder, trying to avoid the cars and lambrettas that use the narrow, cobbled streets as a sort of race-track. Bergamo comes high in the exciting experiences of this trip. Mantua and Verona too.

24 September

I'm hoping yesterday's irritability was charged to my feeling unwell. All right again now. Up to look at the High Town in morning daylight. Dadie inclined to challenge Raymond's view about 'the way'; I thought it politic to stay with Raymond. After lunch Raymond returned to rest, and Dadie and I continued with our non-stop sightseeing, walking down the gradually sloping town wall towards the Pinacoteca. Little boys were eagerly collecting bags and baskets full of shining chestnuts; several fell from the trees as we walked, and down below the wall were neat vegetable gardens sprouting as if it were spring. Why was it that with Dadie I spent two happy hours looking at the pictures in the gallery, comparing impressions, drawing attention and having it drawn, and that he didn't once irritate me? Walked on down to the hotel – a long road, and up to dinner in the Old Town again.

25 September

Another car to Milan and so home.

28 September, West Halkin Street

I've spent three nights in my own bed and hardly feel I've come to my senses yet. Looking back on my extra-long holiday, I feel as if I must have been so relaxed in Corfu as to be semi-conscious, and in Italy almost stupefied by the packed, intensive programme of sightseeing day after day. I slept well and have come back feeling well, yet almost at once London pincers have gripped me, the noise, responsibilities (for myself and some other people), and I sleep less deeply.

Joan greeted me most sweetly with bunches of flowers and dinner on my first night. She has taken in Rose as a lodger and of course loves her.

Both Kees on Sunday looked and said they felt ill. Robert with a heavy cold; Cynthia much too thin and complaining of a pain in her chest but refusing to see a doctor. When I remarked that Rose had had a red nose and purple fingers when she was anorexic, she said, 'Oh, did you know that "cyanosed extremities" was a symptom of anorexia?' I think she has it herself; she once told me she had in the past, but I believe it's with her still.

I think and ponder about the structure of Raymond's character and the strange way his mind works.

5 October

A second visit from the young American, Stanley Olsen, who is writing about the Hogarth Press, was heralded with a nightmare – I had lost Ralph in a huge, horrible liner, and was searching desperately for him, but large pieces of Victorian furniture blocked the corridors. I could find no trace of him but toothpaste and passports. I woke in terror and horror. 'Day's residues'; pictures in the paper of pathetic passports after a fatal air crash – and of course the fact that I knew I must 'search for Ralph' among his letters. There can still, after all these years, be a ghastly shock that breaks like a wave, and this submerged me as I sat listening to a concert of superb Mozart and Haydn, which blended with my tumultuous feelings. What sort of emotions? Pity, terror and beauty.

Joan abreacts her loss of Cochemé very freely. Faith on the telephone referred slightly acidly to this. I see no harm, except that unimaginative people will think it time she stopped talking so much and often about her grief, merely because it is embarrassing and inconvenient to them. And perhaps there's a danger of her feeling her own loss to be special in an absolute way, not merely to herself.

6 October

I'm disturbed by certain reclusive tendencies I've lately found in myself, a desire to withdraw from the world, perhaps be as unaware as possible, a dislike for whatever I'm doing, and a way of doing things as mechanically and unconsciously as I can. All of this is totally contrary to what I believe to be my philosophy of life. Almost the only thing I haven't rejected is the pleasure I get at the orchestra. I was looking forward to meeting Margaret in the pub, first, but there was something rebarbative about her. 'You're looking *absolutely exhausted*', was her first remark. '*Are you?*'

Last night I went to a small dinner given by Ralph Jarvis – present Nancy Shuckburgh, a great friend of Joan's, Robin Fedden, and an old Etonian friend of Ralph's – euphoric, clever and semi-conventional. The Establishment premises lay like a firm skeleton beneath most of the conversation – viz. that we all subscribed to some religion (the Etonian several times mentioned proudly that he had a son who was a Roman Catholic priest), that Eton was the best school and Old Etonians were therefore better than other men; that class distinctions must be preserved and the rich allowed to remain so or get richer, if necessary by soaking the poor; that a classical education, horses and hunting and the arts were all equally valuable and made one an 'all-rounder', than which nothing was better.

One of the reasons I feel a recluse is that most of my contemporaries have moved to the right to support the Establishment, and only among my very young friends do I find those who agree about war and peace, class distinctions, or dislike of conventions. I crave more Bohemian company, or maybe none at all.

The Emperor of Japan is paying us an official visit. This has led to an outburst of old war hatred, and of people on the radio loudly patting themselves on the back for maintaining their hostility. 'I for one shall never forget, and never talk to a Japanese.' This ghastly racialism is to be found now even among many civilised people, whether towards the Irish, Germans, Russians or Japanese. And how on earth can they say such things about the Japanese if they for one second remember what *we* did to them at Hiroshima? How can they talk smugly about forgiveness?

Robin Fedden was fascinating about climbing the Andes – that I really did enjoy . . .

9 October

Weekend in London, fine and still. I feel pretty low and still obsessed with a persistent desire to give up the struggle and turn my face to the wall. Human and other contacts are the only thing that keep me going and I hurl myself from one to the other rather compulsively, wishing I could simply tuck up in bed between whiles. This may be partly the effect of a long struggle to fight off a cold, ending as these always do in a sort of truce.

Stanley Olsen came again yesterday. I do like him, and think his head is screwed on the right way; but one may tend to assume these young addicts of Bloomsbury get it more nearly right than they do. And what *is* right anyway? How can one balance the childishness with the maturity, the rationality with the emotionalism? A reviving 'contact' was the first night of *Aida* with

Desmond, which I greatly enjoyed, though I could always dispense with Act 2 Scene 2 and its dreadful ballet. Towards the end, when the final love duet was being touchingly sung, a couple made their way out, disturbing a Japanese man at the end of the line, who continued rustling his paper bag, to the frenzy of Desmond, who finally got up, darted across the gangway and (I think) hit him!

11 October

I spent Saturday afternoon with darling Sophie, taking her to a pretentious and bad Rambert ballet. We both agreed it was very 'boring' and came away before the end. I brought her back to tea, where she was gay company.

On Sunday I drove down to Marlow to lunch with Alix whom I'd not seen for some time. What a splendid woman she is! I thought of stupid old Lucy Norton's hints that her intelligence is crumbling. It could most certainly run rings round Lucy's. The workings of her mind, the gentle, strong way she builds a sometimes fantastic construction from premises that may be accurate or not (because she is cut off from the modern world) delight me. In a moment we were talking about death – no preliminaries are necessary with her. Her appalling nosebleeds had made her realise that it wasn't death she feared so much (indeed she would welcome it) as dying, and that when the danger of choking in her own blood became urgent, she had to fight for her life. I also feel she's an entirely *good* person; I can find nothing bad in her.

Philip, her brother, arrived for lunch – off delicious cold roast lamb, not touched by Alix. Discussion of the hostility to the Emperor of Japan. They both supported it. I declared they were being racialist. Philip is hopelessly so, won't go to Greece because of the Colonels or to Spain because of Franco. I'm amazed and appalled by this attitude on the part of once left-wing, and still leftish but drifting to the right, intellectuals.

I hate all racialism, and I know Ralph would agree with me, but no one else does. Perhaps it's this feeling out of tune with my coevals that gives me an unaccustomed basic pessimism at present.

I feel that stupidity, bigotry and ignorance have never been more rampant. Even splendid Alix (and of course Philip the sociologist) thought that, in the interests of making more money faster, people should face unemployment, and when I said that having nothing to do and feeling psychologically unwanted was the worst thing in the world for most people, she said, 'Yes, but they must be trained to profit from leisure.' But *how* can one do this to people over forty, suddenly thrown out of work? Is it really better that they should be given money to spend it on lower and lower forms of time-passing occupations like BINGO, which is increasingly driving out the cinema?

Sexual permissiveness seems to have become an issue, and as I'm out of it all I don't trust my judgements. But just as someone (I forget who) was distressed to think of flowers as nothing but sexual organs, I sometimes get a depressing sense that the London crowds are merely dressed-up sexual organs in search of orgasms, and wish I could remember that they also laugh, garden, confide their troubles and tuck up their children in bed at night.

Another rather mad feeling that seems to come from living alone: one thinks of oneself as another person, a sort of *doppelgänger*, with whom one lives at extremely close quarters but is not identified.

This morning, Monday, I feel better. I worried rather about Rose in the night, because she wrote me a sad little note about the horror of London Sunday. She comes to tea, and Margaret (whom I had slightly on my conscience) to lunch. She said on the telephone that Julia had rung her up saying she was going to commit suicide and wanted to discuss the means. Margaret seems to have been rather tough with her and more or less said, 'Go ahead.' Result – Julia has gone to stay with Lawrence and Jenny. She has to leave her flat – maybe she'll settle in with them. But I wonder if such an arrangement can possibly survive her desire to assert herself.

A comic Julia story from Margaret. At Thorington, anxious there shouldn't be a repetition of 'the milk is cold', she put some to heat for Julia's breakfast and went to have her bath. Thundering on the door, Julia cried, 'Where is the milk-strainer?' Margaret shouted, 'On the kitchen windowsill.' The old retainers, Freddie and Bessie, later became involved, declared that Julia had been shown the milk-strainer, and said, 'That! It's too disgusting. I can't possibly use it.' Julia, when this was perhaps unwisely reported back by Margaret, flew in to Freddie and Bessie, rated them soundly and told them they were liars. Lunch-time came, when the retainers usually sit lunching at a side table. Freddie rose to his feet, slowly put on a cloth cap and said he couldn't sit down to eat with someone who called them liars. Somehow or other, Margaret can't remember how, the breach was healed; Julia and the retainers were chattering away and each thinking the other delightful. 'They're *not!*' said Margaret. 'I simply can't abide Freddie and Bessie!' The moral is that Julia is starved of drama and feels happier when she can introduce some into ordinary life, of whatever sort. Also knowing the state of Margaret's kitchen, I expect the milk-strainer *was* in a disgusting state and Julia did say so! I delight in the way small insignificant objects like milk-strainers take a prominent part in emotional situations.

18 October

Back from a particularly nice weekend with Kitty, though it poured persistently all Saturday and I had to take my walk under a large umbrella. That night Gilbert Debenham and his wife Molly, Frank and Billy, came for dinner. The two psychological doctors both firmly denied that sleeping pills did one any harm (so relieving my fear of ruining my memory with them).

Sunday sweet and mild. I submerged myself again in the leafy lanes and from lunch till after six we sat listening to the Caballé-Verrett-Giulini records of *Don Carlos*, partly from outdoors basking in the sun. How intensely moving I find that opera! And the main singers all 'turned their hearts on', but I have a tiny reservation about Caballé, a feeling that she's slightly inhuman.

Dinner at Crichel: Raymond, Desmond and Jack Rathbone. Ever since Italy my sense of guilt has driven me to be as nice to Raymond as I know how, but both Kitty and I thought him rather grumpy. He complained of Desmond not shutting doors and talked almost exclusively to me, resisting my attempts to draw Des in, turning his head in my direction and virtually ignoring Kitty. As I left he said he wanted me to come to dinner in Canonbury and would phone. He isn't happy about our relationship and no more, strictly speaking, am I.

20 October

Answering a letter from Gerald attacking principles in politics (they ought, he said, to be dealt with pragmatically), I said I was all in favour of pragmatism, but that when applied to politics they become as dull as drains and plumbing. That the only aspect of politics that interests me is when principles are involved because this means drawing universals from particulars, general ideas — which are the breath of life — from facts. I realised as I wrote that it was Raymond's failure to find general ideas the breath of life that distressed me about him.

The *Sunday Times* dealt a shattering blow to those prepared to believe it by producing convincing and detailed evidence that the Ulster internees are being tortured to get information about the IRA. The details are sickening and there's been an attempt on some sides to get it enquired into. However one MP said in the House, 'I'm sure a lot of us would agree that where the safety of our soldiers depends on this information, we are not too concerned as to the methods used to get it.' (Some cheers.) I remember Ralph saying long ago à propos of ends and means, and capital punishment as a deterrent, that one must realise that there are some things one would never do *whatever* the end in view – and torture was one of them. At the time it seemed something *no one* would question, but we've descended into barbarism a long way since then. What's more, people are becoming rather pleased with their barbarism.

My private life has been fairly solitary and thin, and my current translation is nearly finished.

But the orchestra last night was deliriously enjoyable . . .

22 October

The pleasure of talking to Robert yesterday, and finding him in agreement on all current political issues – horror at our descent into racialism and torture, desire for a Maynard Keynes to state, without shame and boldly, the importance of principles in politics as in other forms of thinking! I was able (having been tongue-tied before) to thank him for saying he would write something about Ralph, and say he mustn't let it become a millstone, that he could write it after I was dead. He said he very much wanted to do it, and was merely pondering in what sort of way. I told him of

Stanley Olsen's interest, and he said, 'Send him to see me.' As Stanley rang me up this morning, and as he does seem to have taken a genuine interest in Ralph, I mentioned it to him, and I think he might go. Stanley is a bit of a mystery. I really like him and can't help trusting my judgement, but how much he sees things as they are I'm not sure. He's so quick and accurate that I may credit him with too much power to penetrate the mists of time, but he's sensitive and knows how to say things in a way that gives no offence, as he told me on the telephone that he wanted to say how much he liked Ralph, and how a friend he'd told about him said, 'That sounds like a very nice man.'

By the post comes a kind, deferential, soggy letter from Catherine Dupré saying she wants to write 'at length' about Carrington and Lytton. She is aware of 'my feelings that the story shouldn't be fully told', and doesn't want in any way, etc. etc. What a dolt! Hasn't the story 'been fully told' not once but twice? And as if I hadn't invariably told her I was all for the truth being told, and that what I didn't like was a false picture of Ralph being presented. What with one thing and another this question of the presentation of Ralph has arisen as an issue, and I regret not having done more – though I did do quite a lot – to prevent Michael Holroyd (partly on Gerald's say-so) getting him so wrong.

25 October

Noel and I have carried on a ding-dong correspondence with and about Catherine Dupré, from which it transpires that what she wants to do is some awful play for telly or stage, with Jill Bennett as Carrington. In her letter to me she never even said *what* she had in mind, unless of course this was duplicity. Finding to my relief that Noel was as much against it as I am, I have written her a firm letter, reminding her of the Ken Russell battle and making it plain we should arm ourselves again against any fictional treatment of the story. I made a perhaps cruel comment on her remark that she wanted to treat it 'creatively, poetically and interpretively', by saying that I didn't think it possible to improve on Carrington's own account of her story.

By the same post comes a letter from Gerald enclosing a copy of a letter on Ralph's character he had written to Stanley Olsen – the mixture as before. Ralph is represented, bar a few saving adjectives, as an aggressive, slightly absurd philistine. I threw aside the letter in a rage and have not been able to pick it up again. I don't quite know why he sent it to me.

Elspeth Macfarlane to dinner – not too bad. After she had gone I lay in bed, rather idly looking at a Sunday supplement, and saw a photo of an Arab in a white robe, surrounded by soldiers, about to be shot (so I thought), his face brilliant with *excitement*, and a direct sort of anticipation of death. I suddenly saw how it might be possible to feel such an excitement on encountering the dread hand, even while onlookers saw it as a horror. And fell asleep curiously reassured.

Two magic days on Saturday and Sunday, days of almost embarrassing purity and beauty, blue untrammelled skies fading very slowly to a windless evening of rose, orange, apple green with a clear-cut thumbnail moon. I drove down with the whole Campbell[1] family, and was offered the choice of sleeping in their newly acquired Gypsy caravan. Almost ashamed of my romanticism, I jumped at it, rather than the garden house, went to bed early, climbed onto my broad wooden bed, opened the little

---

1 Robin and Susan and their two boys, William and Arthur, had a small house on the shore of the Solent.

window beside it and peered out through its lace curtain at the quiet misty sea. Susan had put in a little oil stove which kept me almost too hot. I slept for hours and hours, and whenever I woke it was to delight in my situation. Robin has somehow put it across to Susan that her shouting at him is the worst thing for his heart. On the whole she restrained herself. Arthur charms me; he was so fascinated by the sunset that he couldn't be torn away from it to go out to supper.

27 October

Last night, entering the tiny Harvane Gallery for a private view of Bloomsburiana, the first person I saw was Catherine Dupré, who (as I knew) would have got my letter that very morning. I went up to her and took the bull by the horns, but I needn't have worried; those horns were made of rubber. Obsession with her own 'creativity', and her natural stupidity, have given her a soft obstinacy which is hard to deal with. I thought my letter was final, but it's obviously not, and she still wants to come and talk about it, and wheedle me with offers of taking me to rehearsals of the Monteverdi opera in which her husband plays the lute. Noel was as firmly against it all as I am, but I fear he's softening. I would like to be adamant; I really rather dislike the Dupré, who dogged me everywhere I went through the small rooms of this exhibition, and I don't credit her with any literary skill.

This morning I woke early, full of frustration and desire to fight this horrid project – the old emotions aroused by Ken Russell are wearily revived.

28 October

Catherine Dupré is like influenza. She produces irritation and fever of an almost physical sort and has given me two bad nights.

I'm struggling to be rational about the subject and not finding it easy; but her soft, gushing schoolgirl manner doesn't mollify me. Then last night, as I was about to leave the house, Stanley Olsen rang up and talked for half an hour in a compulsive way: he seemed to be doing a lot of 'creative' not to say Freudian 'interpretation' of Carrington, and reeled off hypotheses about her relations with Lytton and Ralph and her mother and father – even poor silly old Mrs Carrington didn't escape psychoanalysis – till I felt dizzy. He has obviously been mulling it over till he's stupefied, though exactly what 'it' is I don't yet know, and said he must 'talk about it or burst'. So at last I told him to come and talk to me about it this morning and I expect him any moment. I was perturbed by the way he seemed to clutch at the mental picture he has framed, as if it were dearer than life. It's quite extraordinary what power to grip people's imagination the old old story contains.

Drinks last night with Jimmy and Tanya Stern – Auden, William Plomer, Frank Tait, Jennifer Ross and finally Raymond. He and I went off to dinner and then repaired to my flat and our communion was as relaxed and delightful as I could possibly wish. So what *was all that* Italian miasma about? To myself: take note and beware.

29 October

Stanley Olsen arrived soon after 10 a.m. and talked steadily, or I read what he had written, until twelve-thirty. I take back yesterday's remarks absolutely, and return to my view that he is the most intelligent and perceptive of the Bloomsbury hounds and I really respect his judgement. I gave him one or two small essays of Ralph's I had found, one on the equation of money and shit, which he laughed a good deal over. But he says he doesn't quite feel he's 'got' Ralph and that he sat up until three the night before pondering his character. The difficulty I suppose is that he believes me (I think), and can't fit in what I tell him with the Holroyd – Gerald image. I dropped him off at the end of Parsifal Road and went on to lunch and play trios with Margaret.

1 November

Anne Hill broke her leg and wrist a few weeks ago slipping up on her kitchen floor. I went down last weekend, partly to see her in Ipswich Hospital and – as I hoped – to help look after Heywood. In fact Ruth Gathorne-Hardy was doing this and Anthony and Eddie were both staying. The two brothers are *extraordinary* – I felt as if I were on the stage in a play performed by Gielgud and Richardson. By the time I arrived they were both well away on the evening sozzle, sitting in two armchairs, one on either side of the fire and talking slowly and indistinctly in identical voices. Anthony's lifelong drinking was complicated by his getting cancer of the throat, so that eating was once painful and he has now given it up altogether, doesn't come in to meals but swallows a jug of milk with eggs beaten in it. After about six there are ceaseless requests: 'Since you're up, Heywood, bring me another drop of whisky, will you? Mine's the bottle *under* the table.' Heywood went to and fro like a butler. After dinner Eddie and I got into a fairly drastic argument, starting from agreement about the Colonels, going on to disparagement of almost every other nation, particularly the Germans, on Eddie's part, my accusing him of racialism, whether we believed in democracy, etc. Eddie got crosser than I did. Heywood remained totally silent while this, to me rather enjoyable, artillery sped across the room; Ruth ditto, and Anthony once ejaculated 'BALLS' loudly – but in reference to what I don't know. Anthony apparently always takes a bottle of sherry to bed each night and finishes it. Other people's 'drinking' was talked about as if it was the business of life ('she doesn't *drink*' with evident disapproval).

Both these intelligent men are steadily killing themselves. Anthony (with his cancer) has more excuse. Eddie used to be nervous because of his 'hobnailed liver', but that's all over. He really looks pretty ghastly now, 'like a very old seagull', Heywood said to me with a slight laugh. His memory and mind remain remarkably clear except late at night. Both of them have foot trouble and hobble around like octogenarians. Eddie's selfishness is phenomenal. Twice he said, 'I wish Anne could have broken her leg just *after I went* back to Athens my dear, it's most inconvenient for me.' When I asked him if he would enjoy visiting the Bevans and Harrods, 'Oh, yes, my dear, there's plenty of booze and good food, and they bring me my breakfast in bed, my dear, so that's all right, my dear.' He spent hours planning a very expensive solitary lunch at the Savoy: 'I think I'll have a *woodcock* my dear, but it must be hung and cooked exactly right, and then, my dear, perhaps some *raspberries*, if one can still get them.' Yet on the plus side, beside his intelligence, he has a mild but genuine affection for old friends and took great trouble to be appreciative of Ruth's cooking. He does pretty well nothing all day but read *The Times*, do the crossword puzzle and read thrillers, gets up at about eleven, and goes to bed after lunch till six-thirty. The worst aspect of the old reprobate was his disagreeableness to Anthony, in whom I had begun to see the traces of a human being by Sunday evening, a nicer though less clever one than Eddie. And after Friday night's lively argument, and Saturday night when I fled to the television room with Heywood and Ruth, Eddie got up to pour himself another drink, and Anthony asked him politely to get him one 'while he was there'. 'No, I *WON'T*, my dear, I'm bloody well not going to, my dear. I'm older than you, my dear, and much iller and you must do it yourself, my dear.' He toddled slowly off into the kitchen to get a glass, while Anthony muttered, 'He's the most selfish person in the world.' Feeling, though older than either of them, incomparably more spry, I got up and poured out Anthony's drink and was told, 'Thash the sweeshesh thing you've done.' The other 'sweesh thing' was to ask to see a belt he's elaborately knotting out of fine string for his daughter Rose, and watch him deftly doing it. I was touched by this: one can't possibly imagine Eddie doing anything for anyone but himself. Patrick Kinross says rather acutely that Eddie has decided to make a sort of performance of his own selfishness, and so benefit by it.

One can just carry on the ghost of a conversation with the two old monsters and I became almost hysterically amused by the situation. I had to kiss them both at bedtime.

Ruth: a good kind person, over-emotional and a worrier, very likeable and conversable, has strong reminiscences of her son Jonny. You have only to press a button and everything pours out. She's extremely happy at Snape and feels better in health (she suffers from a painful disfiguring rash) chiefly because of the 'angelic Heywood, and my loving him and Anne so much'. She takes a lot of trouble over meals, and clearly enjoys being away from her incarceration with Anthony. I heard about the break-up of Jonny's marriage, her fears for the two children, doubts about the new girl, and the situation of her Rose. She's rather ludicrously obsessed with the Gathorne-Hardy family, and Caroline Jarvis and Juliet's husband were obviously expected to toe the Cranbrook line. I felt (but didn't really express) some revulsion to this family glorification; however, when I went to bed, in my head was ringing, 'And family pride must be denied, and set aside, and mortified.'

But oh, the goodness and lovability of Heywood. As both the brothers were in bed most of the day, Heywood and I had several marvellous walks in still, warm, brilliant autumn weather. On Sunday we drove to Ipswich and he left me with Anne for an hour, returning to eat sandwiches and drink champagne. Anne looked blooming and serene, and didn't complain at all. But she won't be back to normal for three months.

So now I'm speeding back to London, in a hot train through a summery landscape and wondering what I'll find there.

10 November

The very last bit of my translation went off to America two days ago. The days seem to be fuller without any work on hand – but I have been beset by the Bloomsbury boys: Stanley Olsen and Paul Levy, to each of whom I gave dinner last week. Stanley isn't as clever as Paul but I like him just as much, and I think he likes me. Invited to dinner on Guy Fawkes' night, he spent five hours here! So after correcting his spelling and grammar and answering his questions, I turned the tables on him and asked him some. He's the son of a rich (very rich, I suspect) businessman from Ohio, and left there two and a half years ago because 'the family situation was too dominant'. Apart from his passion for Wagner, he has a girlfriend called Tish and means to take cello lessons. Money seems to be no object with him.

Paul told me that, after getting a dusty answer from both Noel and me about her Carrington play, Catherine Dupré had gone to see him, to look at 'and touch' Carrington's diary, and told him about her project, as something very much 'on'. I dare say nothing will make her abandon it; ambition is a powerful spur, but I've written again emphasising that by doing so she will cause Noel and me 'acute distress'. My idea is that she has such a picture of herself as a kind, Christian, sympathetic person that she may find it hard to fit the two together. But another play, by a certain Peter Luke, is projected, and Paul says even other feelers have been put out. So I dare say the whole thing is hopeless, and possibly 'I do not greatly care' as Carrington used to say. In proof whereof, I had a really narrow miss from being mown down in my Mini by a huge bus – and it shook me not at all.

11 November

My judgement of Catherine Dupré was right insofar as she rang up full of protestations, dismay, 'please trust me', and so forth. But she insists that 'to get it out of her system' she must write her play, though 'nothing more should happen without my consent'. She will then, 'if I don't mind', show it to me – and there followed the bribe as before – tickets for Monteverdi's *Poppea*. So that I don't think she has really abandoned hope, and I awoke in the night to realise that I must not on any account accept her bribe. This is slightly awkward as she offered me a plethora of dates – but I have now written to refuse and feel easier in my mind.

My two engagements yesterday turned out better than I hoped. Rose was delightful and – to my eyes – though thin, seemed alight with life and forward-looking. My old Newnham pal, Dot, was really very friendly and I quite enjoyed my evening with her.

16 November

Sad Tuesday awakening to another sparklingly bright morning. Though there are a mass of 'things to do' on my mental list, I feel the lack of the constricting framework of a piece of work. The river has spread into a shapeless marsh . . .

Last weekend at Crichel alone with Raymond and Desmond,

and with visits from Cecils, Cecil Beaton and Kitty. Wonderfully brilliant days; without the intense usual pleasure I got from them my walks with Moses would have taken the dutiful place of needed work. As for my time, it fills up easily enough. Raymond positively courts me, and even brought up a possible new journey together, to Egypt. We were getting on so well that I considered it with interest.

It can't be said that he and Desmond get on brilliantly, in spite of what is I suppose a basic mutual affection. Raymond kept drawing my attention to 'the heavy weather Desmond makes over every little task', 'his passion for keeping people waiting', 'his appalling hair-do', while Desmond complained – and indeed it *is* extraordinary – that 'Raymond never once went out of doors and enjoyed this marvellous weather, but spent the twenty-four hours stewing, sighing and smoking over his review all morning, snoozing in the smoke-filled room all afternoon and all night.' He says the smell of stale smoke in it is appalling and no fresh air is ever let in and, 'Wouldn't it be a good thing if he sometimes took a little walk?'

The *Sunday Times* is running an admirable exposé of the facts about Ulster; this first instalment took me an hour to read. The others of course – though they spend hours with the papers – didn't read it, and I took Raymond up rather sharply for saying it was biased when he hadn't. I did a little mildish propaganda based on what I had read – but the whole of England is developing a jingo frenzy in which the IRA is 'the enemy' against whom we are 'at war'. There are even cries for 'patriotic censorship'! And I got a letter complaining against 'Liberal do-gooders' and saying that 'if we had been tough and shot to kill from the beginning' the Ulster situation would never have blown up to its present dimensions.

22 November

Two Bloomsbury occasions: on Friday 'An evening with Duncan Grant' at the Institute of Contemporary Arts. I took Joan and we were squired by Stanley, who had an appalling cold but laughed appreciatively at Duncan's jokes. The contrast between Duncan's physical presence as he climbed onto the platform and the film taken of him a year or two ago was distressing – he has got a lot older all at once, but his humour and intelligence seem untarnished. A bad start to the evening, with Claude Rogers[1] making an endless rambling speech composed of sentences which contrived to branch off before they ever reached a full stop, fumbling among a lot of papers, bumbling into his beard. After which all went well, a mixture of Dunconian charm and Bloomsbury muddle. Henrietta, sitting on the platform beside Richard Shone,[2] looked beautiful – and the two of them read extracts about Duncan and his work that were amusing and pointful.

Now I'm lying on my bed trying to recover from the second occasion – the unveiling of a plaque to Lytton on the wall of 51 Gordon Square, a speech from Noel Annan, and glasses of bad champagne two doors along. This took place in the middle of the morning, and I so dreaded confronting Julia that I felt quite shaky beforehand. What a bloody bore it is – I almost feel like trying again to make it up. Especially inconvenient was that Noel Annan asked me to lunch, and suggested Christopher Strachey[3] and Julia as co-guests, so that I *had* to say that Julia wouldn't speak to me. I took greatly however to Christopher who, with his intelligent face and bright brown eyes, looks more Strachey than anyone,

---

1 One of the Euston Road artists.
2 Art historian and critic.
3 Julia's half-brother.

and our three-cornered conversation at lunch was extremely lively. Most of the company were unknown to me — except for the Holroyds, Pansy Lamb, Paul Levy, Raymond and Lionel (who had done his best but without success to keep Margaret from accompanying him). A female dwarf asked me if I'd ever met Lytton. I replied that 'I had known him intimately' but she was deaf and didn't hear. 'I believe there are some very old people here who actually *knew* him,' she said.

'Spotty' John,[1] immensely tall and rather grim-faced, seemed to greet me with the words 'Mister Monster' but I may have been mistaken. Thereafter he was amiable, and suggested a visit. God forbid.

The inevitable keying-up before such social occasions and the rich Greek food and resinated wine we had at the White Tower have quite floored me. What with an extremely social weekend at Stowell (dinner party for eight, trailing skirts and dinner-jacketed, on Saturday, and sumptuous lunch with Ian MacCallum at the American Museum, Bath, on Sunday), I feel it's high time I swam back into the quieter waters to which I'm accustomed.

Catherine Dupré was sitting just behind me at Duncan's 'evening' and made various signs and approaches. I didn't conceal my desire to avoid her. But the other playwright, Peter Luke, writes that his play is with the impresarios. I feel disposed to give up the struggle.

Excursion to the centre of London for the cinema leaves a night-mare impression of noise, garishness, rubbish lying everywhere and young people who ought to look beautiful looking hideous and deformed; it leaves me longing to be surrounded by sheep and green fields and twittering birds.

---

1 Strachey, nephew of Lytton and brother of Dick.

I wrote to Noel about Peter Luke's letter. He replies, 'Let us stick to our guns', but so far he hasn't fired a shot, and I'm sick and tired of the whole thing.

29 November

Stanley gave a party on Friday night, to which I was bidden, and asked me to pick up William Gerhardi on the way – a writer Ralph and I both greatly admired years ago. He lives in a block of flats called Rossetti House; it lived up to its name. I ascended in a shining tin lift to the fifth floor and pressed the bell outside the dead-looking pre-Raphaelite front door. No response. Press again. Silence. I gave a good bang with the knocker and a shape loomed within. The face was somehow familiar: old but spry, tilted slightly forwards, pink, with pale, wide-awake eyes set like headlamps. 'Oh no, the bell doesn't work – it saves me from unwanted callers.' He sent us down in the lift with a stylish swaggering push on the button, climbed into my Mini and off we went. 'Are you a safe driver?' 'Yes, very.' 'Because I want to finish the book I'm writing.' Stanley had warned me that his return to popularity had given him *folie de grandeur*. We talked easily – about the MacCarthys (Desmond had 'given him a rave review' and 'the girl, what was her name?'). I told him what I could about Rachel, remembering that years ago she had fallen for him rather and come the nearest ever to an infidelity to David. Gerhardi tried to get me straight. 'Then there was a lot about you in Holroyd's book?' Later at dinner I heard him talking about that 'extraordinary woman in Holroyd's book who committed suicide'. I enjoyed the party – beside Stanley (whose girl, Tish, had measles) there were Paul Levy, a nice young paintress called Lyn and her man. And a little girl from Gerhardi's publisher who looked stupider than she was. The food was splendid: 'a failed *pâté'*, Hungarian chicken with rice in a creamy sauce. I sat between Stanley and Paul, and conversation throve and even sparkled. Stanley veered between compulsive greed and going off into back-leaning swoons at the thought of some *'exquisite performance'* by Leontine Price or some other singer. It was a jolly evening; I left and drove the publishing girl home before midnight.

Early next morning I drove down to Cambridge with Nadine, who had come up for the funeral of her mother – delightful old Mrs Hambourg. I got to the house of her sister Michal at nine-thirty, and found Michal in a purple nightdress, paunchy Ian her husband and two repulsive dogs like Woolworth brooches, oblong, hairy and hysterical. Nadine was in her compulsively delaying mood. 'I must just write a letter to sack my mother's gardener.' At last we got off to the deceased's house in Maida Vale and collected 'Mother Mary', as Nadine's eldest sister Sonia is now called. Once married to a needy Prince de Bessarabie, she's now an Orthodox Greek nun in France, and dresses in rusty black from top to toe, a black woollen skullcap on her head from which descends a sort of Arabian black cape which meets the voluminous skirts. From this a pale, bespectacled face juts out, ending in a noticeable fringe of beard – and from this singular apparition emerges a charming, cultivated and humorous voice. She's a manic depressive but was obviously in one of her euphoric spells, ecstatically admiring the flat grey landscape through which we drove to Cambridge.

Back to walk into the town for shopping and listen to Monteverdi *Poppea* till bed-time.

30 November

'Mother Mary', as I soon got into the way of calling her, travelled up with me yesterday morning, and I greatly enjoyed her company; she's very clever and interested in everything. I was also amused to go about with a nun and observe with what kindly respect she was treated. There's something winning about her, serenity perhaps, as well as the sense of being already half-buried. Getting home, I spent the afternoon shopping and cooking for last night's highly successful dinner-party: the Campbells, Henrietta and Richard Shone – fondu (a great success with all) and Dublin steak. Georgia in afterwards, sparkling to the top of her bent; talk went on till one-thirty. Everyone was highly and concentratedly themselves, particularly Robin, who was obviously enjoying himself.

Somewhat flattened this morning – but pleased because the evening was so good.

Sunday at Cambridge had included a visit to Jim Rendel[1] and his family – a brisk philosophical argument, and a sight of his dear little girls and backward son.

1 December

Janetta arrived last night and Rose asked me to go to her flat after my orchestra to see her. She looked happy, and is, because Dicky's hypnotist has been seeing Rose and declares that she is on the way to getting well. She certainly seemed so. Janetta had a lot to say about Peter Luke, the author of the other play about Lytton, Carrington, etc. She has championed my cause, with great zeal, and through her brother Mark[2] got in touch with Luke

---

1 My nephew.
2 Culme-Seymour.

and visited him in his house near Málaga. He has had a heart attack, and in spite of its mildness my letter 'nearly gave him another'. He *has* put Ralph in the play, but as a naval officer with another name. Well. Janetta wants me to get in touch with the impresario, and get a copy of the play to read – I think perhaps I will, though I'm doubtful what I ought to do about it. And of many other things.

3 December

The Luke plot thickens. Janetta has told me a lot more about her visit to him. He hedged whenever she suggested I should read the play, showed obvious alarm that I would somehow try to impede it and says that Virginia is the villain – and she has no surviving relatives who might mind. Janetta felt indignant when he talked of his 'six months' hard work being spoiled', when, as she said, many people take six or sixteen years over a piece of work. I don't actually think that anything will stop the play if the impresario likes it, nor that copyrights go for much.

Then, yesterday morning, the telephone rang and it was – of all people – Jane Bomford.[1] 'My great friend, Peter Luke, asked me to get in touch with you and assure you that there's nothing awful about Ralph in his play, and that he's a nice person.' I said, 'I'm sure he is, everyone says so, but that isn't really the point.' And put my view about the distinction between history and fiction, which she seemed to see. I'm going to see Alix and the Carringtons this weekend, and shall discuss it with them. I'm not quite sure how much Noel does mind – quite a lot I think – and of course Carrington is bound to figure more prominently than Ralph. But it has occurred to me suddenly that, as I have inherited

---

1 A friend from Wiltshire.

the Carrington copyrights, it's up to me to fight for him as well as for myself. So, up on to my crusader's charger again . . . but with small hopes and much detachment.

Yesterday, too, I got from Hilary Rubinstein the name and address of Luke's London agent, and the information that the play had only just arrived and in a rough draft. So I at once wrote him a note asking if we could see it.

I feel I have become a different sort of person, now that I have no work on hand or in prospect. I sleep longer, and get up later. On the other hand 'other people', as well as a source of my main pleasure, agitate me and make my heart beat faster. What I liked about my translation was that it was a way of being content while alone; it had the charm a routine task always has for me. I was drawn along by the string of words.

Janetta has been to lunch two days running – it's lovely to see her look so smooth and unworried, and therefore remarkably young.

7 December

I didn't think I'd get caught up in the Luke play, hardly that I would mind about it, but I have and do, somewhat egged on by others, some of whom mind 'for me' as it were (Joan) and others become involved in the drama. I have now had a letter from Luke's agent, who says that 'the very purpose of the play is to highlight Strachey and his contemporaries in an identifiable form' and that the play will probably be called POOR VIRGINIA, *or* POOR OTTOLINE *or* POOR LYTTON! Last weekend I took my dossier of information to Alix and to Noel. Alix said: 'I don't like the sound of POOR LYTTON.' They both sympathise with the desire to stop the project, doubt if it is possible and leave it to me to try and do so. I wrote to Quentin about the involvement of Virginia and he rang up this morning suggesting I contact a lawyer called (improbably) Emanual Wax. I have already done so and await his response, somewhat breathlessly. From the point of view of personal agitation it might have been better to let it rip, and of course I wake in the night . . . Quentin was very warm and comforting; it was like receiving a hug from a bear. Julian is back, and rang up yesterday, sounding exactly the same, thank heavens.

8 December

My present life is made up almost entirely of personal relations and sometimes the miseries of friends are almost unbearable. Among manifold newspaper horrors, such as war in India, I read in *The Times* yesterday that Dot Hambro's eldest son Marc Wallenberg has shot himself in a forest near Stockholm. I've had a pathetic note from her – and last night with terrible vividness her face loomed through the darkness, not as she is now at seventy but as a girl of twenty or so, unaware of the agonies in store, a fully coloured, living and breathing picture accompanied by the sound of her youthful voice.

13 December

Returned in Eardley's car last night from a gentle, grey weekend at the Slade, and went straight round to dinner with Janetta and Robert. It was her last evening and I wanted to see her, yet I think perhaps I ought to have left them alone together. Robert looked knotted and desperate and I had the feeling that his unhappiness had created a false callousness, a shell of indifference impossible to penetrate, on which all efforts at contact rebounded.

15 December

Reading through this year's diary, I'm amazed at its sadness. Whether this is just the effusion of what I had tried to repress, or the naked truth, I don't know. How sad *is* my present life? Sometimes I trudge out, impelled by some inner urge, and find myself stumping, blind and unconscious, down Sloane Street; sometimes I get involved – against my will – in social antics. On Monday I was invited by Andrew Murray-Thripland to a party at the Reform Club. Julian was to have come, but after one or two telephone calls I realised he was in dire distress, and drove round to see him. I think he was suffering from sheer understandable exhaustion after his Australian tour. But he had the desperate person's desire to press to extremes, to tell me he was 'ill', feeling suicidal. His use of 'ill' I've long ago noticed is an emergency exit whether for himself or others; but I was saddened by his haunted expression, and large tragic eyes, and tried to give sensible advice while dreading being too much of a hospital nurse or school-mistress: rest, give up all commitments, take Valium, postpone going back to work by means of a medical certificate till after Christmas. Off I drove again to the Reform Club, and arrived late in its dignified hall. When I asked for Andrew, 'He seems to be a very popular young gentleman,' said the porter. In a room off the hall thirty or forty mostly young people were sitting at small tables round the walls, eating compulsively (as if engaged on writing theses) curried chicken or steak and kidney pie. The popular young gentleman rushed up, offered me a drink, cried, 'The drink has given out', and rushed away again. I was left standing until I spied Raymond sitting by an unctuous Jew and joined them. Later came Pat and Freda Berkeley, pretty far gone in drink.

We drank red wine; I talked to Freda, who was hardly present;

Andrew, looking very charming, was telling everyone how the party had taken shape around his attempt to bring his two mistresses together. He asked Raymond, 'Would you have liked to be married?' Raymond, in a very soft but meaning voice: '*No.*' Andrew admitted he would, and indicated a likely wife, a short, plump girl whose thick brown hair covered her face entirely.

I waver whether to accept this playgirl's life, which doesn't really suit me; I rest and read more but there's too much time and opportunity to be aware of other people. Yesterday Joan very touchingly declared that were I to fall ill, she would come and look after me, and if it was my 'terminal illness' she would see that I didn't suffer. (We had been talking of horrible deaths.) This she said with transparent sincerity, and indeed I believe her, and it's a real comfort to me to know it. She's perhaps the only one of my friends who has no one she's more committed to than me, and this, unexpectedly, turns out to be enormously valuable. I thought I could help her. I see now *she* greatly helps *me*. I was grateful to her for making this comforting promise, and got her to agree that the arrangement would be mutual. I'm only three years older than her, and who knows? But it is a *good* pact to have made. She accepted it as such, but I could see didn't for a moment consider it possible that she might die first. I hope she doesn't.[1]

To a commissioner of oaths today, to swear 'by Almighty God' all kinds of things, true and untrue, about Nicky. Among the untrue ones, that I had been to her flat and found it clean and tidy.

---

1 Joan died in 1995.

21 December

Mary took me to *Figaro* last night – a splendid performance, perhaps the best I've ever been to. Her other guest, a slender, elegant woman dressed tightly in well-cut black, with a profile reminiscent of Cocteau (whose life I've been reading); her name, Lady Daphne Straight.

My hackles always rise, I hope and believe invisibly, when confronted by consciousness of superiority which isn't *real* superiority – i.e. not such as Shakespeare displays in the Sonnets. And I noticed that, though I was the oldest by ten years, they both tended to walk out of the doors first, leave me the back seat in the car and generally treat me rather like an old governess. They prattled away: 'Oh, do you know, Robert wrote to Bobo apologising for being so drunk the other night.' 'Oh, NO! DID he really? How SWEET!' Gossip galore about the rich or noble, Mrs Heinz of Beans, or Lord Lansdowne. Complaints about how booked up the best chiropodist in London was, so that you 'simply have to devote a whole morning to having your hair and feet done'. Or 'Rosie *will* complain of my drinking habits. She says if I didn't drink red wine at lunch I wouldn't have to have my afternoon kip, but I told her that in that case I'd have to go to bed at seven-thirty because I *must* have my ten hours.'

In our box at the opera my companions took care to break the rules and smoke without going into the passage. 'And they won't let one leave one's glass on the edge of the box!' 'Perhaps they're afraid it might fall into the stalls,' I suggested. 'The class war more likely,' said Lady D. The stalls, I see, are the lower classes! I observed Mary's touchingly old-fashioned belief that the waiters were relishing her glamorous superiority, whereas I could see the cold look of calculation in their eyes as to what tip she was good for, and their annoyance that her bringing her own drink made it less. The same with the market lorry drivers as we wound our way out. They, the aristos, fondly believe these men love seeing expensive cars and women with diamonds among them. What fatuous folly!

Last week's opera was *Poppea* with Duncan, Magouche and Joan. Duncan is incredible! The Christmas traffic is appalling at present, so I tried all day to get him on the telephone to say I would fetch him in my Mini. At five I got him; he had only just come in, having been at the Tate since about eleven looking at the Hogarths. 'There were such a lot of them that it took me some time.' He declared he could easily get to the Coliseum by tube. I did fetch him, and he sat through the opera without nodding, came back to supper and was still going strong at one-thirty when everyone else decided it was bed-time and we put him in a taxi. It was glorious music, well sung and moving. I don't think I'll ask Joan to the opera again though, as she keeps her eyes shut ('Because I'm so visual and it was awful to look at') and only liked 'some of the music'.

Sophie has given me a photo of her own sweet face blown up to ten times lifesize. I have pinned it on my bedroom door, and it gives me enormous pleasure.

Dadie has been to lunch here – as splendidly life-enhancing as I knew he would be. I got Mary to come and have a drink first, a great success.

22 December

Suddenly heavy-hearted, I sat down to my typewriter and began free-associating in the shape of an unsent, unsendable letter to Julian. Amongst a lot of trivial rubbish, there suddenly popped out straight from the unconscious, 'Will ye no come back again?' from the old Scotch song. No – that's just the trouble. He never will. At the moment the wooden determination of those who would rather be dead lies heavily on my mind. Yesterday I went to a curious function in memory of Dolly Hambourg. The proceedings began with old Mark Hambourg playing Dolly's favourite bit of Beethoven *outre-tombe* on a scratchy record. Then eulogies – quite good – from Tom and Gerald Moore (who included some funny stories). A final piece of Schumann by Michal, who was obviously moved herself. Yet the whole thing, with its evocation of a personality and its obliteration, was strangely affecting, even to me, who liked and admired her.

23 December
What I think terrifies a lonely person out of his or her wits is the awareness of a thin steel barrier between every individual and the next. It sometimes seems impossible, and not even desirable, to penetrate it, except in the relationship of love. But which sorts of love? Sexual, and that between parent and child at its best. In friendship permeability is subject to unexpected variations, and when it is lost, panic follows. Then again the barrier is sometimes breached without effort – sometimes through conviviality, food and drink.

24 December
Or, as yesterday, when I was 'taken out of myself' as it is ludicrously called, by talking to Stanley. Our conversation was about metaphysical speculation, and whether the taste for it increased with age or not. He – at twenty-four – thought it did. I assured him he would find it wouldn't go on much longer, also that most people stop altogether in middle age, and also move further and further to the political right. He says even his contemporaries are rapidly doing so. His failure to act on his socialistic beliefs

appears to worry him. I said I thought the sin against the holy ghost was not to stand up for one's beliefs in *speech*. I enjoy talking to him much as if he was someone of my own age. He has had his long bob shortened, which makes him look thinner, and less like my private nickname for him – the Wombat. A nice friendly creature with an independent will of its own.

Christmas is upon us, oh Lord preserve us.

Christmas Day at the Cecils'

Can one have too much even of good talk? Yes. For me at any rate, though apparently not for any of this family – they talk and talk and talk torrentially, all at the same time, hardly able to wait while others hold the floor. It's as if some current was flowing out of them all the time. Don't they long, as I do, sometimes for a pause to put something back into what must be an empty receptacle? Music, a book, or silence. But a lot of it is stimulating, interesting, amusing, *if only* there were time to digest it. Naturally stories get repeated, by David anyway. He remembered our conversation about Hamlet and revenge last Christmas, as I do. I called it an 'argument'. D: 'Not an argument, a discussion.' F: 'But that's what I mean by an argument – I *love* arguing.' D: 'Ah, you use it in a purist sense.'

Well, I do believe thinking and talking to be two of the highest activities, but as with a meal, digestion is a necessity. I've been reading the Reith lectures on communication – mild, well-meaning and honest explorations, which insist that communication must be founded on a common ground of feeling and judgement, and must be more than an Ancient Mariner's 'desire to get something off one's chest', and that as such it is possible – a desire most people feel and that can be gratified.

26 December

And what a lot of each day here is spent in communication. When and how do they curdle within them the thoughts that they want to communicate? People often say how 'solitaries' become so garrulous when they meet others. But the batteries of great talkers who live with others are always flashing their lights and never recharging. I heard David say ruefully to Jonathan, 'I'm beginning to repeat myself. It's awful. You must stop me.' Indeed his loquacity sometimes quite worries me – I feel he'll collapse, pale and drained, after such marathon talk. All that so far happens is that the quality gets somehow thinner. With six of us in the house there are often three conversations going on at once, full lick and *fortissimo*. I am getting used to it, but I think I miss my normal silence. A record is the only thing to stop talk, or retirement to one's room. On a walk it goes on in a sustained duet.

Yesterday, we went over to Crichel before lunch for a drink with six bachelors, and for another before dinner to the Trees, Andrew Devonshire's handsome sister and her flashy husband (who appeared in a bright cherry-coloured velvet evening suit, bulky and genial). Elizabeth Cavendish, Betjeman's 'Feeble', was also there. David has twigged that there were difficulties in Australia.[1] I was interested that the forceful Feeble said she had been knocked out for three weeks by the thirty-four-hour flight home.

It's delightful to witness the happy relations within this family. Hugh (with Mirabel) and Laura (with Angelo Hornak) have their extra-family supports; hour-long telephone calls go on; each starts up when the telephone rings. As for Jonathan with his broken marriage, I think it has matured him, but I wonder how painful it is. Vivien rang him last night and he came back, leant

---

1 Where Betjeman had been with Julian Jebb.

on the mantelpiece and poured himself out a whisky. The lack of irritation, friction or non-comprehension between them all astonished me. I came in yesterday upon a talk about religion – Hugh holding forth in his deliberate way, punctured by very encouraging grunts, but few words, from Jonathan. I was interested and wanted to find out where Hugh stood. He seemed to want to justify his position somehow, but his approach to ideas is like a potter with a lump of clay on a wheel, often reversing so that the lip of the pot vanishes and he begins again.

Paper games in the evening; wild, childish and salutary laughter; Rachel striking her unexpected note of inspiration.

27 December

After absurd near-panic on Christmas Eve (how was I to last out for five whole days of constant contact with five other people?) I have settled down to feel I could enjoy it for ever. It was only a momentary queasiness.

Each day I have walked out into the monochrome grey-brown countryside with Rachel, and each has its social occasion, when all six of us squash into the car and drive off for miles through the darkness to some large house with lit windows, holly and Christmas cards, butlers and – last night – an immense throng standing up and shouting face to face. We went into a room to arm ourselves with drinks and there was Cecil Beaton, who now has a habitual tease about my being 'the most popular guest in England, who has to be booked weeks ahead', looking at me sideways with little snake's eyes and smile, and wondering what on earth makes people ask me. Then I was adrift, no known face in sight. I had something approaching a conversation with deaf 'Duchess' Ashley-Cooper about Carrington's Letters, Holroyd and the Johns, in which I sensed but couldn't analyse some strongish emotion. Back after not too long a session in the social lists to cold supper and a quiet evening. David read a chapter on Queen Elizabeth to Rachel, Jonathan and me. I thought it good. Poor Rachel, tired out with household responsibilities, kept nodding her brown head over her sewing. As for David, I really feel he will need a long convalescence after all this non-stop talking. Does he keep it up always? *Is* the spider left with no more web material?

28 December
We have gently slipped into the last day here. Yesterday afternoon, David and I went out and paced gently through the gardens of Cranborne Manor, where there was much to delight the eye, even if David's was turned inwards onto the landscape of his thought: neatly trimmed plants in clean dark earth, some precocious polyanthus in flower, rooks swinging in the branches of the magnificent beeches, the beautiful grey face of the Manor theatrically lit by the pale sinking sun. 'A little sleep now, I think,' he said as we got in after a flurry of rain. But not a bit of it. From my room above the drawing-room, where I retired to read and be alone, I heard animated non-stop talk between David and his children below. It's like a myth; it's also beyond anyone's capacity, as David proved later on.

People came to have a drink, the Goldings and a young brother and sister, musicians. I talked to William Golding about Russia; he's a short, squarish, bearded man, smelling rather like an old labourer, doesn't drink at all because he can't in moderation, and has a twinkling blue eye. I dare say both David and Jonathan had drunk too much, but at dinner they got into a *row* – a one-sided row, if such a thing is possible, because I've never heard Jonathan lose his temper. But the difference between his tempo and David's was increased until Jonathan's words drifted off and slowed almost to a standstill. David's face became red and contorted, and he almost screamed: 'Well, *DO* let me finish! . . .' Rachel got involved on Jonathan's behalf and clamoured for him to be heard. David sprang up and said, 'I'll go away if I mayn't speak!' What *was* it all about? It veered towards the existence of poverty and whether the gap between rich and poor was widening or not. David was passionately optimistic and thought two years' unemployment would lead inevitably to happiness for all. Everything, too, was related to Hatfield in the days of his youth, just as all schools are to his own Eton days, America only to the nice time *he* had there. On the whole I think all the young and I were on one side. Hugh said little; I interposed once or twice about the damaging psychological effect of unemployment. 'But it's going to get BETTER! It's going to be all RIGHT!' David shrieked and I said gloomily that I hoped so, but saw no signs of it at present. The argument continued in one way or another till bedtime. David, full of compunction as he always touchingly is, went and sat by Jonathan, who revealed interesting things about the wild waste of public money by the BBC – a woman designer sent twice by air to Rome, and put up in a grand hotel, to buy lace for a cardinal's robe which wasn't even used. The cardinal made himself some out of two paper doilies and anyway it didn't show. Jonathan, as far as one could gather from his slowly developed thoughts, felt that it was wicked for this waste to be allowed when so much poverty and unemployment existed. There's no doubt the speed and non-stop quality of David's talk has inhibited and slowed up that of both his sons, which doesn't mean they don't think.

Rachel persisted in telling me how prosperous the Cranborne villagers were and how 'they don't ever take holidays. They don't want them.' It was rather a frustrating conversation and I doubt if it modified anyone's views at all.

30 December

Winter has struck. Big flakes are falling between me and the stucco façade opposite. I came up from Dorset yesterday with Jonathan and Laura and sank into a semi-coma most of the afternoon. Joan came to supper in the evening. As usual I'm inclined to feel guilty about the part I took in the 'rich-poor' argument. On Tuesday night we all went to eat mashed-up turkey on our knees with Frank and Billy. The other guests, Billy and Jenny Hughes. Billy made his contribution to the current theme by saying as he came into the room that he had just been made a judge and therefore was very much richer than ever before 'but it goes absolutely nowhere'. I liked him. He reminded me of my visit with Ralph to his flat, and how he had pointed to the Greville diaries and said, 'That's the best-indexed book in existence,' and Ralph said, 'I indexed it.'

INDEX